Sport, Power and Culture

Sport, Power and Culture

A Social and Historical Analysis of Popular Sports in Britain

JOHN HARGREAVES

Polity Press

First published in 1986 by Polity Press
in association with Blackwell Publishers Ltd.

Reprinted and first published in paperback 1987
Reprinted 1991, 1993, 1995, 1998, 2005, 2007

Polity Press
65 Bridge Street
Cambridge, CB2 1UR, UK

Polity Press
350 Main Street
Malden, MA 02148, USA

ISBN: 978-0-7456-0153-3
ISBN: 978-0-7456-0507-4 (pbk)

A CIP catalogue record for this book is available from the British Library.

Typeset by System 4 Associates, Gerrards Cross, Buckinghamshire
Printed and bound in Great Britain by Marston Book Services Limited, Oxford

This book is printed on acid-free paper.

For further information on Polity, visit our website: www.polity.co.uk

For Carl and Jane

Contents

List of Tables

Acknowledgements

I should like to thank, in particular, Mike Mann for his patient help and incisive comments on an earlier draft of this work, and also John Thompson for his extremely helpful suggestions on how to make it more amenable to a wider reading public.

Foreword
Stuart Hall

The topic of sport has acquired a certain popularity in the publishing world in recent years. But the majority of studies – useful as they are – tend to be confined to the internal structure and history of a particular sport. One alternative to this approach is often to set sport in the context of 'leisure' activities. However, while 'leisure' is an important valuable concept, placing sport in that context often results in rather slack or loose formulations, which lack either a sense of the organic relationships between sport and wider social questions or a sense of the tensions and pleasures which are intrinsic to its pursuit as a social activity.

John Hargreaves' study has the considerable merit of treating sport as a *social* phenomenon and setting it squarely in the context of power and culture where, in my view, it properly belongs. The book is enriched by its historical framework, without which the topic makes little sense. Fortunately, the historical treatment does not simply provide a chronological and evolutionary frame for the study, but a context in which serious theoretical issues can be posed. These issues relate, especially, to the way sport has been articulated in different historical periods, to the relations between classes; to the role which sport has played in the re-education and re-formation of the popular classes and to the 'stake' which sport represents in the general relationships of power in society. A related issue which occupies attention in the later chapters, is the commercial penetration of sport and the pressures of massification, spectacularization and fragmentation which have accompanied its development in the era of mass culture.

John Hargreaves' treatment of these themes is enhanced by his awareness of how they intersect with questions of gender, ethnicity and individualism – and by the extended conception of power which he deploys. For once, the relationship between sport and hegemony – the maintenance of a particular structure of power and social authority through society – is organic to the treatment, not merely parachuted into place.

Sport, Power and Culture thus raises serious and urgent questions about the relationship between sport and the configurations of power in contemporary British society and represents an overdue and welcome intervention in the field.

1

Approaching Sport and Power

Introduction

There are few activities which have secured a more central place in the national culture of countries like Britain and the USA than sport. Loved by millions, it peppers our daily discourse with rich anecdote, vivid terminology and striking imagery. Sporting activities feature prominently in the broadcasting programmes of the mass media and they constitute a weighty component of the leisure and entertainment industries. They generate jobs for many people, fortunes for the stars and profits for the business interests involved. Sport stimulates young men to dream of escape from boredom and deprivation. It is eulogized by educators, philanthropists and social reformers, appropriated by politicians and promoted by the modern state. And yet, precisely because it is so deeply ingrained in our type of culture – precisely because, in other words, our understanding of sport is so impregnated with common sense – sport is, in one particular respect, problematic. As a socio-cultural and historical phenomenon, sport remains profoundly opaque: it has proved strongly resistant to critical analysis, and by far the most intractable aspect is the question of the relationship between sport and power. It is this aspect, therefore, that we wish to investigate with reference to the development and the contemporary character of sport in Britain, but much of what we have to say applies, with appropriate elaboration, to societies which are culturally similar.

We are, therefore, not so much concerned with giving a comprehensive account of sport as such, nor with analyzing all respects in which sports are related to other aspects of society, but with understanding the way in which sports as cultural formations may, in certain respects, be connected with the power apparatus. We do not, indeed we cannot, attempt to match the technical expertise of the variety of sports specialists, or the enthusiast's knowledge of the rule and lore of sports. Nor is it necessary to do so for our purposes. We wish to probe issues concerned with the way power is structured that lie at the intersection of political theory and the sociology of culture. In particular, we are concerned with the relation between sports and working-class culture, and the extent to which sport has played a role in accommodating the British working class to the social order.

For the majority of people, even the majority of social scientists, common sense denies the possibility of a relation between sport and power; the issue rarely, if ever, reaches the agenda in a serious form, let alone is pursued by systematic investigation; for common sense decrees that the character of sport is obvious enough. How could such a benign pursuit be of any consequence at all for the ways in which power is wielded? Even to propose such an investigation seems to impugn the integrity of sport and of its prac-titioners and administrators, and to look for a conspiracy at work within an institution embodying some of the finest values and standards and the source of much innocent enjoyment. Of course, given the increasing occurrence, over the last few years, of boycotts of major sporting events and bans prohibiting teams or individuals from participating in them, almost everyone nowadays is aware that governments and pressure groups meddle in sport, and that on occasion sports are thus pulled into politics. On such occasions common sense strides in to declare 'sport really has nothing to do with politics', that any such connection is purely fortuitous, indeed unnatural and highly undesirable.

We are going to argue that common sense is mistaken, indeed that such a perspective on sport, plays an important part, albeit unintentionally, in reproducing the sport–power relation. Unfortunately, social science and political theory have also accomplished relatively little in elucidating the relationship. The prevalent view in the sociology of sport for example, is that, broadly speaking, sport performs a positive function. It provides meaningful activity for individuals by allowing them to express themselves and to acquire stable personal identities, thereby integrating them into the structure of society and it stabilizes the social order by reinforcing common norms and values. The fact that certain satisfactions are derived from sports, which are not readily derived from activities central to people's lives, such as work, is seen as compensating them for such unavoidable disappoint-ments and constraints and for the general pressures which modern life exerts.[1]

On the other hand, when more critical commentators have noted the sport-power relation, it has usually been in the context of an elitist polemic against modern sports, which dismisses their popularity and the prevailing enthusi-asm for them as a pathological obsession, a symptom of cultural decline and of the degradation of the masses.[2] The 'bread and circuses' model of social control springs readily to the lips of such critics. In some cases something similar to this basically conservative *kulturkritik* is rather crudely grafted onto a Marxist framework to produce an account of sports in which they are seen as ineluctably functioning to reproduce the types of labour power required by capital, and to indoctrinate the masses with the dominant ideology of capitalist society.[3]

Now, while sports are undoubtedly satisfying, they can promote social integration, and they may be used to control people, that is to say, both their harmonizing and their controlling and exploitive aspects need to be taken into account, when they are taken separately, and when they are put in the context of the kinds of arguments that usually support these propositions, sport is depicted in a one-sided, fundamentally misconceived way. Sporting activity, we contend, can never be adequately explained purely as an instrument of social harmony, or as a means of self-expression, or as a vehicle for satisfying individual needs; for this ignores the divisions and conflicts, and the inequalities of power in societies, which if we care to look more closely, register themselves in sports. Nor can their social role be explained simply as a means whereby the masses are manipulated into conformity with the social order, capitalist or otherwise, for to do so is to regard people as passive dupes, and it ignores their capacity to resist control and to stamp sports with their own culture. Unless we have adequate concepts with which to understand the character of sport, the social and historical context of sporting activity, and the power network which impinges on sports, it is not possible to understand the sport–power relation.[4] We are going to argue then, that sport, in specific conditions, is an important, if highly neglected constituent of power structures, and that the reproduction of the sport–power relation is systematically concealed in the routine operation of that relation.

Sport, Power and Culture

When we use the term power, we are referring not to an entity, the mere possession of which enables an individual or collective agent to dominate another, but to a relationship between agents, the outcome of which is determined by agents' access to relevant resources and their use of appropriate strategies in specific conditions of struggle with other agents.[5] Power is thus conceived here not as the exclusive possession of any single agent (the capitalist class, the political elite, men, etc.); nor is it situated in, or generated at, any single location or level of the social formation (the economy, patriarchy, or whatever).[6] We reject, in particular, the common-sense notion that the exercise of power is to be equated with political activity as it is formally constituted, that is, the activity of government, political parties and matters with which the state concerns itself, since in our view the power network extends well beyond this sphere into the interstices of civil society. We are going to argue that the sport–power relation is constructed on the terrain of both civil society and the state. The latter is distinguished from civil society by the fact that it successfully claims the monopoly of legitimate force, it co-ordinates the social formation by providing a forum for the expression and representation of interests, and it provides a set of procedures for settling conflicts between them and for executing collective decisions. Civil society, in contrast, refers to the dense network of voluntary associations and institutions, and the informal social relations which regulate every day life – economic, political and cultural – which, although they are subject to the law and, therefore, fall within the jurisdiction of the modern state, exist autonomously, in the sense that they are neither possessed nor managed by the latter. Our over-arching theme will be how modern organized sports, as we know them, emerged simultaneously, and subsequently developed with, the expansion and elaboration of civil society in the nineteenth and twentieth centuries; and how in the twentieth century the state intervenes progressively in sport, concomitantly with its increasing propensity to intervene in civil society as a whole.

Power in societies like ours is diffused and circulates throughout the social body. It is precisely this 'capillary' quality that has enabled power to be expanded so effectively in the modern age, to be applied routinely at appropriate points in the social order, and to be reorganized, refurbished and elaborated periodically. Although power is inherent in the structure of social relations, it is not identical to this structure. If it were so, there would be no need to employ a separate concept of power, since in that case every social relation would, by definition, partake of its exercise; whereas the question of how, why, and by whom power is exercised, and its relation to sport, is to us an empirical question.[7] What is true, of course, is that its exercise requires resources, access to which is usually unequal. However, this can not be the sole determinant in a power relation, except in the limiting case, otherwise agents with the greatest command over scarce resources would always come out on top in history. The other vital ingredient is how available resources are deployed, that is, power relations are also determined by the kind of objectives agents pursue and by the strategies they employ to achieve them. The latter are worked out and developed through discursive practices in response to the experience of struggle. That is to say, outcomes depend on the ability of agents to develop an appropriate language, to institutionalize reflection on their situation and to generate knowledge which allows them to act effectively in response to other agents' actions. Power and knowledge are thus two sides of the same coin: just as knowledge generates power, power enables the process of knowledge-creation to be institutionalized, and knowledge to be applied, developed and reproduced routinely. Power networks are actually constituted through a whole variety of systematically connected, that is, 'articulated' elements, through which effects are produced on 'power subjects' (those over whom power is exercised). In general terms they encompass, of course, economic, political, and cultural institutions, but when we look in detail we find they consist of all kinds of disparate elements: discourses, architectural forms, the arrangement of space, time budgeting, regulative decisions, laws, administrative measures, scientific statements, and philosophical, moral and philanthropic propositions. What we are interested in is not only the unequal structure of access to resources that advantages dominant groups in their attempts to appropriate sports and programme them for their purposes, but also the differential capacity of dominant and subordinate groups to create appropriate discourses and develop appropriate strategies in relation to the uses of free time and the significance they accord to sporting activity.

Power relations take different forms: the compliance of subordinate groups may be obtained through the use of physical violence, or in the knowledge that is likely to be used against them; or by other types of coercion, such as economic sanctions or the threat of these; through the assertion of authority, or the prestige enjoyed by agents; and through agents' persuasive powers; or through some combination of all these means. Power may be exercised with or without the resistance of power subjects, and with or without their knowledge. Also, it can be exercised effectively simply by an agent deciding to withhold action rather than by taking positive measures to coerce, command, or persuade others. Throughout this study we will be attempting to specify the exact conditions in which each of these forms characterizes sport–power relations.

Power relations are rarely total in their scope, or totally one way in their effects, for agents can never perfectly predict and control the whole environment of their operations, and least of all the actions of other agents and or the responses of power subjects. If ever there was an 'iron law' in human affairs it would seem to be that the exercise of power over people engenders opposition and resistance. So, programmes designed to have specific effects usually succeed only partially, fail often, and have quite unanticipated consequences. In this sense power relations are permanently poised on the brink of failure and they therefore require perpetual attention, adjustment and development, even in 'normal times'; and they tend to undergo strategic elaboration or radical reconstruction when crises occur in the established order. This means that power relations are by no means necessarily structured as a zero-sum game, that is, so that 'winners' gain exclusively at the cost of 'losers'. Power relations, especially in modern democracies, can be expansive, so that all sides, dominant and subordinate groups, gain something in the course of struggle and out of the process of accommodation that tends to take place between them. This is not to say that perceived benefits are distributed equally – it is to emphasize that just as agents rarely obtain their objectives totally, neither do they necessarily come out empty-handed. When considering subordinate groups' involvement in sports, one of our major themes will be the ways in which they manage to evade and subvert controls, the respects in which the sport–power relation enables them to resist pressure from dominant groups and to make tangible gains for themselves, as well as the ways in which it reproduces their subordination.

We will be making this point with particular reference to the question of how class relations enter the picture, in order to assess the role of sport as a factor in the composition and recomposition of class relations in Britain. By class relations we mean an unequal type of social relation tending to structure relations between major segments of the population, on the basis of their respective members' common experiences and perceptions of economic, political and cultural processes. Classes are composed, constantly reproduced, and, at key points, recomposed or reconstituted through economic, political, cultural and ideological struggle.[8] Since class is a process, classes are rarely, if ever, completely unified, homogeneous entities. We are interested in the way these internal divisions, and the differential involvement in sports that is associated with them, interrelate. We will argue that, in fact, such divisions within classes constitute one of the most important aspects of the manner in which sports make an input to the power network.

One of the most frequent mistakes made in the analysis of class formation and reproduction is to treat classes as preconstituted 'historical subjects', or as things-in-themselves, rather than as the achieved effects of a continuous process, consisting of the interaction of many elements, both of a class and a non-class nature. Accordingly, we treat class and non-class divisions in relation to sport and power, not by reducing the latter to class, or by opposing this or that factor to class as more or less important, but instead as affecting each other mutually, and as undergoing the process of construction together. Thus we argue that class and gender divisions are constructed together by examining how sport plays a part in the construction of both simultaneously. The composition and general character of the British working class has been, traditionally, affected powerfully by gender divisions which, as is generally acknowledged, are reproduced by the structure of the working-class family. We contend, in addition, that both gender divisions within this class and the character of working-class culture in wider terms are significantly determined by the pattern of working-class men's leisure, and that sports, occupying as they do such a prominent place therein, help to reproduce both the class and gender division within the class.

In relation to class power and sport our central thesis is that sport was significantly implicated in the process whereby the growing economic and political power of the bourgeoisie in nineteenth-century Britain was eventually transformed into that class's hegemony in the later part of the century. By hegemony we mean the achievement by a class, or by a class fraction or alliance, of leadership over the rest of society, in accordance with its perceived interests. It is a power relation in which the balance between the use of force and coercion on the one hand, and voluntary compliance with the exercise of power on the other, is shifted so that power relations function largely in terms of the latter mode.[9] Power resides more in the ability of the hegemonic group to win consent to, and support for, its leadership, and on its ability to pre-empt and disorganize opposition, so that the major forces in society are unified behind the hegemonic group and forceful, coercive measures against opposition to the pattern of hegemony acquire legitimacy as well. Hegemony is achieved through a continuous process of work: potential resistance is anticipated, organized opposition is overcome and disarmed by broadening and deepening the base of support. Thus alliances with subaltern and subordinate groups are brought off, concessions to and compromises with potential as well as actual opponents are made. This type of relation, then, is characterized above all by mutual accommodation between opposed groups which, nevertheless, simultaneously secures the hegemony of one of them. We will argue that bourgeois hegemony and its subsequent elaboration in the twentieth century, notably that following the Second World War, was achieved on the basis of the recomposition of the working class, accompanied by a pattern of accommodation in which certain forms of involvement in sport play a significant part. In making this suggestion our major thematic concern will be that in this process the working class and other subordinate social categories (blacks, youth) are *won over* to sports rather than forced into, or manipulated into, involvement in them.

We have identified several 'turning-points' at which the power network has been strategically elaborated in response to perceived threats to the social order, from the point of view of dominant groups.[10] The concept of a 'turning-point' has been chosen to indicate a moment in history when its movement takes a significant shift in direction: when changes in power relations quicken, the power network undergoes reconstruction and elaboration; and a new pattern crystallizes, to be followed by a period of relative stability, during which the changes work themselves out more fully. Thus the successive periods we have identified are marked by continuities and discontinuities with the preceding pattern, by forces propelling change and by countervailing tendencies, by resistance to change and by struggle, and by acquiescence and accommodation on the part of those affected. We will be considering four turning-points and the periods they inaugurate: around the turn of the nineteenth century, the mid-nineteenth century, the mid-1880s and the 1950s. Change is continuous, of course, but it reaches a critical state at such conjunctures. If the onset of each phase is compared with the end of the period, we argue that a transformation can be observed to have taken place in the structure and meaning of sport and its relation to the power network. Our main theme here is that the outcomes at each stage are not planned or foreseen: they are the result of the complex interplay of forces.

Our analysis of the sport–power relation is very firmly premised on the twin notions that sport is, above all, best categorized as a cultural formation, and that cultural elements constitute absolutely fundamental components of power networks. The fact that, in contrast, sports are conventionally subsumed under the rubric of leisure activity, and that the latter is represented as the sphere, above all, in which individuals enjoy the exercise of free choice and personal expression, we see more as an ideological notion than the insight into the nature of leisure in capitalist society that it purports to be. It is surely not so much a question of the presence or absence of freedom and constraint that defines and characterizes leisure, but the specific nature of the freedoms and constraints that are manifested therein, when compared with other sectors of social life. When we refer to 'leisure' it is, therefore, in a descriptive rather than an analytical sense.

The fundamental importance of culture can be appreciated if we bear in mind that social relations, as such, of whatever kind, are culturally constituted, in the sense that they embody signifying practices, or rules of signification, through which social agents generate ways of giving meaning to their experience. To put it another way: there would be no experience without culture. Yet for our purposes we need a more substantive idea of what constitutes cultural relations, and hence cultural power, in contradistinction to the other main types of relations and the power that they generate. Each of these types of relations have their own components and dynamics, which means they cannot be explained simply in terms of the way other sets of relations function. Thus economic relations structure the production, distribution and consumption of goods and services; political relations mobilize interests and structure conflict and accommodation between them. However, the cultural realm covers a somewhat vaguer area, and it is consequently more difficult to categorize.[11]

Certainly, it is not to be confused with ideology. Ideology, whose specific function is to misrepresent social relations and so to legitimize the established power structure, is reproduced at the economic and political levels as well as at the cultural level.[12] Consequently, the position we take on sport as ideology is that it is neither an ideological institution, in the sense that some institutions, such as political parties, journals and churches are, by providing over-arching structures of support and belief for the status quo, nor is it completely innocent ideologically. Like any other social entity, it may take on an ideological function in specific conditions. We will thus be concerned with identifying those conditions and respects in which sports do, indeed, aid in the reproduction of power relations by misrepresenting the nature of major inequalities in Britain. We will focus, in particular, on the way images of class, gender and race relations and images of the nation are projected in certain aspects of sporting activity.

When we refer to culture in the substantive sense, then, we mean first those activities, institutions and processes that are more implicated in the systematic production and reproduction of systems of meaning and/or those not concerned mainly or immediately with economic or political processes, but which instead encompass other kinds of vital activities. We are referring here to major institutions, such as religion, education, science, the arts, the media of communication, the family, leisure and recreation, as well as sports – and, in fact, to much of the routine practice of everyday life. Secondly, we find it useful to employ the ethnographer's substantive sense of culture as a 'whole way of life' of a particular group of people. Culture here refers to the way different threads of similarly placed individuals' lives – work, leisure, family, religion, community, etc. are woven into a fabric or tradition, consisting of customs, ways of seeing, beliefs, attitudes, values, standards, styles, ritual practices, etc., giving them a definite character and identity. It is thus we speak here of working-class culture, men's and women's culture, black culture, bourgeois culture and youth culture. Cultures in this sense are profound sources of power, reproducing social divisions here, challenging and rebelling against them there, while in many ways accommodating subordinate groups to the social order. We will be at pains to develop the theme throughout this study that the function and significance of sports varies with the type of culture in question, and even does so within cultures. We will be arguing that it is precisely because sport plays different roles in relation to different cultures that it is able to reproduce power relations.

We contend that, in addition, the linkages between sport and power cannot be elucidated without reference to two other forms of culture – popular culture and consumer culture. As the term implies, popular culture engages 'the people', and although, therefore, it is not the product or possession of any one specific group, popular culture does overlap to a perplexing degree with working-class culture and the culture of subordinate groups as a whole. While expressing in its content and idiom the experience of those whom it engages, like its political counterpart 'populism', it does so ambivalently, facing simultaneously in a radical and in a conservative direction – for popular culture as we know expresses a certain critical penetration of the power structure, while also manifesting a complicity in it. The long historical association between sports and popular culture, culminating in sport becoming a major component of the national popular culture is, we argue, highly significant for the character of sport.[13] Accordingly, one of our major themes will be the ambivalent relation between sport and power, exemplified best perhaps, in that mixture of respectable family entertainment, violence, rebellion and chauvinism that characterizes modern-day professional football.

Consumer culture, by which we mean the way of life associated with and reproduced through the operations of consumer capitalism, clearly in many ways also overlaps with working-class and popular culture, to the extent that many aspects of the latter, notably sports, seem to have been in effect appropriated by consumer culture.[14] We will be exploring the significance of the increasing tendency of sport to become one more commodity, and attempting to specify the extent to which sporting activity, as an aspect of working-class and of popular culture, remains autonomous. In particular we are rather sceptical of the notion that sport has been absorbed into a manipulated form of culture supposedly exercising a uniformly conservative influence over 'the masses'; and we will be attempting to pinpoint ways in which, as far as commodified sport is concerned, it also exhibits an ambivalent tendency to, on the one hand, accommodate subordinate groups, and on the other hand, to stimulate resistance and rebellion in certain ways.

The Autonomy of Sport

The extent to which a given cultural formation is enabled to feed the power network also depends crucially, on its own particular character, that is on those autonomous features which distinguish it from others as a specific type of cultural formation. The realm of sport encompasses a bewildering diversity of radically different kinds of activity, which defies a watertight definition – from the local hunt, and pub darts match, village cricket, intercollegiate rowing and little-league football, to professionalized mass entertainments like the Football League, the Wimbledon Tennis Championships, heavyweight boxing and horse-racing. Some of this activity plainly has little if any connection with power. Despite the complexity, in our view sufficient distinguishing characteristics can be identified which enable us to analyse how, in specific conditions, the sport–power relation may be constituted.

First, sports to one or other degree embody an irreducible element of play. Play is a type of activity having no extrinsic purpose or end, and as such it is a form of activity which enjoys a universal appeal.[15] Sports play is not always unalloyed by other motives or considerations – financial gain, prestige, etc. – and in specific instances (politicized and professional sport for example) play may be by no means the most important element.

But the ludic impulse is, nevertheless, always present to some degree at least, existing in tension with disciplined, organized aspects of sporting activity. Secondly, sports play tends to be highly formalized: in many cases it is governed by very elaborate codes or statutes. Sports play in this sense is far from being spontaneous: it is by convention rule-oriented, and to have no rules would be a contradiction in terms. Whether the rules are, in fact, being followed, is therefore an ever-present issue in the conduct of sports, and in this sense we could say that not only are sports rule-oriented – they can be rule-obsessed. Rule-structured play, like play in general, 'suspends reality', but in this case through the acceptance of formal codes ordering the use of space, time and general behaviour. In choosing to structure their activity thus, both participants and onlookers are indulging in a form of 'play-acting', and in this respect the activity can be said to be 'unserious' or set aside from normal life. Play-acting is also involved in sporting activity when 'display' before an audience is one of the objectives. In addition, many sports were associated historically with the great festivals and to varying extents are still conducted in a spirit of festivity, a spirit which, by 'turning the world upside down', suspends while simultaneously challenging reality.[16]

Thirdly, sports involve some element of contest between participants. The rules which structure sporting contests, however, unlike those that structure competition and conflict in the real world, deliberately set out to equalize conditions of participation, that is, they are intended to be neutral, so that no one party to the contest has an advantage over the other(s). Since a contest within neutral rules makes the outcome inherently uncertain and in principle unpredictable, the very point of the activity is negated when either the rules are biased in favour of one or other party, or when the contestants are matched unevenly, for then the outcome does indeed become predictable. The uncertainty of the contest's outcome and the attendant tension it creates lends a unique excitement to sports, compared with other activities involving play, and it is probably one of the main reasons why sports become so often the subject of intense interest and emotion. Paradoxically, the deep commitment which sports often arouse also makes them deadly serious affairs as well as unserious ones.

Three other attributes of sporting activity which have received much less attention are crucial in any consideration of the sport–power relation. The play-acting, contest, and uncertainty elements ensure that sports are an intrinsically dramatic means of expression, and an audience in addition transforms them into a form of theatre.[17] We argue that sports fall within the province of 'the popular', and in so far as they take on the attribute of a dramatic performance they can be said to constitute a form of popular theatre, arguably the most popular contemporary form of theatre. Also, sports often seem to involve their participants, the audience and commentators, in much the same way as a theatrical performance: participants are enabled to put on a show and in a way, play a part; onlookers can identify with contestants; and both players and audience can project their thoughts and feelings. Sports can thus constitute regular public occasions for discourse on some of the basic themes of social life – success and failure, good and bad behaviour, ambition and achievement, discipline and effort and so on.

Secondly, strongly associated with the dramatic element, sporting activity is frequently characterized by ritual practices. Ritual activity is rule-governed behaviour of a symbolic character which draws the attention of its participants to objects of thought and feeling which are held to be of special significance. These may be multiple and occur at different levels of meaning. Ritual symbols 'condense many referents uniting them in a single cognitive and affective field. Each has a "fan" or spectrum of referents which tend to be interlinked by what is usually a simple mode of association, its very simplicity enabling it to interconnect a wide variety of signification'.[18] Ritual symbols may very powerfully denote, and connote as well, what is important to participants. Plainly, the ritual of official state occasions and that surrounding the major state institutions in Britain – the Coronation, the State Opening of Parliament, Remembrance Sunday, the ceremonial of the law courts, and so on – constitutes a powerful collective representation of the social and political order, focusing people's attention on the national symbols in a manner designed to invoke their loyalty, that is, it helps to define as authoritative certain preferred ways of seeing power and society. But we contend that much activity of a ritualized nature is effective in performing the same function precisely because it is not normally defined as 'political', and in our view, in specific conditions, many aspects of sports come into the category of 'political ritual'.[19]

Sports are extremely rich in symbolization and undoubtedly possess the capacity to represent social relationships in a particularly striking, preferred way. Notably, this is accomplished through the elaborate pageantry and ceremonial, even at the local level, with which organized sports surround themselves – the parades, opening and closing ceremonies, victory ceremonies, the special accoutrement worn by contestants and officials embellished well beyond technical necessity, the sacred connotations of sports settings, etc. We argue that not only the great national sports events, like the Football Association Cup Final, take on the character of a political ritual, when the Queen, the Prime Minister and other figures of state are in prominent attendance, the national anthem is sung, military bands march and play, 'Abide with Me' is sung and so on, but also that, for example, school sport and local community sport can function to symbolize or encode preferred views of the social order and thus legitimize power relations.

This should become clearer when we consider a further absolutely central characteristic of sports. Although the degree of physical input varies from sport to sport, the primary focus of attention in sport as a whole is the body and its attributes – its strength, skill, endurance, speed, grace, style, shape and general appearance are tested and/or put on display. This need not imply that the mind is not involved: judgement, motivation and aesthetic awareness are integral to physical performance; but it is the body that constitutes the most striking symbol as well as the material core of sporting activity. The primacy accorded to the mind in Western civilization has ensured that social analysis has been largely confined to the mechanisms for the transmission of values, norms, attitudes, emotions, ideologies, or whatever; and consequently the body has been almost entirely eliminated from social-science discourse.[20] Yet control over the appearance, treatment and functioning of the body is an important aspect of social order in all societies, and the elaboration and refinement of such forms of control has been critical in the emergence and development of modern societies.[21] Bodily appearance, posture, movement, gesture, facial expression, eye contact, adornment, smell – these elements constitute a message system or language structuring social action.[22] The body is, then, an emblem of society, and the ritual practices governing its usage symbolize and uphold fundamental social relationships and bind individuals to the social order.[23] Changes in body ritual and general body usage indicate fundamental changes in social relationships and interference with them has serious implications for social and cultural reproduction. The more the social situation exerts pressure on individuals the more the social demand for conformity tends to be expressed by demands for physical control. The greater the conceptual distancing between social and physical bodies, the more threatening is the loss of control over the body and body processes to the social order. Just as the child in becoming a native speaker learns the requirements of society, so the child learning the body code also learns the social requirements. In so far as body appearance and usage are integral to the conduct of sports, these considerations point to the ways in which sports as ritual practices may function to symbolize and uphold the social order and thus feed the power network.

We argue not only that the body symbolizes power relations, but furthermore, that power is literally incorporated or invested in the body, most obviously perhaps through such practices as gymnastic exercises, musclebuilding, nudism, practices glorifying the body beautiful, and insistent, meticulous work on the bodies of children, hospital patients, keep-fit enthusiasts and sports participants. Such work reproduces the social body: it exemplifies the materiality of power and culture in the sense that social relations are the outcome of material operations on the bodies of individuals carried out with the aid of a vast economy and technology of control. The body is not the object of consensus – it is the site of social struggles, indeed, we can say there is a battle for control of the body.[24] In holding that sports constitute one of the main arenas where that struggle ensues, we take the view that the restrictive, relatively ponderous forms of control perceived as a prerequisite for the efficient functioning of industrial capitalism in the nineteenth and earlier twentieth century are no longer needed, and that sports are increasingly implicated in a new, currently emergent form of control.[25] Under the impact of consumer culture especially, the restrictive deployment of sexuality for example, is attenuated and sexuality is now deployed more through techniques of eroticization. Instead of repression we have control by stimulation. The body is clearly an object of crucial importance in consumer culture and its supply industries; and sports, together with fashion, eating and drinking outside the home, cooking, dieting, keep-fit therapy, other physically active leisure, advertising imagery, and a battery of aids to sexual attractiveness, are deployed in a constantly elaborating programme whose objective is the production of the new 'normalized' individual.

To thematize sport as an object of struggle, control and resistance, that is as an arena for the play of power relations, is of course ultimately to thematize its achievements with respect to human freedom and implicitly to raise the question of the transformational potential of sport in this regard. Societies like Britain and others to which organized sport spread from these shores, would be, in a genuine sense, unquestionably different places in its absence.[26] Whether they would be better places without sports depends on one's value standpoint. We do not attempt to address this important, vexacious question although plainly our study is value-oriented in its choice of problem to investigate. We consider the achievements of sport instead, with specific reference to the effects on the power position of subordinate groups and, in particular, its effect on the trajectory of the British working class. Broadly speaking, we consider sports somewhat of a mixed blessing from this point of view. Logically, we do consider it to be part of the analyst's task to identify those points at which involvement in sport contains a potential for going beyond the present power balance. In our conclusion we tentatively suggest a number of ways sport–power relations may generate a potential for evening-up somewhat the present unequal power balance in Britain. Whether one wishes to recommend them as points to which pressure should be applied, and develop strategies for doing so, is a matter of one's political commitment. For what it is worth, it seems to us that Britain would be a better place if such a change were to come about.

Given the underdeveloped state of knowledge concerning this field, in particular the absence of anything like adequate data covering a full range of sports giving details of the relationship between participation and social-group membership; and given the limitations on what can be accomplished within the compass of a single investigation, it would be neither appropriate nor possible to examine the entire spectrum of sports and all their facets. In selecting our material from the world of sport we have cast the net as widely as possible in the direction of those popular sports with features that are to a greater or lesser extent relevant to our themes. Thus cricket, football, some athletic events, and horse-racing crop up continually. Other sports, such as golf, boxing, hunting, motor sport, and swimming are featured less prominently; and some minority sports or sporting activities with a more tenuous connection with our themes are scarcely mentioned. Into the latter category come games like hockey; water sports; outdoor pursuits like rock-climbing; some indoor sports like ice skating, badminton and squash; and new sports like hang-gliding. A wide coverage to include these, and also some of the popular sports we have not had space to deal with, like professional wrestling, angling, weight-lifting and table tennis, (and lately, skiing), would, no doubt, make a more complete, interesting picture from some points of view. But we have no reason at the moment to think that including them would do anything other than add details which would not fundamentally affect the analysis. In this sense, although inevitably our selection is somewhat arbitrary, on balance we would argue it produces better results than concentrating on a more limited number of sports, which necessarily could not represent the vast heterogeneity of the domain, or attempting to include all sporting activity and thus risk a super- ficial coverage of the subject matter. We have adopted instead the strategy of focusing on those aspects of sport in Britain which engage large numbers of people, and examine how they intersect with other major institutions through which power is mediated and exerecised. Thus in examining the relation between the economy and sports we focus progressively on consumer culture. In examining the place of sport in working-class culture we focus on the working-class community, media sport and the state schools. In examining state intervention and politicization we focus on the schools, the Sports Council and government policy. How the six autonomous elements of sport that we have adduced figure in the sport–power relation is woven into the analysis throughout.

2

The Repression and Reform of Popular Sporting Forms

Sport and Popular Culture
Prior to the Industrial Revolution

The Puritan-inspired attempt to reform popular culture with the objective of encouraging instead a way of life strictly in keeping with the tenets of the Protestant ethic, receded with the Restoration. Attacks on such popular boisterous, disorderly sporting pastimes as football and May games and on cruel sports such as bear-baiting and cock-fighting abated accordingly.[1] Some of the Puritan social attitudes were taken over by the Church of England, but it was far too thoroughly integrated with the ruling class to exert much authority over the mass of the population.[2] The system of control, therefore, lacked the authority which had previously been conferred on it by the churches' command over the leisure of subordinate groups.[3] True, efforts to reform manners in the Puritan tradition continued but they were generally not effective.

Secondly, as the seventeenth gave way to the eighteenth century, economic processes associated with the development of capitalism were progressively eroding the basis of paternalistic control over labour: non-monetary usages or perquisites were steadily translated into money payments; the sector of the economy which was independent of a subject relationship with the nobility and gentry was enlarged with the extension of trade and industry; and there continued to exist petty forms of land tenure which together with the varied sorts of by-employment available was an additional source of independence from gentry clientage.[4] Furthermore, for the greater part of the eighteenth century the mode of production had yet to develop to the point where there was a sharp distinction between work and leisure. Work was still governed, to a large extent, by the rhythms of nature – time of day, the weather, the seasons – and in addition was regulated by the guilds. Where, as in many cases, the power of the guilds had been eroded, it was regulated through the journeyman's capacity to exploit his market position; and in the case of other categories of labour it was mediated also by local custom and tradition.[5]

Consequently, from the Restoration to the onset of the Industrial Revolution popular culture bloomed. Not only had the old festivals and the activities surrounding them largely survived, they were elaborated and extended through an accelerated process of commercialization, in particular, through the activities of publicans, hucksters and entertainers. The gap that had been opened up by the Puritan recession which followed the Restoration was filled by 'a creative culture-forming process from below: folk songs, trade clubs...corn dollies...wakes...rushbearings and rituals...the exuberant revival of popular sports...These occasions were, in an important sense, what men and women lived for.'[6] There was Shrovetide football, in which rival armies of participants battled it out through field, street, even in rivers and under bridges; there were foot-races and pedestrian contests; there was bull-running through the streets of certain towns.[7] Some sports became festive occasions in their own right from the early eighteenth century, and experienced considerable commercial development and a growth in professionalization, in town and country alike.[8] Gambling, and the opportunities entrepreneurs found to make money by obtaining franchises to operate at sports gatherings, was the major fulcrum of such development. Professional cricketers, who were engaged to work on the gentry's estates, were playing in teams run by aristocratic gamblers, in well-publicized matches watched by thousands of people. The folk game had been transformed by the gentry after 1660, and under their patronage it developed subsequently. The first written rules were adopted as early as 1727, the game spread beyond the south-east of England, and by the mid-century one centre was accepted as authoritative, the Marylebone Cricket Club (MCC).[9] Never so genteel as cricket, horse-racing – apart from aristocratic Newmarket – was usually associated with local holidays and fairs, where meetings attracted travelling shows, gaming booths, beer tents, cock-fights, boxing and wrestling and open-air dancing. Gambling was again the motor of development in the direction of increasing organization and specialization: professional jockeys emerged in the early eighteenth century, rules were formulated, a racing calendar established, and by 1750 there was an authority which acted as the supreme arbiter, the Jockey Club at Newmarket, once again under aristocratic control.[10] Similarly, prize-fighting developed under the aegis of the aristocracy with its penchant for gambling on sports, and it also attracted a large following.[11] With the commercialization and professionalization of such sports the sports celebrity emerged as a new type of social figure: jockeys and prize-fighters, for example, became household names, and even in some cases entered the higher reaches of society.

The key to the ruling class's permissive connivance in, and patronage of, this robust, often turbulent and pagan popular culture, lies in the relations between Whig oligarchy, Tory gentry and subordinate groups. Thompson has argued persuasively that the Whig oligarchy's paternalistic attitude to expressions of popular culture was a key feature of the pattern of control, which, he maintains, rested primarily on a 'cultural hegemony' and only secondarily in an expression of economic and political power.[12] A plebs is not a class with a consciousness and organization capable of cohesive political action and revolt. It could nevertheless, manifest its presence in the shape of the mob, and therefore it had to be taken seriously, that is, it had to be accommodated by the ruling class. Although it is simply untrue that the ruling class in the eighteenth century in Britain was without a standing army at its disposal, it was inadequate for purposes of internal control because it was incapable of using force swiftly enough. The price the ruling class paid for a limited monarchy and a weak state was the licence of the crowd. There was, as Thompson puts it, a reciprocity of relations between rulers and ruled, which was more active than the relations suggested by the formula 'paternalism and deference'. In a sense they needed each other, they watched each other's performance, and moderated each other's behaviour. It would have been possible to transform popular culture fundamentally and discipline the crowd if there had been a unified, coherent ruling class, content to divide the spoils of power amicably among its members. Such cohesion did not exist before 1790: there were tensions which went very deep. The Tory lesser gentry developed an active alliance with the crowd against the hated courtiers, great landed magnates and monied interests – the Whig oligarchy which monopolized political power. The oligarchy's control was more effective, Thompson suggests, by virtue of the fact that it was indirect: tenant farmers and various middlemen like the miller, for example, themselves economically and politically subordinate, tended to take the brunt of lower-class hostility to the system, when, for example, the poor organized as a mob and engaged in food riots.[13] Secondly, the oligarchy's low visibility in this respect was coupled with a high visibility in others where they met the 'lower sort' of people on their own terms; and sports provided many opportunities for them to do so. On such occasions a studied and hegemonic style was adopted by the oligarchy, a 'theatre of the great'. The appearances of the great were formidable affairs having 'much of the studied self-consciousness of public theatre...ceremonial sword...wig and powder, ornamental clothing and canes...rehearsed patrician gestures and hauteur of bearing and expression, all were designed to exhibit authority and exact deference...[as were] the pomp of the assizes and the theatrical style of the courts; segregated pews, late entries and early departures from church...'.[14] And also, we must add, gatherings involving popular sporting activity.

The success of the theatre of the great depended not upon day-to-day attention to responsibilities, but upon occasional dramatic intervention – the prizes given out by the great at a sporting contest, for example, were on a par in this respect with the gift of the roasted ox for a festival, liberal donations to charity, an application to the justices for mercy on behalf of the accused, a proclamation against forestallers and so on. Appearances at, and participation in, popular activities offered numerous opportunities for performances of this kind. The conduct of prize-fighting, horse-racing and cricket demonstrated a division of labour and of consumption between aristocrats and gentlemen, the rich and the powerful, on the one hand, and the 'lower orders' on the other. In horse-racing the horses were the property of the ruling class and although the riders were professionals, they were simply employees from the lower orders. Already there were separate enclosures at race meetings for the purpose of parading wealth and superior status.[15] In cricket the aristocratic element not only financed and led the teams, but monopolized the more prestigious playing roles on the field: they battled while their professional employees from the lower orders bowled, fielded and ran for them. In prize-fighting individuals drawn from the plebs battered each other, while aristocrats sponsored, gambled on and generally patronized these performances. The Tory squirearchy's involvement in sports, on the other hand, was less a studied intervention than a genuine expression of this group's way of life. Notoriously lacking in culture in the received sense, they retired to their country seats, self-consciously anti-Puritan, nostalgically promoting cakes and ale, sports and the bucolic virtues in general, against the perceived money-grubbing sordidness and effeteness of London society and the Court circles. Whether contrived or otherwise, by patronizing, identifying with, and sharing in the enjoyment of popular sports and pastimes, the oligarchy and the gentry cemented social bonds between themselves and the local populace; and their manner and style of participation symbolized and reproduced the social hierarchy.

The theatre of the great was not without its coercive side, and one can hardly find a better illustration than hunting, the sport which, above all, symbolized the landed oligarchy's economic, political and cultural supremacy. In so far as hunting inevitably involved members of the local community, in the economic activities it generated, or as participants in the festivities, it served to integrate the local community. On the other hand, since the game laws more or less gave exclusive rights to hunt increasingly to one class, whether on its own property or elsewhere, and since the great landed estates of the oligarchy were being increasingly enlarged through enclosures of wasteland, common land and smallholdings, not only was the ruling class all over the country increasingly infringing on local traditional rights, freedoms and pleasures, thereby offending local people, but also this encroachment directly threatened the livelihood of that section of the rural population that traditionally relied on taking game as an important contribution to its means of subsistence. The result was sporadic eruptions of violent conflict while organized poaching enjoyed a good deal of local support in challenging the law, offenders against which, who had not even injured or killed anyone, could be executed or transported for life.[16]

What distinguishes this period from the subsequent one in terms of the mode of control is that the ruling class was not threatened by anything like an organized class opposition on the national scale. Opposition was localized and fragmented, and outbreaks of disorder, although fairly frequent, were sporadic and uncoordinated. What the ruling class feared and had to cope with was, in the main, anarchy, loss of prestige and 'hegemony' at the local level. Controls tended to be particularistic and multilayered rather than diffuse, and the oligarchy, therefore, did not exercise a hegemony in the proper sense of the term. The careful attention paid to maintaining cultural supremacy and to minimizing the use of coercion remained firmly implanted in British political culture, but the strategy of permissive, paternalist connivance in various aspects of popular culture no longer received the support of dominant groups as a whole in the period which followed.

Repression and Reform

The period from the last decade of the eighteenth century to roughly the mid-nineteenth century was one of unprecedented change: the transition to industrial capitalism and the spread of the factory system, an associated expansion of trade and commerce, a rapid rate of urbanization, an explosion in population growth, the rise of the new class of industrial capitalists, the emergence of an organized, combative working-class movement and growing demands for political change.[17] The dominant classes felt threatened with social and political disorder, by Jacobinism in the early part of the period, and after 1832 by a more class-conscious, organized labour movement which Chartism represented. The whole period is marked by a relatively heavy reliance on repressive means of maintaining social order.[19] From the middle of the eighteenth century the dominant classes were beginning to withdraw from the established structure of relationships with subordinate groups, to attenuate cultural links and to regard the whole way of life of the latter with suspicion, if not active hostility. By the turn of the century and down to the mid-nineteenth century there was an active determination among sections of the dominant classes to change the way of life of the mass of the population, if necessary by repressive means.

It was from Evangelical clergymen, Nonconformist preachers, Sunday-school organizers, factory employers, modernizing land-owners, philanthropists, utilitarian-inclined ideologues and state officials, that the chief support came for the movement aimed at monitoring, controlling, reshaping, delegitimizing and where necessary forcefully suppressing popular cultural forms deemed as dysfunctional to social order. The objective of inculcating the lower orders with the bourgeois virtues – a consuming work ethic and its associated time discipline, frugality, sobriety and respectability, respect for constituted authority, self-reliance and the pursuit of individual self-interest – was not entirely new. What was novel was the propitious conjuncture which enabled social forces to be marshalled in a more cohesive and effective manner. An important feature of the movement's power base in church and chapel, local and national state, and in the economy, was the co-ordination of its different elements through interlocking membership of key institutions: factory employers were often prominent Methodist laymen, especially active in Sunday schools; the local clergyman could be the local land-owner and magistrate; and the factory- or land-owner could be the Member of Parliament (MP). What tended to mark it more as a movement for cultural supremacy was the formation of a series of closely associated campaigning organizations, whose specific object was to control the free-time activities of what were perceived as the threatening lower orders. Organizations like the Sabbatarian Lord's Day Observance Society (LDOS), the various temperance bodies, the Society for the Suppression of Vice, and notably, in relation to popular sports, the Royal Society for the Prevention of Cruelty to Animals (RSPCA), were able to generate a mass base of support for their activities.[19]

Popular sporting activities categorized as 'disreputable' formed one of the main targets of this movement. The most basic way in which popular sports and popular culture in general were circumscribed was through the rearrangement of physical space. This was brought about by a combination of factors: the last great wave of Enclosure Acts; the new urban ecology in which a rapidly increasing proportion of the population was confined; and the repressive way this environment was managed by the authorities. Attempts to use the existing space for physical recreation purposes tended to be interpreted by the authorities, and by the more respectable elements, as potentially disruptive of urban routine and law and order.

Sports and popular cultural forms were constrained, secondly, by the new economy of time.[20] The balance between free time and work time shifted drastically in favour of the latter. By 1834, for example, there were only eight statutory holidays remaining out of the numerous holidays enjoyed sixty to seventy years before.[21] The pressures and limits exerted by the economy on popular cultural expressions is demonstrated in the dramatic increase in the absolute number of hours worked per day or per week. The exact extent of the increase is disputed by social and economic historians, but there cannot be much doubt that for many people virtually the sole purpose of existence was to work. Also, the pace and rhythm of work changed significantly: it became far more intensive than previously, punctuality was insisted on, there were fewer breaks and much more continuous effort was demanded, so that the opportunity for recreational activities to be interspersed with work declined. Thus, not only was there less time for sporting activities, but the arduous hours of physical labour are likely to have reduced the capacity and inclination to engage in physically demanding pastimes. In contrast to the previous era, early industrial capitalism induced a much more rigid separation of work from free time, very much subordinating the latter to the former.

The reproduction of labour power and the general problem of labour discipline was obviously one reason employers, as such, played such a prominent part in the movement to exert moral influence and control over how workers spent their free time: 'To the fines, beatings, dismissals and monetary incentives of employers were added the Protestant Ethic and indoctrination in bourgeois values.'[22] But, employers included, it was more the diffuse fear of social disorder and of contagion which sprang from a perceived propensity to dissoluteness among the lower orders, that led the movement as a whole into attacking, and attempting to curtail, the opportunities provided by public gatherings for outbreaks of disorder and displays of undisciplined behaviour. So, not only was a campaign mounted to ban 'cruel' and 'disorderly' sports, by organizations like the RSPCA, but a campaign was also waged against a range of popular institutions and activities of which sporting activity was an organic part – festivals, fairs, Sunday enjoyments, pubs and beerhouses, the use of streets, byways and open spaces. The movement ceaselessly prosyletized for 'rational recreation' that would be 'improving', educational, respectable and more refined than the boisterous and dissolute pursuits of popular culture. The alternative model offered was a more privatized family-centred recreation and wholesome entertainment, catered for by respectable institutions under the supervision of dominant groups.[23]

The repressive manner in which the attempt to spread bourgeois mores concerning the use of free time, – that is, involving the use of physical force and coercion and the extent to which popular sporting activity figured in it – has been overlooked in much social history. Children and youths were literally rounded up by clergy and the locally appointed authorities and taken to Sunday school; and factory employers in many areas literally ordered their employees to attend.[24] Even near the end of the period, in 1842, boys at Aylesbury were being fined by the Beaconsfield Bench fifteen shillings, or six weeks in jail, for playing cricket on Sunday.[25]

Traditional festivals and the activities associated with them were a prime target. 'Saint Monday', celebrated at the ale house with bar games, pugilistic contests and animal fights, was legally prohibited in some places. Two Birmingham apprentices in 1836 were given a month's hard labour for keeping it.[26] Between 1788 and 1840 repeated attempts were made by Sabbatarians, the RSPCA, and their supporters to suppress festivals like the Stamford bull-running. The struggle over this particular festival, especially towards the end, developed into battles between a section of the local populace and troops and constables, until it was finally suppressed.[27] Similar struggles took place over attempts to suppress Shrovetide football: the Derby struggle went on from the later eighteenth century until it was suppressed with the aid of dragoons and special constables in 1846;[28] and the banning of Leicester football under the local Improvement Act of 1847 again provoked riots and was only quelled in 1848–9 with physical force.[29] Many local games and pastimes were similarly suppressed.[30] Wakes, pleasure fairs and hiring fairs, which provided a major setting for sports, incurred the implacable hostility of the reformers and were whittled down gradually in number. The great pleasure fair of St Bartholomew in East London, still going strong in 1834 after years of resistance, finally succumbed in 1855, legislated and regulated out of existence.[31] The campaign against cruel sports succeeded in getting sports like cock-fighting and cock-throwing legally banned in some places by the early 1800s; and bull-baiting, over which the RSPCA had been very active, was banned under the Cruelty to Animals Act of 1835.[32]

The new police forces which were implanted in the working-class communities from the 1830s onwards were to act as, in the words of Storch: 'domestic missionaries of the bourgeoisie', who embarked on an entirely novel and uncustomary surveillance of the entire range of popular leisure activities: drinking, brutal sports, foot-racing, fairs, feasts and other fêtes.'[33] In 1836 Leeds police were instructed to suppress cruelty to animals in sports and the council requested the mayor to direct the police to give information 'as shall lead to the conviction of all persons as shall continue to profane the Lord's Day and to pay particular attention to drinking places on Saturday nights, to strictly enforce proper closing time and to observe those who resort to the public house or use sports in the time of divine service.'[34] The Improvement Act of 1842 gave police the power to enter unlicensed theatres and arrest those within, to prosecute publicans who managed houses where cocks, dogs, or other animals were fought for sport.[35] Their appearance at sports gatherings, such as the Lancaster races holiday in 1840, was interpreted as an attack on traditional freedoms of assembly and provoked serious disturbances.[36] In the 'Huddersfield Crusade' of 1848, the infamous Superintendent Heaton 'made a strenuous effort not only to monitor and control but to smash the locales of working-class recreational life by direct intervention at every opportunity'.[37] Publicans were prosecuted for permitting Sunday drinking, gambling and illegal sports. He even attempted under an obscure ancient statute to prosecute three men for watching cricket on Sunday and not attending church when bidden. Numerous prize-fights were broken up in the area and there was a crack-down on holding sweeps on the St Leger horse-race.

The other side of the coin to repression was the attempt to persuade the lower orders to mend their ways through simple instruction, much prescription and heavy didacticism. Also, a modicum of the amenities that were needed was provided by employers, socio-religious organizations and philanthropists, in order to wean away working-class people from dissolute sports and drinking. Samuel Gregg provided a playground for games, music classes and regular tea-parties on his industrial estate. The Ashworth brothers at Bolton provided an annexe with a school, museum, music-hall and ballroom. Stanfield and Briggs near Huddersfield provided playground and gymnasium facilities together with a club-room and choir. Benjamin Heywood, the Manchester banker–philanthropist, in the 1830s opened his Lyceums to attract the working class, with sports as part of a regimen of social evenings and excursions; and after the Chartist agitation of 1842 they were used as an instrument of class reconciliation and community welfare.[38]

Novel as it was, the factory system was not the complete cultural rupture with the past that some imagine. Since industrial capitalists usually had strong roots in the dominant classes of the eighteenth century anyway, it would be surprising if they had not also inherited the cultural capital of their predecessors. In fact, it is precisely where the factory system was most advanced and well established that paternalist relations between employer and employee were strongest.[39] In the Lancashire cotton towns the factory dominated the local community and tended to engross the social life of factory workers, and to place them in a position of extreme dependence on the employer. Sporting activities and facilities were part of a range of services provided by employers, including schools, Sunday schools, treats and outings, through which they exercised a supervision over their workers' lives outside work. They were part of a system of local control in which employers were even powerful enough to discriminate against employees on religious and political grounds. The paternalism operated, then, at two levels: firms were privately owned and controlled by locally well-known, influential, high-status families, and secondly, contrary to received wisdom, the transition to industrial capitalism did not fundamentally alter the traditional working-class family structure. In fact, it was preserved and pressed into service in the factory, where the division of labour replicated and reproduced it; for the father exercised authority over wives, mothers and children in their work roles.

After 1830 few working-class people can have escaped some contact with the Sunday school and countless numbers attended before that date. By 1850 there were two million members and there was scarcely a child that had not been touched by them.[40] These institutions catered as well for large numbers of adults. They soon turned to amusement and recreation as a counter-attraction to those activities of which they disapproved and to categorizing sporting activity in terms of its respectability or otherwise. In Bolton in the 1820s bun and tea-parties were organized as a diversion from the race-meetings. The Easter Monday annual 'folly fair' in Blackburn was counteracted by a day of respectable sports in the country. Often Sunday schools combined with temperance associations in an attempt to dominate popular holiday festivities with demonstrations of strength, using marching bands, flags and decorations. In the long battle over the Newcastle races, processions with brass bands were thus put on followed by a 'treat'; in 1802 a Whit walk was organized against the Kersal Green races; Wigan Sunday School Union in 1844 put on a rail outing against the local races; against St Barnabus Fair Macclesfield church schools organized an excursion to Trentham Park, Staffordshire, where boys played 'the more noble game of cricket.'[41] By operating to provide an alternative world of recreation for the lower classes, in which sport figured prominently, the temperance movement, Harrison suggests, may have constituted the single most important agency of 'recreational improvement' at this time.[42] For the pub was probably the most important recreational institution for the lower classes and as such it was a hub of sporting activity.

The humanitarianism of bourgeois advocates of reform like the MPs Slaney and Ewart, state functionaries like Tremenheere, Chadwick and Kay Shuttleworth, and the journalist–historian Cooke-Taylor, had its ulterior, as well as its genuine motives. They were aware that repression and a few scraps-worth of amenities was insufficient, and that if it was not supplemented by something more substantial, in the longer run problems of social control would be encountered. Slaney thought that if relief were not forthcoming 'the working classes will fly to demagogues and dangerous causes...it is alike wise and benevolent to provide, in regulated amusement for the many, safety valves for their eager energies'.[43] The fear was Chartism. Chadwick, in 1842 in his evidence to the Commission on the Health of Towns, advocated improved recreation facilities, arguing that open spaces and sports were essential for diverting the lower orders from political disaffection. Cooke-Taylor reflected in the early 1840s: 'There must be safety-valves for the mind; that is there must be means for its pleasurable, profitable and healthful exertion. This means it is in our power to render safe and innocent: these means in too many instances have been rendered dangerous and guilty'.[44] Under Kay Shuttleworth's tutelage the state-aided schools seem to have paid rather more attention to custodial problems, such as whether the height of the walls around schools was sufficient to keep the children on the premises, than to providing playing space and encouraging sports.[45] But Cooke-Taylor warned: 'The lectures of the classroom will be utterly ineffective when they are counteracted by the practical lessons of the playground...moral education...is really acquired in hours of recreation.'[46]

There was agreement, among reformers at least, of the need to provide more recreational amenities in towns. The Select Committee on Drunkenness in 1834 had already included among its recommendations open spaces for healthy and athletic exercises, together with walks, gardens, libraries, museums and reading-rooms. Some reformers in addition were keen to establish a cultural supremacy by setting an example and establishing a presence in recreation which would 'engender a moral vigilance, a police of public opinion.'[47] Thus, the attitude to popular sports among such influential shapers of public opinion formed part of a reassessment of the social function of recreation in general, one which from the 1840s onwards was to view recreation provision increasingly in terms of its efficacy for social control. The movement for reform was also not without its working-class advocates and we will return to this point in a moment.

The Effects of Repression and Reform

It is difficult to be certain about the overall effects of the movement to reshape the sporting forms, for it is as easy to romanticize the degree to which working-class people resisted as it is to exaggerate their quiescence. Certainly it is a gross exaggeration to claim, as Hearn does, that the critically significant capacity to play among the working class was eliminated by the mid-nineteenth century.[48] Neither did participation in sports mean working-class people were 'embourgeoisified'. However, this is not to say that sport played no part in the pattern of working-class accommodation to the new social order. By the mid-century significant changes had occurred: some forms of popular sports had been curtailed, though they were hardly reshaped as yet into their modern form; work culture and especially the culture of the factory, did overshadow sporting activity more (the 'dull compulsion' of the capitalist mode of production, as Marx called it); sports were tending to become more orderly and organized. Working-class people were forced, as well as persuaded, to accommodate 'from above', but the process of accommodation was also eased 'from below' by certain features of the cultures in which working-class people were involved. We have to look more closely at the interrelations between work, religion, popular culture, working-class radicalism and dominant group strategies.

The movement to change the way of life of the lower orders and to control popular cultural forms like sports met certain obstacles which tended to limit its effectiveness. Firstly, in terms of the economic processes involved, the pattern of industrialization, the accompanying changes in the nature of the work, and the degree of urbanization developed unevenly over the country. The majority of the labour force, in fact, was not yet employed in factories and escaped subjection to factory discipline and its effects on non-work life. Furthermore, whether inside or outside the factory sector, workers managed to retain a significant degree of power and control over their labour: not only were employers often resisted successfully, but autonomy was frequently retained through the practices whereby employers delegated their authority to other agents, notably skilled workers and foremen, and subcontracted work tasks. In this way authority in industry was to an extent shared between employer and worker.[49] Nevertheless, the effects of the factory system rippled outwards, transmitting the character of the factory culture beyond the sector of factory employment. The factory put the small workshop under intense competitive pressure, to which it had to adapt or go under, thereby forcing it to change work patterns. Also, changes in the tempo and quality of industrial work as a whole were brought about, in the main, through capitalist control of credit, supply and distribution, in this period.[50] So, we could say that the dull compulsion of industrial labour, rather than factory labour, *per se*, is likely to have had some effect on the character of non-work life, on popular culture and on popular sports.

Having said this, it does nevertheless seem to be the case, as Joyce and others have argued, that economic styles and forms of coercion and control were slow to develop and were by no means necessarily the most important form of control. Indeed, much of nineteenth-century management itself, particularly in this period of early capitalism, was extra-economic, and control of time by work discipline was inseparable from wider social and moral reform. Work such as Joyce's tends to support our stress on the importance of the cultural dimension of control and the importance of compulsion by political means. In this period then, the attempt to reconstruct popular cultural forms and the institutions that nurtured and sustained them was part of a co-ordinated and sustained movement to exert control over the lives of members of subordinate groups, of a predominantly propagandist and repressive kind, that paved the way for economically based controls and that only became nationally extensive later.

The cultures under attack possessed certain strengths of their own which limited the impact of reform and repression. Empirically, of course, these 'counter cultures' overlapped considerably, so it is necessary to analyse the separate strands and the way they contributed, both to the resilience of working-class people's response and also to the ways they limited that response.

In terms of working-class religious culture, Methodism succeeded in appealing to working-class people because it was itself deeply rooted in popular culture and working-class communities. Membership of the more democratically organized Methodist sects in particular, seems to have provided one of the few opportunities for working-class people to acquire some stability and to exercise some independence.[51] As Thompson points out, even though the Evangelical movement and Methodism were used extensively to discipline the working class by dominant groups, the Puritan character structure, once established, had a dynamic of its own and could not be made to serve solely church and employer. At Peterloo, in the agricultural labourers' rebellion, the Pentridge Rising, the Plug Riots and the Chartist agitation, Methodism combined with rebellion and was not necessarily against the use of physical force to obtain justice. Even the Sunday schools, which were very much a creature of the Evangelical movement and the Nonconformist revival, in which the Methodists were particularly prominent, were not simply tools of the dominant classes. In them working-class people could become literate and thereby advance the cause of their class; and they were to some extent secularized under working-class people's influence.[52]

However, the participation of working-class people in religious institutions put them also under the direct control and influence of dominant groups more than some commentators have imagined, as well as contributing indirectly to that control and influence. Joyce argues that church, chapel, day school and Sunday school were social and political centres that were also part of the work culture and that formal religious adherence as revealed in the 1851 Census of Religious Observance was less important than the informal ways religious activity engrossed social life. Not only did religious institutions form a vehicle for political intervention in workers' lives and religious affiliation provide a basis for discrimination by employers, they actively engrossed working people's recreational and sporting lives. It was participation in Evangelical and Nonconformist institutions that very effectively mobilized many working-class people behind the rational recreation movement, and Methodism, the Sunday schools, and the temperance bodies were in the vanguard, striving to reorganize working-class people's recreative and sporting activities.

Methodism as a whole had a propensity to accommodate to the status quo and if in some places Methodism readily combined with outbursts of radical activity, it can hardly be credited with them. The contribution of Methodism to working-class radicalism is extremely complex and Thompson has attempted to capture this complexity by characterizing the relation between the two in terms of a 'reactive dialectic'. Tensions were generated within Methodism, especially within the sects, between on the one hand the theological tenets of submissiveness and the sanctification of labour, so dear to the hearts of authority and employers, and on the other the independence and self-respect conferred by sect organization in particular. He argues that 'it would be just as ridiculous to describe the participation of rebellious Methodist lay preachers and others in extreme radical agitations as a "Methodist contribution" to the working-class movement, as it would be to describe the practice of "free love" among Antinomians as a "Puritan contribution" towards sexual liberation. Both are reactive cultural patterns.'[53] And Methodism became more politically conservative and progressively developed stronger links with the middle classes in the 1830s and 1840s.[54]

'The sects' radicalism was deeply ambivalent. Many were avowedly politically neutral and Methodism in nearly all its varieties was strongly anti-intellectual and anti-rational. The sects, with their fanatical hostility to play and the pleasures that many working-class people enjoyed, like drink and popular sports, as Hobsbawm and Rude observe acutely, made them, despite their apparently archaic chiliasm, a modernizing, anti-traditional force internal to the working class.[55] The function of Methodism was, then, on the whole, to detach one part of the class from the rest.

The Sunday school movement, in which Methodism was the most successful component, was particularly closely associated with efforts to engross working-class people's free time and their participation in sporting activity. Although it is correct to say they were much less part of the cultural apparatus of the dominant classes than is often supposed (they were genuinely popular and heavily involved working-class people as members and as teachers) to suppose, as Lacquer does, the schools were unequivocally a source of independent working-class culture, is to overstate the case. He ignores the way the schools were an integral part of the culture of work, which involved more than an assault on the morals of the pupils and an attempt to inculcate the middle-class virtues of 'self-help' and 'improvement'. In addition, as Joyce points out: 'the schools were an agency of a party politics organized by the middle-class party hierarchies and the political clergy. Scholars were institutionalized in a political culture far removed from independent working-class politics'.[56] National, regional and local organization was directed by those outside the working class. Although older scholars and teachers had a say in the daily running of the schools, centrally produced school literature and propaganda certainly shaped the teachers' effort, and ultimate authority was always in the hands of the usually socially superior lay superintendents (Nonconformists) and the local parish priests (Anglican). The Nonconformist-dominated temperance movement worked in the same direction. The attack on the drink culture around which so much sporting activity in which working-class people were involved took place, failed to stop the working class as a whole from drinking and it can hardly be credited with eliminating popular sports. But what it did achieve, as Harrison usefully points out, was the division of the working-class movement by setting the teetotal, anti-traditional-sports worker against the sporting drinking workers.[57]

Secular–radical working-class culture descended from the old radical, rationalist tradition of the previous century, and it served to isolate certain sections of the class from the politically conservative influence of religion, the more fanatical, repressive aspects of the temperance movement and the bourgeois rational recreation lobby. Above all this probably applied to the skilled craftsman or artisan outside the orbit of the factory culture and that kind of employer influence. Among such working-class groups traditional sports and pastimes often survived and developed, albeit sometimes in a more respectable sober form. In contrast to Manchester, for example, in the industrial area around Birmingham, Saint Monday and the sporting activity associated with it continued to be celebrated by skilled workers into the 1860s.[58]

Working-class culture manifested itself in the creation of a range of independent institutions around which free time and sporting activity could be organized and enjoyed: trade unions and trade societies, friendly societies, burial societies, improvement institutes and so on. They were in many ways concerned with self-discipline, respectability and improvement, but the meaning of these terms was not necessarily the equivalent of the bourgeois conception. Thompson and others have argued that these conceptions were oriented to the interests of the collectivity, not the individual's. Discipline was necessary in the interests of the advance of the class as a whole. Such conceptions arose and were elaborated on the basis of working-class people's own experience, and even if they were handed down from above through contact with bourgeois institutions, they are likely to have been reinterpreted in the light of that different experience.

But despite its anti-religious orientation, the fact that working-class secular–radical culture shared the antipathy of working-class religious culture towards popular culture, meant its sporting and recreational activities were consequently more ordered, disciplined, respectable affairs, little different, it seems, from what the socio-religious organizations and the rational recreators had on offer for the working class.[59] They too thus reinforced the cultural fragmentation of the class. If, as Thompson suggests, a general moral primness embraced the vanguard of the working class, and if we regard the radical–secular culture as the most advanced expression of the class, this primness seems to have blunted the radicalism and to have functioned inadvertently to accommodate the radical working class to the emergent social order. Cultural conformity often went hand in hand with political reformism:[60] Some working-class leaders, like William Lovett and Thomas Cooper, shared a Puritan dislike of drink and crude amusements, Lovett preferring recreation and study, Sunday opening of museums and art galleries, correct diet, proper exerecise and personal manners. Cooper was against dancing and theatre-going. Lovett's 'People's Halls' were therefore eminently respectable affairs designed not to offend the bourgeoisie and to prove their trustworthiness, as were Owen's 'Halls of Science', which were teetotal and Christopher Thomson's Artisan Improvement Societies. The Co-operative Movement's secular Sunday schools were remarkably similar in tone to the religious ones.[61] These institutions placed a heavy emphasis on discipline and propriety. Consequently, there tended to be an accommodative bent in the activity of those institutions, specifically created by and for working-class people, and around which sports and recreation would be organized, that is, the trade societies, friendly societies, co-ops and so on. These were often penetrated and/or patronized by dominant groups, for example, in Lancashire employers were customarily invited to patronize friendly society functions. The activities of such institutions also often took place within a broader cultural–political context not under the control of working-class people, which could transform independent working-class cultural activity into a conciliating, integrative mechanism. For example, local trade unions and friendly societies often participated in the highly ritualized local ceremonies and festivities which were held under the aegis of the town corporation.[62]

Popular culture under attack proved remarkably resilient: there was vigorous resistance to enforced change, a significant degree of continuity was maintained and innovation went on nevertheless, showing that there was no necessary fit between culture, the mode of production and the new social order. The rather frequent resort to legislation, the length of time it took to get legislation passed, and the inability to render it effective despite frequent resort to police force, troops and militia, suggests popular resistance was stubborn and widespread. The fact that even many cruel sports like cock-fighting, ratting, and dog-fighting, lived on all over the country, together with other popular sports strongly disapproved of by the improvers, such as pedestrianism, prize-fighting and folk football in certain localities, and that it continued to be necessary to repress popular sports and the festive occasions associated with them in the period which followed, is further testimony to the resilience of these popular cultural forms.[63]

Popular culture in some ways very effectively rendered working-class people immune to the Protestant ethic and norms of bourgeois respectability. Paganism flourished within this soil and the irreverence about religion went hand in hand with a constant tendency for the bourgeois proprieties to be overrun by the demand for amusement, when working-class people came into contact with leisure and recreation institutions provided for their improvement. Heywood's Lyceums could never compete effectively with other entertainment outlets like the free and easy commercialized singing-rooms. Where working-class people took part in sporting activities organized for them by their patrons, they were quite capable of using them as opportunities to satisfy their needs without necessarily committing themselves to their patrons ideologically. A free Sunday outing was a free Sunday outing and nothing more than that. If it is remembered that working-class people were treated with suspicion and sometimes open contempt by their 'betters', and the ethos of the improving institutions was relentlessly didactic, then they could not have been that attractive and ideologically effective. There was, in truth, a mutual awareness of a gulf and a great unease on either side of it, which by no means made for easy ideological integration.

Many sports then, successfully resisted reconstruction, while others experienced substantial growth and development. Sometimes this was under the patronage of the rich, but not always. Horse-racing expanded and developed, both as a class-exclusive social event and as a popular sport, especially under the impetus of commercialization and gambling. Newmarket was the scene of select upper-class meetings, but elsewhere the sport was still associated with local holidays, travelling shows, gambling booths, beer tents, cock-fights, boxing and wrestling. Financial support came from the race-horse owners, sweep-ticket holders, the richer element who paid for entry into the stands, from hoteliers, publicans, victuallers, brewers and other financial beneficiaries of racing; and it came also from local gentry and other notables, like the local MP. Race-meetings at Ascot and Epsom were major social events, attracting support from different social groups beyond the locality, but many were also local meetings for the lower classes. The sport developed further with the coming of rail transport, making it easier for horses to be transported to meetings. The many meetings that did survive were not yet, in general, organized on a regular basis, but survive and prosper they did.[64] The Jockey Club consolidated its control of flat racing from the 1790s, and in the 1830s attempted to make racing more socially exclusive by restricting entry to the Ascot Gold Cup to its own members and to the membership of exclusive London clubs. This seems to indicate a degree of conflict within the dominant groups over the entry of new bourgeois elements, like John Gully, the son of a publican, himself a racing entrepreneur, prize-fighter and industrialist, who became MP for Pontefract in 1832. In the 1840s with its upper-class patrons maintaining their patronage and control, the sport was rife with corruption. Although social mixing was restricted to the race course and even there mixing was somewhat limited, this sport, like prize-fighting, and despite Lord Bentinck's reforms, continued to bring together the upper-class gambling element and the 'dissolute' plebian element in society. Riots and violence were not uncommon, especially over welchers and disappointments at the race results. Gambling spread further afield with the development of betting lists run by bookmakers and publicans in the towns and cities. The state was early involved in the sport also, because of the importance of maintaining bloodstock for military purposes. It therefore subsidized racing for most of the century by putting money up for King's and Queen's Plate races.

It was precisely during this period of repression of 'brutal' popular sports, i.e. between 1780 and 1820, that the much denigrated sport of prize-fighting was at the height of its fame and it continued to flourish in the 1830s and 1840s although its upper-class patrons were beginning to withdraw. Gambling, corruption and violence continued to characterize the sport and reform had to wait until well after the mid-century. Similarly wrestling and pedestrianism flourished despite disapprobation and persecution.[65]

The aristocracy and the gentry maintained their monopoly over the controlling bodies in cricket. Matches between elite teams led by notables attracted audiences of as many as 20,000 in the 1820s and 1830s and other big matches were inaugurated around this time – the inter-varsity match and the 'gentlemen versus players' matches again attracting thousands. Again, the game did not depend entirely on upper-class patronage, for commercial interests took advantage of its popularity and developed it further. Thomas Lord, the owner of the ground that became the home of the MCC, was actually a publican–entrepreneur, in the game wholly for profit, and he actually sold the ground in 1825. In the second quarter of the nineteenth century the game began to acquire a more complex organizational structure, players developed more elaborate techniques and the status and rewards of professional players from lower social origins rose. The latter development occurred to a great extent as a result of the initiative of William Clarke, a socially mobile cricketing entrepreneur and player, who formed his own professional touring team in the 1840s, playing matches which attracted thousands all over the country.

Yet popular as it was, dominated as it was by older, more backward-looking ruling-class elements, exhibiting more cultural continuity with the pre-industrial era, exemplifying the relaxed, leisurely, rural, aristocratic virtues rather than the values of hard work and efficiency, cricket did show signs that the older ruling group in control was prepared to accommodate to the forces of reform. Already it possessed a decidedly more respectable ethos than other popular sports we have examined. One clear sign that it had managed to distance itself from too close an association with the more dissolute, disorderly elements (a relatively early sign of bourgeoisification), was the elimination of gambling in 1825 at Lord's Cricket Ground. Also, in so far as it allowed the new, as well as the old, dominant groups to patronize local cricket teams, of which there were many all over the country, it enabled both groups to extend their spheres of influence in local communities and to attain a degree of control over potentially disorderly leisure activities.[66] Cricket continued to emphasize the exclusivity of dominant groups which controlled the game and ran the teams and their superiority over the professional players who sprang from the people.

Popular culture and its disreputable sporting forms tended to alienate the more organized, respectable working class involved in religious and secular–radical culture, and so it too bore its share of responsibility for the class's lack of cohesion. The religiously affiliated were threatened by its paganism, its disorderliness and lack of sobriety – to them it represented temptation and sin. To the radical–secularists it was anti-intellectual, shallow and amusement-obsessed and dangerously chauvinistic – at best it seemed politically agnostic and at worst reactionary, and as such it was seen as retarding working-class advance. It was, no doubt, all these things, but it was also something more. It was rumbustious, disrespectful of authority, anarchic, playful, anti-utilitarian – in a word it was anti-bourgeois. To see popular culture as unequivocally playing into the hands of the masters was mistaken and the proof is that a considerable proportion of them thought otherwise. From the rational recreators point of view it threatened to turn their tidy world upside down. Its ambivalence then, was responsible for fragmenting not only the working class but also the dominant groups as well.

The dominant classes were not united monolithically behind the campaign for reform. Popular culture was, in fact, quite vigorously defended, notably by upper-class, anti-Puritan, mostly Anglican, Tory traditionalists, who abhorred a good deal of the modernizing, more rational social order of industrial capitalism. They associated themselves closely with certain aspects, in particular some of the major sporting forms such as horse-racing, prize-fighting and the various blood sports, and with the gambling and the world of entertainment associated with them. Their defence of the rights of the people to enjoy themselves in the old ways was not without appeal to anti-Evangelical Whigs and middle-class radicals.[67] Among the traditionalists, popular culture, especially its sporting forms, was regarded as a social cement, a useful safety-valve, and attacks on it were seen as not only attacks on their pleasures, but also as undermining a fundamental basis for social unity. It was from this quarter that the ideologically influential conception originated – later to be taken up more by the rational recreators and absorbed, in particular, into the ideology of athleticism – that popular sports were class conciliatory, promoted the martial qualities and patriotism and prevented effeminacy.[68] It was in sports above all then, that the essence of Englishness, what distinguished us from the effete, inferior foreigner, was encouraged and expressed. Sports could thus be made a rallying point for chauvinistic and nationalistic sentiment, an association that was to crystallize later in the century. As Joyce has pointed out, this cultural division cut across the industrial-employer class as well, helping to give rise to two separate yet paternalistic styles of factory-owner/employer:

the one Tory, Anglican, bucolic, the simple, sporting man-that-knows-the-people; the other Liberal, Nonconformist, temperance, and social-improver-for-the-people. Associated with this division within the dominant classes, the effects of the temperance lobby were strongly counteracted by the very powerful drink lobby. At the same time as the drink culture and the sporting forms associated with it were subjected to attack, the commercial interests comprising the brewers, publicans and associated entertainment interests, were busily promoting them and, incidentally, popular sports, with a good deal of success.

Disunity within the dominant classes with regard to popular culture and sports certainly reduced the effectiveness of the movement to reconstruct how working-class people used their free time, but it must not be thought that this necessarily weakened the overall power and influence of the dominant classes over subordinate groups. On the contrary, these sorts of divisions enabled the dominant classes as a whole to respond more flexibly to subordinate groups, to mobilize their support, to subject them to cross-pressures and to trade off divisions within the latter.[69] On the one hand, lined up against disreputable sports were the Evangelicals, Nonconformists, Liberals, Liberal-Nonconformist employers, the rational recreation/anti-cruel sports/Sabbatarian/temperance complex, who manage on this question to harness to themselves the more respectable working class involved in working-class religious and secular–radical culture. On the other hand, defending sports and the people's rights to enjoyment were the Anglicans, Tories, Tory-Anglican employers, the brewers, the drink trade and entertainment interests, and the aristocratic, bohemian element of the 'fancy', who managed to harness the more plebian, rougher working class to their wagon. The working class is thus divided and cross-pressured by a bewildering array of power and influence. Simultaneously, just as these centres of power and influence had to a significant degree accommodated to each other politically, they did so culturally over the question of their own sporting activity. That the rational recreators' attacks on popular culture were directed specifically at the lower classes and not the upper-class patrons is clear from the selective nature of the targets chosen. Where similar or the same activities were indulged in and patronized by, the upper classes, unlike the remnants of the Whig oligarchy's 'Old Corruption', which the new bourgeoisie attacked unequivocally as a political threat to its interests, these practices were not attacked, but instead were more or less tolerated as part of the price of accommodating the older ruling elements. It was not so much the activities in themselves that were repugnant to reformers, but the life-style of the lower orders that was seen as a threat. Hunting, for example, was simply ignored by the anti-cruel sports lobby, and its upper-class supporters were left in peace to go on killing animals for fun. Similarly, the Betting Act of 1853, in banning street betting alone, in effect singled out working-class gambling for legal prohibition and left those rich enough to belong to clubs like Tattersalls, where betting continued, and those who could afford to bet on credit, free to gamble as they wished. A noteworthy indication of the reformers' connivance in this area was the fact that gambling debts were recoverable at law, whereas wages and certain other essentials were not. The class-biased sentiment was made explicit in Lord Brougham's *obiter dicta* in 1844: 'Gambling has much more fatal consequences and is far more injurious to morals among the inferior classes than among the superior classes.'[70] The same bias can be seen in the way prize-fighting with its brutality, corruption and criminal connections, escaped effective control for a long time because it was patronized by an upper-class, aristocratic element. Similarly with drinking, which in no way warranted the magnitude of the attack mounted on it, for in fact, Britain was at the height of its industrial power when drinking was at its peak around 1870.[71] The concern about drinking was motivated by the recognition that so much of working-class culture, which was a beer culture, was organized around it. Trade unions and political groups traditionally held their meetings and discussions in pubs. Here then, was an institution in which working-class people were in danger of evading surveillance by their superiors for a major slice of their free time. Consequently, the beerhouse and the pub became one of the most closely supervised and regulated institutions in British society, hemmed in by a plethora of petty restrictions and subject to continual harassment by the authorities.

By the end of the period, in the 1840s, where the culture of the factory had taken a grip, the dull compulsion of work and associated urban routines was enabled to take a firmer hold because of the continuity that existed between pre-industrial culture, characterized by paternalistic relations between ruling and subordinate classes, and the culture of the factory under early industrial capitalism. Employees were supervised–patronized both in their work and non-work lives and integrated through the superimposition of work culture, religious culture and leisure cultures. The layering of cultures overcame the resistance and tendency to independence of sub-ordinate groups that was expressed to one or other extent in these cultures. That is to say, it positively favoured a bourgeois 'social hegemony' at the local level.

Secondly, the integration of the working class into the new social order rested on the fragmentation of the working class. The sources of fragmen-tation were economic and political as well as cultural. We have focused on the latter, pointing out the disjunction between the cultures in which working-class people were likely to participate and the way sporting activity helped to mediate fragmentation, reduce the class's cohesiveness and its independence.

Thirdly, differentiation within the dominant groups interacting with the pattern of fragmentation among the working class, enabled 'cross-class' alliances to be formed, further disorganizing the working class. Culturally fragmented, placed in a dependent relationship with dominant groups, an accommodation between classes was the outcome. The working class had yet to establish itself as a sufficiently cohesive independent force, coterminous with society. The ruling class did not need at this stage to take diffuse, trans-societal integrative measures of a kind which could reasonably be classified as 'hegemonic' in function. So the extension of the franchise to the working class for example, was to follow later. The economic, political and cultural controls over popular sporting activity cannot, therefore, be categorized in terms of their role in a hegemonic system at this point, although they were, nevertheless, an integral part of the way the class was integrated at that time.

3

Consolidating the Bourgeois Model

The mid-Victorian period was characterized by economic expansion and relative economic and political stability.[1] By the mid-point of the century the transition to industrial capitalism had been accomplished. Although Britain was not to become a preponderantly urban industrial society with class loyalties and class conflicts set in a genuinely national framework, until the last quarter of the century, a significantly larger proportion of the population lived in towns and was engaged in some form of industrial employment. The major political threat in the shape of Chartism had collapsed, and a more orderly entry of the working class into politics was initiated with the extension of the franchise in 1867.[2] A shift had occurred in economic, political and cultural relations within the power bloc. The bourgeoisie exercised hegemony over the landed aristocracy, although the latter continued to dominate important sectors of the state.[3]

The Role of the Public Schools

The importance of the public schools in the development of sporting forms and in articulating them on the power network in this period can hardly be exaggerated. A reconstructed form of sport became the norm in these schools spreading throughout a network of voluntary sport and recreation associations dominated by public school men. These institutions played a crucial part in the formation of the ruling class in the second half of the nineteenth century. Their specific function was to accommodate and unify the older, landed 'patrician' ruling class and the rising bourgeois elements.[4]

The success of a class alliance is dependent on appropriate socialization of the offspring of the parties concerned, and it was under the tutelage of evangelizing intellectuals, of whom Thomas Arnold, Headmaster of Rugby School, is the legendary epitome, that the public schools became a major *locus* for working out the terms of that alliance; and it was above all in the sports culture of these institutions that those terms were expressed and put into practice. Arnold's aim was to create an enlightened ruling class of educated men 'who would resist the ''crimes of Toryism'' and the greed and vulgarity of industrialists on the one hand, and the socialistic claims of the oppressed on the other'.[5] Education at Rugby, where he was Headmaster from 1828–42, was therefore designed to turn out 'Christian gentlemen', men who were disciplined, socially responsible and self-reliant enough, not only to govern themselves but the lower orders as well. The concept of the 'Christian gentleman' gave primacy to moral excellence and character training without neglecting the intellect. The concept of the gentleman retained its anti-democratic traditional connotations of honour due and privileged right to rule, but it incorporated a new demanding version of *'noblesse oblige'*: the new notion of 'service' required those who were privileged to earn their position by paying continuous attention to duty and by displaying ordered, disciplined, restrained conduct as an example to the lower orders. Those who did not fit into Arnold's world were ruthlessly excluded.

Arnold himself is said to have had only a casual interest in games, but there is no doubt he did positively encourage them nevertheless, carefully preserving a place for the traditional games he found established at Rugby by according them an official, important place on the curriculum. His main innovation seems to have been to create a new system of authority relations, whereby the head and his staff strengthened their control through a reformed prefect–fagging system, and to incorporate games into the new regimen. This new order enabled him to both preserve the traditionally established relations between older and younger boys, and also to eliminate aristocratic domination and to curb the general unruliness in the school that went with it. In particular, it militated against the relatively disorderly sports the aristocratic element patronized. In this sense Arnold can be said to have deliberately encouraged and favoured the development of more rationalized bourgeois forms of sport and helped create the climate in which the games cult could flourish later. A major development was the transformation of popular folk football into a 'gentlemanly' sport possessing a code which differentiated it sharply from the uncouth game played by the lower orders. There was an increasing differentiation and growing complexity of the game as it was played in public schools like Rugby, which culminated in the first attempts at codifying the rules formally, and the bifurcation of the game into its soccer and rugby versions by the mid-1840s.[6]

The actual way football was transformed in the public schools was an unintended consequence of Arnold's reforms, but the receptivity of these schools and their clientele to the transformation of traditional game forms and their awareness that games could be used to inculcate the kind of virtues which Arnold and his successors had pinpointed – loyalty, *esprit de corps*, self-sacrifice – does not seem to have been accidental. The public schools' role can be seen as part of a 'civilizing process', but it is necessary to be precise about the nature of the norms and values permeating their sporting practices and the relations between the dominant groups which formed their clientele.[7] The rapidity with which Arnold's ideas spread is an indication not only of the respect and authority he commanded, but also of the degree of social support among dominant groups for those intellectuals who articulated successfully and seemed attuned to their social needs. When he emphasized 'moral excellence' and 'character training' in the education of his 'gentlemen' he showed an acute perception of the need for the new ruling class to develop a firm identity as a prerequisite for wielding authoritative power. The dominant classes accepted his broad programme, but significantly, the cultivation of the intellect as a major aim was downgraded and primacy was given to the games cult instead. The 1856 Rugby School *Yearbook* declared: 'We are not students in England. Great Englishmen (generally speaking) are great in some departments of practical life, great statesmanship, jurisprudence or war. Their nature is abhorrent of the study. With the Germans it is otherwise.'[8] The denigration of the intellect in the post-Arnoldian era entailed by the flourishing of the games cult, of course, distorted his insight into the importance of cultural supremacy in a vulgar, philistine manner, but it was, nevertheless, highly effective. The sentiments expressed in what was to become a bible of nineteenth-century public-school and ruling-class sensibility, Thomas Hughes *Tom Brown's Schooldays*, written in 1856, though they purport to be in keeping with Arnold's, are in fact more truly representative of the manner in which the latter's ideas were taken up after 1850. The author, speaking through Squire Brown, requires of education:

> Were I a private schoolmaster, I should say, let who will hear the boys their lessons, but let me live with them when they are at play or rest...Shall I tell him [Tom] to mind his work, and say he's sent to school to make himself a good scholar? Well, he isn't sent to school for that – at any rate not for that mainly...I don't care a straw for Greek particles...What is he sent to school for? Well, partly because he wanted to go. If he'll only turn out a brave, helpful, truth-telling Englishman, and a gentleman, and a Christian, that's all I want....[9]

Hughes takes games like football and cricket as the epitome of what he wants from education, for they are an occasion for inculcating and displaying the virtues of Victorian bourgeois morality, leadership, compliance with authority, patriotism and militarism: 'and over all is old Brooke, [the captain] absolute as he of Russia, but wisely and bravely ruling over willing and worshipful subjects, a true football king. His face is earnest and cheerful as he glances a last time over his array, but full of pluck and hope, the sort of look I hope to see in my general when I go out to fight.'[10]

The cult of athleticism which gripped the period was instrumental in several ways: it fed into the growing concern about the health and fitness of the nation for national defence; it met the growing demand among dominant groups for a form of leisure activity which was complementary to work; and above all it was a way of disciplining or 'normalizing' the male youth of the dominant classes to enable them to take their places in the modern social order. In this period Arnold's moral earnestness passed into the doctrine of *'mens sana in corpore sano'* and the related conceptions of 'manliness' which were associated particularly with the 'muscular Christianity' of authors like Hughes and Charles Kingsley. In the 1830s the notion of *'mens sana'* was almost unknown, but by 1860 it was everywhere. By 1858 it was held that boys active in strenuous sports are less liable to indecent behaviour than lonely meditative ones. Middle-class readers of Baily's, one of the new sporting journals, were being urged that 'they may rise to the ranks of gentlemen if...they would cultivate in themselves healthy minds and bodies "taught to endure, disciplined by obedience, self-restraint, and the sterner duties of chivalry".' Kingsley in his novel *Two Years Ago*, links good character to physical fitness and size. George Lawrence's novel, *Guy Livingstone*, contributed to the myth of the athletic hero who combined physical massiveness with aristocratic hauteur and with a righteous, brutish nature. Lesley Stephen believed the highest poetry 'is the product of a thoroughly healthy mind...no man can be thoroughly healthy in mind who has bad digestion'. George Meredith believed in his own case how: 'a joy in a healthy body creates an increased lucidity of mind.'[11]

Evolutionary theory in the shape of some of Herbert Spencer's ideas were influential on the muscular Christians. Although Spencer saw evolution in terms of the triumph of the mind over physical force, he nevertheless believed 'the first requisite of life is to be a good animal...[and that] all breaches of the laws of health are physical sins', and like others at the time he doubted the merits of book-learning.[12] Evolutionism provided a way of moralizing about human conduct as if it were a matter of obeying natural laws. According to Kingsley's social Darwinism for example, the only way to profit from what he called the 'terrible laws of natural selection' was to understand and obey them: to curb the beast in man, paradoxically one must cultivate the animal.

In equating moral rectitude with physical well-being, Kingsley, Hughes and their followers provided a powerful ideological underpinning for the public schools games cult and the related sports movement of the mid-Victorian era. Football and cricket became virtually the chief vehicles of a moral education, and athleticism became the dominant ideological motif of the cultural integration process that was going on in these schools and at other levels.

Heads of older, established schools, like Mitchell, Keen and Warre of Eton, became enthusiastic supporters of athleticism; and heads of newer schools like Thring of Uppingham, Cotton of Marlborough and Almond of Loretto, opportunistically saw the cult as a short cut to equal status with them; and it was often the *nouveaux-riches* manufacturer parents in particular who pressurized the schools to develop in this direction.[13] The sports cult is sometimes explained as a pragmatic response to the problem of keeping lively boys occupied during the considerable time they were in the care of these schools, but there is plainly more to the phenomenon than this.

In the public schools a new disciplinary technology was discovered and developed, which was deployed for the first time on the sons of the dominant classes themselves. Like the workhouses, asylums, hospitals, prisons, barracks and factories of the era, these schools closed off the individual from society, subjecting him to the uninterrupted gaze of authority. Young adolescent males were 'normalized' by subjecting them to detailed, minute, continuous, comprehensive surveillance in Spartan conditions. Unlike these other institutions, however, what was unique about the public schools was their discovery, development and deployment of the new athleticist technology. As C. L. R. James notes, putting it in more conventional terms, the idea that a moral education could be imparted through games, and what they thereby imparted, was their one original contribution to 'educational theory' and practice. Athleticist discourse, the knowledge produced in athleticist practices, and the techniques that were developed, represented an entirely new disciplinary strategy: by extending the gaze of authority beyond work and rest into the world of play, the body was made uninterruptedly visible and control was thereby extended over the 'soul' of the individual (the 'character' in athleticist discourse).

The centrality of games in the curriculum of the 1860s is indicated in evidence given to the Clarendon Commission by the schools themselves. At Eton between four and a half and six hours a day were devoted to work compared with between five and seven hours a day to cricket. At Harrow up to twenty four hours per week went on cricket and at Rugby fifteen hours.[14] What became a 'games mania' was not without opposition from a minority opinion among the dominant groups: Matthew Arnold, Ruskin and Wilkie Collins condemned athleticism for its class connotations and for encouraging what they saw as antisocial behaviour; and even the Clarendon Commission admonished the schools for spending too much time on sports, but the criticism was to little avail.

By closing off their pupils from the immediate influence of the family and by rigidly segregating them from females the formation of the ruling class in these institutions was achieved in a thoroughly male-dominated culture. That is, one of the main cultural supports of the ruling-class alliance and of ruling-class identity was a rigid gender division and chauvinist masculine identity. It was the family that was allocated the task of 'normalizing' ruling-class girls, and the public schools with their athleticist technology were responsible for the boys and young men. Athleticism produced and reproduced not only ruling-class identity, but it thus also constituted one of the most powerful sources of gender division among dominant groups.

This cult then, expressed in many ways the characteristic mode of understanding of the nature of social existence that developed among the dominant classes. In organized sports the scions of the ruling classes absorbed a uniquely British 'bourgeois ideology' and rehearsed the practices that were necessary in order to integrate successfully into the social order. It was in games primarily that one learned how to be a gentleman and through them that the model of gentlemanly behaviour was exemplified and spread. Participation in school sport was a way of learning to be the kind of individual who would fit in with the class ally and learn how to rule over subordinates. Confidence and self-reliance, learning how to take the initiative and responsibility, how to control aggression and yet act decisively in a determined manner, the necessity of conforming to the established way of doing things, and above all, loyalty to one's group, were all being taught. Games were a medium whereby common under-standings among the dominant classes about the nature of social existence could be developed and stated in a condensed, striking form, notably the idea that ordered struggle, in which some are destined to win and others to lose, is a normal and inescapable feature of social life.

The schools' stress on the efficacy of team games, rather than the more individualistic sporting events that were to become more popular in the following century, was exactly appropriate; for team games allow a fine balance to be struck between the utilitarian rationality and individualism that had gained ground among the middle classes, and the necessity for the latter to conform to an already well-established order which tended to place definite limits on such an outlook. This tension was managed in the way adherence to rules, as such, was venerated, and also in the way the cult of leadership and team-work was sponsored in public-school sport. The very definition of playing fair, that is of being a good sportsman or 'sport'; was to play according to the rules: even if one thinks a decision is wrong, one is obligated to accept the umpire's or the referee's decision without question. To do otherwise is 'bad form', a terminology pregnant with meaning. The elementary conception of justice and equality present in the orientation to rules encouraged in schools sport corresponded closely with the prevailing ideology: just as abiding by the rules made one a good sportsman, so abiding by the rules of the established political and social system made one a responsible citizen. Just as in games the judgement and the decision of the umpire was taken to be impartial, so the administration of justice was assumed to be so and the legal framework was taken to be neutral and fair.

The value accorded to leadership in games articulated the need felt within the dominant classes to maintain respect for established authority, and the value accorded to team-work articulated the need for co-operation with, and social acceptance by, one's class ally. The latter was some source of anxiety to both the rising industrial bourgeoisie, uncertain of the extent to which it was accepted by the more polished patrician ally, and for the older ruling-class element as well, whose position was being undermined by the development of industrial capitalism. If the team's chances of winning are not to be jeopardized, competition against the opposing side requires team-work and co-operation with one's own side. The style of games-playing in the public schools placed great stress on the role of the appointed leader in relation to team-work: the leader's function is to lead, in the sense of building up morale and binding the team together by example. The leader both gives shape to and also expresses the group will; and it is in this restricted sense that he is said to 'represent' the team, and therefore loyalty to the leader is equated with loyalty to the group. This conservative understanding of the nature of team-work, representation, co-operation and comradeship sees the individual's personal worth primarily in terms of the extent to which he fits in with, identifies with, and serves the pre-ordained order. The cult of leadership was intimately associated then, with the prevailing anti-intellectualism already noted. More specifically it was associated with the fact that the games-playing products of these schools were destined to be members of the governing class, leaders of the professions and imperial administrators.

The public schools were not only political devices in this sense. What this type of education uniquely sought to achieve in fulfilling this function was a form of ideological indoctrination by which 'vast sections of a schoolboy's life were roped off from their exercise of individual reason.'[15] It sought instead to inculcate a reverence for established authority, an unquestioning faith in tradition, a self-abnegation and a loyalty to the group. This was accomplished through a system of informal, unwritten ethical constraints and a plethora of ritual practices, which provided a very powerful means for expressing a specific morality and tradition. The practices, in fact, closely paralleled the character of the 'British Constitution' as enunciated by Bagehot at the time. Such a system 'instilled conformity not by explicit dogma but by etiquette and custom, devices that played on community mysticism and the aesthetic notion of ''good form'' rather than reason'.[16] The public school made gentlemen of the rising bourgeoisie at the expense of their potential liberal rationalism and the main vehicle was the games cult and all the ritual surrounding it. An ideology was encoded in the practice of public-school sport which was to become an important component of British political culture; and it was also to have long-lasting effects on the character of sport in Britain. The public-school model of sport had an ultimately wide-reaching and indirect influence. Not only was it disseminated by public-school and Oxbridge men over a relatively long period lasting well into the next century, via their direct presence in sporting institutions, but also some of its main features were institutionalized in other sectors of society which mediated sport for the majority of the population, notably the state schools in the following century.

The Expansion of Reconstructed Sports and Ruling-class Integration

Under the impetus of athleticism a whole number of sports were reconstructed or introduced under the aegis of public-school, Oxbridge, muscular-Christian, amateur gentlemen. These became more differentiated activities, with their own elaborate, codified rules and procedures. The scale and complexity of organization increased: ruling bodies emerged at the centre to co-ordinate individual sports, adjudicate disputes and formulate policy. New playing techniques were invented and developed and new types of equipment came into use. Roles in sport, both playing and administrative, became more specialized. These sports became less like gladiatorial contests and more like scientific exercises in improvement – matters of safer, measured, exact, ordered achievement. Controlling bodies were formed for a number of major sports to co-ordinate the activity of the many sports clubs of different kinds that had sprung up all over the country – the Football Association (FA) in 1863, the Amateur Athletic Club in 1866, the Amateur Swimming Association (ASA) in 1869, the Bicycle Union in 1866 and so on. Major competitions were inaugurated – the FA Cup (1871), the Amateur, Professional and Open Golf Championships (1858–1861), the Oxford and Cambridge Boat Race (1849), County Cricket (1873), etc. And new major organized sports like tennis, gymnastics, croquet, bicycling and mountain climbing, caught on rapidly.[17]

The remarkable reconstruction, innovation and scale of expansion of organized sports was a major cultural achievement of the mid-Victorian era, which laid much of the foundation on which working-class people would participate later and for the development of sport world-wide. Britain's global economic and political supremacy was accompanied by a global supremacy in this particular cultural field as well, and organized sport accompanied the flag and international trade all over the world.

Although it became widely accepted at this time among the dominant classes that sports could unite classes and heal divisions between them, reconstructed sports functioned primarily to unify the dominant classes. In fact, participation in reconstructed sports sharply differentiated the dominant classes from subordinate groups. The former accommodated to each other culturally by disavowing certain forms of sport altogether as not fitting for 'gentlemen' and attempted to exclude the lower orders from those sports deemed appropriate for themselves. The rules of the Amateur Athletic Club, the Amateur Rowing Club and the Bicycle Union in the 1860s explicitly excluded 'mechanics, artisans and labourers' and the numerous sports clubs in the country catering for the middle and upper classes were busily excluding the majority of working-class people in one way or other. The linchpin of the system was amateur-gentleman status.

The way in which the cricket authorities resisted the challenge to amateur-gentleman supremacy illustrates the differentiating function of much reconstructed, organized sport at the time. When compared with other sports in this period, such as football, the process whereby cricket took on its modern structure seems to have played a unique role at the national level in unifying the power bloc and differentiating its constituents from the working class. The lower classes had never been excluded from active participation in cricket controlled by dominant groups: the professionals were simply ascribed an inferior status. Between the 1840s and the 1870s professionalism however advanced to the point where dominant groups' control over the game was challenged briefly. The independent teams of professionals, such as Clarke's All England XI were of lowly social origin, nakedly money-conscious, individualist and opposed to the Marylebone Cricket Club (MCC). Some of the clubs, like Surrey, expanded their membership very rapidly, relying heavily on professional players for their successful performance. There was even an attempt to set up a 'cricket parliament' to replace the MCC, which had tried to exert authority over the professionals without much success. The latter, as a highly skilled body of workers whose services were in demand, established a considerable degree of control over their market and work situations. Their cohesion proved to be relatively weak however, as bickering broke out between northern and southern teams over the issue of who should captain foreign tours. The watershed was reached in 1866 when the northern professionals dissociated themselves from all cricket played in the south, a move that was taken as a challenge to gentlemanly control. An article to this effect in *The Times* explicitly drew an analogy between the attitudes of professionals in cricket and those of industrial workers, likening the conflict to a battle drawn on class lines.[18] The response from the patrons of cricket was to assert their authority over the game in parallel with the way they asserted it over society. Ranks were closed, professionals banished from

Lord's Cricket Ground, they were attacked by their own county clubs, and the northern players were given pariah status.

It was in the newly formed county clubs and not the MCC that the basis of accommodation between the different elements within the dominant classes who controlled cricket was reached, and that enabled the professionals' challenge to be repulsed. The aristocracy, the county gentry and the most prosperous section of the urban bourgeoisie combined and were able to oppose successfully attempts to make cricket completely amateur or professional. It was possible because of the relatively greater cohesiveness of the dominant groups and because the professionals failed to gain sufficient public support, mainly as Brookes suggests because they lacked geographical identity and suffered from internal schisms. A deeper reason for the failure to gain requisite support was that the class from which it would have come, the urban working class, found it hard to identify with a game whose ethos and organization were more rurally based, and the class at this point lacked the basis for the independence it was to show later in relation to football. The dominant groups were able to capitalize on public disaffection with professional cricket, marshall support for county cricket, and inaugurated the County Championship in 1873 as the alternative. Each of the nine clubs taking part in the latter incorporated the invidious distinction between amateur gentlemen and 'players': amateurism and *'esprit de corps'* triumphed over the professionals' individualism and instrumentalism. The analogous position of the place of the professionals in cricket with that of the trade unions in commerce and industry at the time was plain. As Brookes concludes:

> Both sport and commerce were spheres in which the presence of members of the Victorian ruling class was a particularly dominating one; both were activities which lay at the heart of their identities and self-conceptions. Professionalism and the growth of trade unions constituted a challenge to the hitherto unquestioned assumption that this domination was in the best interests of society. In the case of cricket the impact of the professionals' challenge was intensified by reason of the fact that it coincided with the rise of the game to the status of a 'national sport'. If there was something peculiarly British about cricket, it could not be supplied by a largely working class body.[19]

Cricket was thus of tremendous symbolic importance to the ruling class: this game, above all, expressed for Britain's rulers the essence of Englishness, an essence, incidentally, tinged with incipient chauvinist sentiment. Epitomizing Englishness and the class balance was, of course, the figure who became a national hero and a cult in himself, W. G. Grace.

No sooner had the dominant groups closed its sporting doors than some working-class people were knocking on them for entry. The new sports clubs and organizations functioning as a sociability network for dominant groups spontaneously attracted a following among subaltern groups. One of these was the lower middle class; the other was the skilled manual worker stratum, the artisans. Gray notes, for example, a growing enthusiasm for healthy recreation among this group of workers in Edinburgh, which was reflected in their choice of leisure pursuits and above all, for football, and their propensity to join voluntary associations run by dominant groups catering for these tastes.[20] To an extent this tended to segregate skilled workers during a proportion of their leisure time from the rest of the class and to encourage social contact with those above them in the social scale. 'Mechanics clauses' soon fell when it became clear that the artisan was not the lout he was reputed to be among the middle and upper classes, but rather an eminently respectable sports enthusiast who harboured no ambitions to challenge gentlemanly amateur supremacy. Almost immediately then, bourgeoisified sport inadvertently began to bridge class divisions through initiatives from below.

However, bridges also began to be built by initiatives from above and working-class people began to experience the impact of athleticist technology in a different way. Under the auspices of the 'urban gentry' the hegemonic project was being tried out, not on the class as a whole but on it group by group. These bourgeois intellectuals – members of statistical societies like the Social Science Association and of Royal Commissions, writers and readers of the quarterly press, organizers of charity and of social discipline – were drawn from the churches, the professions, the Civil Service, Parliament, socially concerned 'ladies', intellectually gifted protégés of the wealthy and from established wealth; and they were concerned with the administrative and ideological organization of society.[21] Theirs was a complex relationship with the dominant groups on the one hand, and with more broadly based social strata on the other. Their paternalism was strongly tinged with utilitarianism, vulgar political economy, rational recreation and evangelicalism; their fear was of social disorder; and their programme was social harmonization.

The strategy they arrived at was basically to reach the working class in a more positive manner and more on its own terms. Simple evangelism and heavy didacticism tended now to give way to an approach based on the appreciation of the evident demand for amusement registered by working-class people. Amusements were not seen as a safety-valve: work still took priority, disorderly forms of recreation were still proscribed and the correct model of behaviour was still the moderate, polite gentleman who observed decorum, but amusement was now seen as a legitimate functional need. The tactic of securing an upper- or middle-class presence in working-class recreation to establish fraternal, harmonious relations between the classes was now developed and applied more systematically.

The most favoured model was the club, or small institute, which it was hoped would attract, in the words of the Reverend Solly, founder of the Working Men's Club and Institute Union in 1863, 'the more prudent, worthier members of the working classes...(away from) their reckless drinking, cowardly, and dishonest neighbours'.[22] The working mens' club movement was the most outstanding example of this strategy in action, it secured the heavy backing of the ruling class, and it attached large numbers of working-class men.[23] Lord Brougham explained the policy of the movement to the Social Science Association in 1865 thus: 'Nothing can be more erroneous than the notion prevailing in some quarters that the object of these clubs is for education...the primary objects are relaxation and amusement.'[24]

Reconstructed 'orderly' sports began to be seen as one of the chief instruments of cultural integration and the attempt to spread sport downwards to the working class, with the rational recreators taking over the theme that sports created social harmony, got under way. Thomas Hughes' advocacy of athleticism along these lines was put into practice when he launched an athletic programme consisting of cricket, gymnastics and boxing classes at the London Working Men's College.[26] One of the most common agents of access to working-class communities was the athletic clergyman, cricket at first being the most favoured sport for this exercise in social fraternity, with football a close second and overtaking it in popularity later. By 1867, for example, a third of the local cricket clubs in Bolton were connected to a religious body.[26] Many of the Football League Clubs of today had church origins in this period.[27] Local employers were increasingly prepared to found teams and provide facilities: 'Pillars of the local community would often be pleased to help working men fill their newly-found regular leisure time with recreation that was healthy and harmless and satisfying to local patriotism.'[28]

The Volunteers, a paramilitary organization founded in 1859, was extremely sports conscious, in fact sports provided the chief means of recruitment; and it is significant that after some initial opposition from the officer class, by 1879 this body was overwhelmingly artisan in social composition.[29] Middle- and upper-class support stemmed from belief in the benefits of healthy recreation; and the objectives of the organizers were clearly class control. John McGregor, Captain of the London Scottish Volunteers, made it explicit when he listed the objectives and benefits to the Social Science Association in a paper on 'The Moral, Social and Hygienic Effects of the Volunteer Movement': 'Discipline, cleanliness, order, punctuality, promptitude and obedience have been imparted to them in such a manner as could not have been done by any other means whatever ...[volunteering made men]...less idle and dissipated and more respectful of authority.'[30] Such objectives linked up a number of other institutions dispensing sports to the lower classes under the control of dominant groups – the Young Men's Christian Association (YMCA), local schools, Sunday schools, and mechanics institutes.

The strategy failed to make a deep impression for a number of reasons. The reformers were not able to mobilize sufficient support among the dominant classes to establish a substantial enough presence in working-class recreation. The dominant classes, including the proponents of rational recreation, were far from willing to provide the same facilities for mass participation in sports as they enjoyed themselves; and nowhere is this attitude revealed more starkly than when it came to the question of state provision. In schools catering for the working class, drill not sports was seen as appropriate by reformers like Chadwick, and it alone qualified for a grant from the Board of Education.[31] Consequently, physical space in these schools continued to be drastically limited compared with the extensive acreages available to those who were being trained to be leaders of society at the public schools. Secondly, participation in the institutions of rational recreation still depended on meeting the patrons' criteria. Church-going was commonly required by church-sponsored sport when the majority of the working class were not attenders,[32] and access to employer-provided facilities tended to be restricted to those judged as reputable employees. Thirdly, sport of almost any kind was often expressly prohibited in the public parks and other open spaces. Lastly, and probably most importantly, again as in the previous period, a good proportion of popular sporting pastimes managed to escape reconstruction, or were only partially reconstructed, and were developed further.

Continuities and Developments in Popular Sports

If the ruling class as a whole was not particularly interested in achieving hegemony over the working class, and if reconstructed sports functioned primarily to unify the former, we must not lose sight of the fact that the sporting activity of the lower orders was still subject to fairly rigorous controls. Outbreaks of warfare continued over police interference in working-class recreation. In the later 1850s the new West Riding Police provoked riots and bitter opposition by mounting a concerted campaign against customary patterns of working-class recreation: roads outside Wakefield 'habitually infested with young men given to footracing' were being cleared by the police; gambling on the public highway – a traditional Sunday morning activity of working-class youth – was severely repressed; sporting pubs on the outskirts of towns like Leeds and Huddersfield were suddenly descended on and forced to close during divine service; and near Bradford there was a crackdown on cock-fighting and gambling, with large numbers of arrests and severe fines.[33] In 1866 it was possible for a man to be arrested and prosecuted in Bolton for race-running in the streets, on the grounds of 'indecency' because his legs were showing.[34] At the end of this decade Yorkshire Chief Constables were campaigning to restrict pub licensing hours on the grounds that the pubs harboured 'pests of society' and dog fanciers, race-runners, prize-fighters and others taking part in 'demoralizing games'.[35] And the same sort of thing was going on in the south of England as well. In an attempt to prevent Londoners from going racing *en masse*, 'saturnalian' horse-race meetings in the suburbs were banned by Act of Parliament in the early 1870s as a threat to law and order. Activities with close affinities to sports were treated in similar fashion: in 1871, 150 local fairs were suppressed by Act of Parliament.[36]

The degree of continuity that was maintained with the old popular cultural forms made healthy exercise and bourgeoisified sports relatively unattractive and helped insulate many people from the tenets of rational recreation. The permissive connivance in and patronage by a section of the dominant classes in popular sports continued to be an important supporting factor. Animality, excess and boisterousness seem to have remained notable features of popular recreation in the mid-Victorian period. The last of the big bare-knuckle contests, the legendary and brutal Sayers–Heenan fight, took place in 1860 and attracted an enormous amount of attention (the Prime Minister himself, Lord Palmerston, was in attendance);[37] public executions continued until the same year; elections were celebrated as popular holidays-cum-licensed brawls; Derby Day, Boat Race Day, and August Bank Holiday were days of Bacchanalia; sports like 'ratting' were extremely popular; alcohol consumption reached its peak in the mid-1870s; the 'beano' or 'spree' or 'blow-out' style of conviviality lived on.[38]

Although some major sports escaped thorough reform and reconstruction due to the influence of their aristocratic patrons, they did, nevertheless, experience some definite changes in that direction. The gaming element, however, remained absolutely central to some major sports and the association between aristocratic and plebian 'dissolute' elements in society remained strong. In 1865 boxing, the 'noble art of self-defence' came under more orderly rules, introduced with the help of an outstanding sporting aristocrat, the Marquess of Queensbury. Rounds of fixed duration were laid down and gloves were increasingly worn to prevent injuries becoming too serious.[39] Horse-racing's rather limited clean-up in the 1840s continued under Lord George Bentinck's successor, Admiral Rous: punctuality in starting and a new starting system, the numbering of horses and more careful weighing-in and weighing-out were introduced; and racing became more regular and frequent. By 1870 the Jockey Club had further tightened its control by threatening to withdraw recognition from meetings unless additional prize-money was put up, a consequence of which, whether intended or not, was the closing of many small local meetings. Despite the reforms corruption remained a serious problem throughout the period.[40]

Some historians are inclined to argue as if there was an absolute unilinear decline in the old pastimes of this period. Hobsbawm, for example, asserts that professional races, walking and rowing contests virtually disappeared and Best asserts that the spread of football and cricket 'made it clear they were the true representatives [of majority taste] compared with pugilism, badger-baiting, etc.'.[41] Yet the picture seems more complicated and the evidence for continuity in popular culture, in the shape of a great underground of popular sport, is somewhat stronger than these claims suggest. Take pedestrianism, for example. Although more or less abandoned by the 1850s by its former patrons the aristocracy, who had put up their footmen against each other for money, this eccentric, undisciplined, bizarre sport (competitors walked backwards, raced in weighted clogs, picked up stones, trundled barrow-loads of bricks in the style of the old festival contests) remained extremely popular: 'The elite among the professionals bearing heroic and flamboyant names like "The Gateshead Clipper", "The Norwich Milkboy", "The Crow-Catcher" and the like – raced for championship cups and belts before crowds of several thousands at major pedestrian enclosures in the big cities.'[42] The matches, often promoted by publicans and on which there was heavy betting, were so unruly that respectable citizens were outraged and encouraged police harassment. Or take rowing. Commencing on the river Tyne in the 1840s and in the 1860s on the Blyth and Wansbeck, rowing between individuals and teams for money stakes attracted thousands of betting onlookers and enthusiasts until the mid-1880s. The Tyneside local hero, Harry Clasper, was a miner, and in effect, a professional rower. Opponents came from far afield with their supporters, for example from London came the costers (street traders) bringing lots of money for gambling. Thousands of people were involved and rowing was much more popular than football. At Clasper's funeral in 1872, 130,000 people are said to have turned out, including local dignitaries, with foremost rowers as pallbearers, and the coffin was carried up the Tyne, which was lined with supporters, and followed by tugs.[43]

There are obviously important regional variations in the pattern of sporting activity and more evidence is needed before firm conclusions can be drawn. Some evidence available does suggest that particular kinds of working-class communities like the mining communities of the north-east of England, were immunized fairly effectively against reconstructed sports.[44] There, under the impact of legislation, brutal sports faded out, but they did not give way to bourgeois organized sport: there was strong continuity with traditional recreation forms and recreation developed in a different direction. The organized forms of sport that emerged in this period and became established in the 1860s and early 1870s were deeply rooted in mining culture and rural life – bowling, which was the most popular sport, pedestrianism and handicap racing, quoits, pigeon-racing and shooting, dog-racing, rabbit-coursing, and rowing. Thousands of miners and their families gathered at commercial sports grounds and at the chief centres of sporting activity, the inns, run by publican sports entrepreneurs. The participants were almost exclusively miners, as competitors and spectators, and the organization and the values symbolized in the proceedings were the reverse of the amateur–gentleman spirit. Competition was always for prize-money, rather than the amateur paraphernalia of cups, medals, etc. The object was unashamedly to win – to lose was catastrophe; and heavy betting provided the rationale. In communities where livelihood depended on the ability to perform hard physical labour and where economic insecurity was the norm, physical recreation dominated free time: 'it provided the meaning of life, more important by far, after survival needs had been met, than other aspects of life.'[45] Proficiency in sports conferred status in the community on the individual and each community had its champion in the various sports, who represented it in competitions involving other, similar communities; so sports were one of the main ways these communities held together. In Newcastle dominant groups reacted by castigating such sports gatherings as a threat to safety and to law and order, and accordingly in 1877 a by-law was passed arming magistrates with discretionary powers to prohibit bowling on the Town Moor. One opinion-maker commented: 'That fully 90% of the men who frequented that Moor on Saturday, for the purpose of bowling and racing and rabbit coursing and other such like dangerous and immoral pastimes were pitmen, and pitmen who were simply the scum of the neighbouring villages.'[46]

This is an example of local conditions producing a relatively self-contained, insulated working-class community sports culture sharply differentiated from that of dominant groups. On the other hand, Joyce argues convincingly – on the basis of a very thorough study of the character of class relations, work culture and politics in the Lancashire industrial town – that up to the 1880s the working class remained effectively integrated through the superimposition of work culture, religious culture and community life in general, that is, in such cases the class was not self-contained and there was no sharp break between working-class culture and that of the dominant class. Furthermore, and significant as a harbinger of things to come, he shows how popular sports were appropriated, incorporated into the political culture and harnessed to democratization of the political system as it developed in this period.[47]

The nature of popular culture and especially the centrality of popular sports therein, afforded dominant groups opportunities to exploit it for political purposes, and new ways of harnessing sports to politics were developed during this period under the stimulus of pressure for political change. What Joyce has shown in detail for one region no doubt has features peculiar to that region, but it indicates what is likely to have been the case in at least some other places as well. The political culture, that 'grand participatory theatre of politics' as he terms it, was saturated with sporting activity and the symbols of sport: the latter functioned as an aspect of a political system in which working-class participation was of a symbolic, ritualistic character, and in which real power and control resided firmly in the hands of local, regional and national oligarchies. The formation of political clubs, co-ops, and friendly societies was a central feature of the elaboration of local political party organization that accelerated in the 1860s with electoral reform, the extension of the franchise and consequently the need to gain popular support. These organizations, especially the clubs, were highly successful in tapping working-class people's political allegiances and in encompassing their leisure and social lives within a framework of politics. Popular sports figured prominently among their activities: billiards, bowls and the bar, dog-breeding and coursing were typical and the clubs were centre pieces of election campaigns. In the campaign and in the election the emotion and imagery of the race-course and the fair day was incorporated in the general saturnalia that surrounded these occasions: 'Election day was a celebration of allegiance and a popular sport of the greatest participatory intensity. . .proceeded by a welter of broadsheets, songs, placards and ''squibs'', the motifs of which were often sporting. . .the parties as opposed football teams, or the much used billiards and horserace handicap fictions. . .pigeons, dogs, especially bulldogs, were often tied with political colours.'[48] Elections were conducted as 'speaking matches' in which the game was at least as important as the contest. Sport was particularly important in mediating the political personality of the candidates and the respective parties' appeals. Candidates were presented as, and played up the role of being, 'good sports' and their largess in the community around election time generally included gifts of money to cricket and football clubs. In many ways though, participation in popular sports affected masters as much as men.

On the whole, the Tories tapped popular culture – especially the sporting component – more successfully than the Liberals, and the Tories, brewers and butchers formed a powerful alliance that was strongly associated with sports. Beer and Britannia was often more than a match for rational recreation. The major symbols which functioned to equate Toryism with Englishness and patriotism and which became symbols of British national character, the John Bull figure and the bulldog, had strong sporting connotations and were appropriated from popular sports culture. With the advance in rivalry between the great powers and with the extension of the franchise, dominant groups and the political parties found it convenient to tap the widespread suspicion of foreigners and outsiders and to identify their own interests with the 'national interest'; and so appeals in terms of the national good, often mixed with chauvinism, became an increasingly important element in the emergent pattern of hegemony; and sporting imagery and symbolism played a certain part in this kind of appeal.

The great degree of regional and local variation in working-class culture exhibited in the patterns of participation in sports, points up the absence of working-class cohesion at the national level. What Joyce reveals in the case of the Lancashire towns is likely to have become more typical of the country as a whole in this period, given that between 1850 and 1880 the factory system had spread more widely, if still unevenly, over the country. Furthermore, the differential attachment of sections of the working class to religious culture, secular–radical culture and popular culture remained a significant factor fragmenting the class, in particular the propensity of working-class people to affiliate differentially to sporting forms played an important part in this process locally.

One of the main sources of fragmentation, the heterogeneity of labour, still very much pertained, notably the superior position of the skilled craftsman. While we agree in general with Joyce that theories (such as Foster's) of the role of the 'labour aristocracy' are inadequate in themselves as an explanation of the integration of the working class, there is evidence that the pattern of participation in leisure and sports among skilled workers or artisans, did differ in certain respects from the pattern in the rest of the class. No doubt, as Joyce suggests, there were many similarities also, but he tends to pass over these differences too lightly. There are some indications that the rational recreation movement and bourgeoisified sports did register a greater impression as far as skilled workers are concerned. Their superior economic position and their outwardly more respectable style of life in many respects rendered them more readily able to participate and made them more acceptable to their patrons and controllers. Also, in the countryside football and cricket appealed more to village tradesmen, craftsmen and young farmers than to village labourers, who could neither afford the time nor the equipment to play.[49] It was implicit in the mode of organization and the ethos of rational recreation and bourgeoisified sports that the more respectable segment of the working class was always more likely to become attached, although it was not necessarily in the programme of the controllers. The relatively greater involvement of this group did not necessarily bourgeoisify it, but it certainly paralleled the already significant gap in other aspects of its life-style, such as housing, diet and clothing, that existed between it and the rest of the class.

Lastly, wherever we look – the gentleman–amateur controlled network, sports provided by patrons of the working class, commercialized popular sports, or local working-class community-based sports – sports culture seems overwhelmingly a masculine culture. Middle- and upper-class women took up some sports like bicycling, croquet, and tennis, in a 'ladylike' manner, that is a manner compatible with their ascribed segregated role. Working-class women seem to have been almost entirely left outside sports save perhaps those that centred on working-class communities, and even here there seems little evidence of as active a participation and control as that enjoyed by men. The new disciplinary technology of athleticism and organized sports seems only to have impinged marginally on females in so far as they experienced 'drill' in the schools. Plainly, more work needs to be done on the effect of women's and girls' participation in sports at the time, but until evidence emerges to the contrary it seems reasonable to conclude that, in addition, sports culture produced further fragmentation by fostering gender divisions among working-class people.

The 'double armoury' whereby the working class was sewn into a system of cross-class alliances – the more respectable and upper working class tending to be more closely stitched to the liberal bourgeoisie in an alliance of the 'industrious classes' against the remnants of 'Old Corruption'; and the other elements tending to be more closely associated with the Tory radicals and Whig patricians against the political economy of the liberal bourgeoisie – continued to limit working-class cohesion and reduce its independence. We must note significant developments concerning sports in relation to the hegemonic project. The main measure at this time was, of course, the extension of the franchise to the urban working-class male (which meant, in effect, the skilled workers). While the bourgeoisie dominated the power bloc and did not strive to achieve a hegemony over the working class as such, we have seen the project being tried out with respect to sporting activity in two ways: the 'urban gentry's' initiatives along rational recreation lines, and secondly, the major political groupings' use of sports culture in election campaigns and to maintain a permanent footing in local communities. Such moves were made in relation to specific groups, one at a time, and whether intended or not, the main target turned out to be skilled workers and the more respectable workers. Moves to press sports into the service of the hegemonic project, that is, to bridge the class divide and win working-class support, were to become more characteristic from this period onwards.

4

Sport and the Remaking of the Working Class

The period from the 1880s up to 1914 saw increasing class confrontation, the threat of political instability at home and anti-imperialist rivalry abroad. By about 1900 the main features of a modern capitalist economy were diffused throughout Britain and the scale of industrial conflict and settlements broadened out to the national level. The emergence of the Labour Party and other socialist groups, the new unionism, and the greater militancy of labour in general, expressed the growing independence, organization and power of a more homogeneous extensive working class.[1] Although the value of real wages had risen and with the spread of the Saturday half-holiday and the 55-hour week, there was now more free time for workers, Booth's and Rowntree's surveys revealed a seemingly ineradicable mass of poverty, indicating the presence of an even wider gulf between the classes than had hitherto been realized among dominant groups.[2] This together with agitation for Irish Home Rule and for women's suffrage combined to produce among the dominant classes a widespread sense of an impending clash at home; and the intensity of rivalry between the great powers heightened the sense of threat from abroad and stimulated an outpouring of jingoistic sentiment.[3] The need to promote social harmony through policies of class reconciliation and to be prepared to face the foreign enemy became predominant themes in social and political commentary.

Hardly yet a full electoral democracy in today's terms, Britain, had, nevertheless, embarked on the era of mass politics. Civil society expanded and elaborated at every level into a more or less unitary entity, in which the working class was integrated in a subordinate position. That subordination was now based on the extensive participation of working-class people in civil society and on accommodation between nationally extensive classes. Rule was based on consent rather than the exclusion of working-class people from national life and on localized, particularistic forms of control and repression. In Gramsci's terms the basis of the dominant class's hegemony over the working class was achieved in this period.

It was also in this period that sports took on their modern dimensions as mass entertainment forms and that certain sports, notably football, became a firm part of working-class culture. The heavier concentration of population in urban areas, increased income and leisure time for the working class, better transport, the development of a mass-circulation press, and the technological advances made in sports equipment (the invention of the bicycle, etc.), were all important prerequisites for the expansion of sports, but in themselves these factors do not account for the specific pattern of development in relation to the power structure. Demand from working-class people for more extensive participation, the centrality of sports in haute-bourgeois culture and in the formation of the identity of dominant groups, attempts to discipline the working class through sports, bourgeois women's desire for more independence and a more emancipated leisure, the activities of leisure entrepreneurs, and the appropriation of the symbols of popular sports by the political elite – all played their part in the deployment of sports and its articulation on the power network.

Missionizing, Conciliation and Discipline

A more sustained and variegated attempt was made by a section of the dominant class to adapt, extend and deploy athleticist technology as part of a programme of class conciliation and control, using a 'philanthropic strategy'. To the sports-oriented missionizing institutions of the mid-Victorian era already implicated in this emergent programme – the Volunteers, the working men's clubs, the local political clubs, the Young Men's Christian Association (YMCA), the Sunday Schools and other socio-religious organizations, and employers' philanthropic efforts – were now added a series of new missionizing movements, agencies and their attendant discourses. The appearance of the settlement movement, the boys' club movement, other socio-religious organizations like the Band of Hope, the uniformed youth organizations (Boy's Brigade, Boy Scouts, Girl Guides, cadet forces, etc.), sport in the state elementary schools, the hygienist movement, and the growing concern with physical fitness and training at the War Office, among the military and in imperialist circles as a whole, signalled an important development in the strategic elaboration of power at this level. Perceived gaps in the circuit of power were being filled in, the lines connecting civil society and the state were being laid down more firmly, the gaze of authority was being extended further into the everyday lives of the lower orders. Now more consciously political, the ideological impetus and the organizational capacity were provided, in the main, by the urban gentry. The programme could not have achieved its effects without the practical support of subaltern intellectuals and social categories forming a bridge between dominant and subordinate classes. Important in this respect were the lower clergy and lay preachers, lower-middle-class quasi-professionals like elementary schoolteachers, medical auxiliary workers and others involved in youth and community work, especially bourgeois women and women of the middle classes in general. To some extent upper-working-class individuals figured in this role as well. Neither the strategy nor the objectives were monolithic, nor was the discourse univocal; yet the effects, despite the differences between groups, tended to work in the same direction. Whatever the religious or political message – Christian–Socialist, Church of England–Conservative, Liberal–Nonconformist, or whatever – the twin objectives were class conciliation and disciplining the lower orders into conformity with bourgeois norms of respectability; and sporting activity was central to this project throughout this period. One clear indication of the churches' involvement in the deployment of sport as part of this kind of enterprise is their success in promoting football. A quarter of Birmingham's teams were church-connected in 1880, and in Liverpool in 1900 local teams originated almost exclusively from church organizations. A significant proportion of the clubs which later formed the core of the Football League were sponsored by socio-religious bodies – among them were Bolton, Wolverhampton Wanderers, Aston Villa, Birmingham City, Swindon, and Tottenham Hotspur.[4]

The strategy depended on entry being gained to working-class communities and so, from the later 1870s into the Edwardian era the rash of settlements, clubs, institutes, branches of national uniformed youth organizations, elementary-school and church-based groups, which broke out in the main urban centres, relied heavily on organized sports and other forms of physical recreation to attach working-class people. The settlement movement was probably the most systematic and elaborate attempt to do so.[5] Inspired by the social teachings of a group of reforming Oxford intellectuals – Toynbee, T. H. Green and Jowett among them – the rationale was to become comprehensively involved inside working-class communities: involvement in sport and recreation, charitable work, clubs, local politics, university extension teaching, etc. replaced proselytizing and indoctrination. Practitioners like Canon Barnett, the founder of Toynbee Hall in East London, conceived of their settlements among the urban masses as civic centres from which civilization was to be dispensed. The urban gentry would use their influence and their wealthy social connections to work for social harmony and to heal the class breach. The annual report of one of these establishments, Oxford House in East London, is revealing on the objectives:

> Colonisation by the well-to-do seems indeed to be the true solution of the East End question...for the problem of how to make the masses understand

their spiritual and social solidarity with the rest of the capital and of the kingdom: how to revive their sense of citizenship with its privileges which they have lost and its responsibilities which they have forgotten. Among these privileges should be education and rational amusement and social intercourse, and these can best be supplied by local clubs with their various guilds, classes and societies. Among the duties, on the other hand which require to be revived, thrift and patience stand pre-eminent.[6]

Given the public-school, athleticist background of the missionaries, clerical and otherwise, the primacy of sport in their programme is understandable. At the Clifton College Settlement in Bristol for example, in 1883 a working men's club was started, with reading-rooms, library, meeting-room, billiard saloon, refreshment room, a magnificent gymnasium with showers and washing facilities, football and cricket teams and a cycling club.[7]

Once entry to working-class communities had been gained, a second strategic feature – best exemplified again, perhaps, in the settlement movement – was the way the missionaries aligned themselves with the local working class on certain issues. The Reverend Harvey for example, pioneer of the Clifton College Settlement, associated himself with workers' struggles over wages, conditions and welfare through the mutual improvement society he started at the settlement, and by 1886 he was arbitrating industrial disputes and sat as Chairman of the Co-operative Education Committee. Similarly, at Toynbee Hall the settlers ran campaigns for open spaces, for the appointment of the first school board doctors, for classes for the handicapped and for free school meals. Such activity led the leader of the Bermondsey Labour Party, Alfred Salter, to attribute the end of the class war there to their influence.[8] The missionaries' ability to make such contacts was enhanced by the fact that much of the leadership of the labour and co-operative movements in the 1880s and 1890s was supplied by men who had received their early training in such Bible classes or mutual improvement societies as those of the Clifton College Mission and Toynbee Hall. Some of the university and public-school men who descended on working-class communities at the time, later exercised an important influence over the Labour Party and British socialism and on the development of the Welfare State. The future Prime Minister, Clement Attlee, worked in the Stepney Boys' Club set up by his school, Haileybury; Tawney and Beveridge were resident for a time at the turn of the century at Toynbee Hall.

Financed and patronized by the urban gentry and their allies, officered by God-fearing, earnest middle-class men, the clubs, institutes and other organizations catering for working-class boys and young men projected an image of the ideal normalized youth as being organized and disciplined. With minor variations the formula for producing such youth was the same everywhere: 'Football in Fulham, boxing in Balham, and ping-pong in

Putney', as one commentator put it.[9] The underlying concern with respectability deemed appropriate to their clients' station is exemplified in the boys' club movement's disciplinary code. Religion, orderly behaviour, cleanliness, temperance, non-smoking, 'manliness', 'self-control' and individual improvement were the watchwords in the clubs proliferating in the urban centres; and their targets were the more amenable boys. For example, the target group was identified in London as the 120,000 boys who fell between the 'hooligans' and 'decent boys'. The concern with control is to be seen in the technology of surveillance incorporated in the design of club and institute buildings, and the use of space, furnishing and decoration: frosted windows, or windows fitted with blinds and curtains to avoid attracting 'loafers' and 'roughs', a single entry and exit to control admittance, glazed upper halves of interior doors to prevent users escaping the gaze of authority, iconic photographs of sports teams in prominent positions: 'Attention to small details such as these will do much to foster the good spirit and to remind the members continually that the place is not merely a playground, but in the best sense of the word, a club.'[10] Similar organizations like the Band of Hope, a temperance body with three million members in 1900, achieved their greatest success with children of stable families with a steady, if little, income.[11]

On the other hand, the uniformed youth organizations that began to appear in the 1880s were a break with the Sunday School, club and mission approaches, more in tune with the growing militarism and imperialist sentiment of the period.[12] Once again religiously inspired and obsessed with physical fitness, they recruited strongly from the ranks of skilled labour and the more respectable kind of youth. The Boys' Brigade's aim was: 'The advancement of Christ's kingdom among boys and the habits of obedience, reverence, discipline, self-respect and all that tends towards Christian manliness'.[13] The formula of sports, uniforms, bands, street processions and a summer camp was highly successful with boys and young men up to the age of seventeen, and it was rapidly copied by the Church of England, the Roman Catholic Church and the Jews. Working-class cadet forces started in the 1880s and the one associated with Toynbee Hall impressed social-reforming ladies like Octavia Hill with their potential for control:

There is no organisation which I have found influence so powerfully for good the boys in such a neighbourhood [Notting Hill]. The cadets learn the duty and dignity of obedience; they get a sense of corporate life and of civic duty; they learn to honour the power of endurance and effort; and they come into contact with manly and devoted officers... These ideals are in marked contrast with the listless self-indulgence, the pert self-assertion, the selfishness and want of reverence which are so characteristic of the life in the low district.[14]

From their inception in 1908 under Baden-Powell, the Boy Scouts rapidly became the most successful of the uniformed youth organizations. Less authoritarian than the Boys' Brigade, motivated by an amalgam of muscular Christianity, imperialism, anti-urban open-air naturalism, and crude anti-socialist social-Darwinism, they deliberately played down military-style discipline as off-putting to their clientele.

Sports were still largely excluded from the state school curriculum. In 1895 within a mile radius of Charing Cross, 30,000 children were in schools without even a yard or playground. Although the various elementary school codes placed an increasing importance on the physical well-being of children from 1890 onwards, in practice variations on military-style drill for disciplinary, rather than therapeutic purposes, were the norm.[15] Individual, more enterprising school boards, like the London School Board, were exceptional in getting sports onto the curriculum in the face of Board of Education parsimony. Swimming in particular, which was promoted for public health reasons, was given a major stimulus as a competitive sport in London in this way. But the really significant way the state schools promoted sporting activity among working-class people was through the extra-curricular initiatives of teachers, who took on themselves the role of youth workers, as a strategy for controlling their pupils' free time, with the objective of making them more amenable to school discipline. In 1885 teachers were thus responsible for the formation of the South London Football League and by 1890 there were highly competitive schoolboy leagues up and down the country. Indeed, elementary school teams were another source of origin of Football League clubs, and in these ways the state schools were a vital link in the growing popularity and development of the game as a feature of working-class culture.

The increase in the statistics for juvenile delinquency between 1890 and 1914 can be attributed directly to this kind of redeployment of power to organize the free time of young working-class males, that is it produced the 'delinquent' as the independent, 'anti-social' youth who resisted organization.[16] Over the five years ending in 1908–9 an annual average of 177,500 people, including thousands of children, were summarily convicted for minor offences and committed to jail.[17] Their commonest crimes were playing in the street, throwing stones and snowballs, gambling, sleeping out and trespassing, for which stretches of between three days and one month in jail were awarded. A study of St Ebbes in the city of Oxford confirms that from the 1890s a major proportion of non-indictable crime was of this kind and that voluntary youth workers, not the police, were the most vociferous element in urging stronger control over non-conforming youth.[18] Drawn from subaltern groups like teachers and clerks, strongly committed to bourgeois norms of respectability, the voluntary workers, especially the women among them, were particularly sensitive to behaviour which seemed to challenge their authority. In the continuous battle to delineate the model adolescent, those who challenged the norms were abruptly expelled and stigmatized as 'trouble-makers', or dealt with by the police, with the result that by 1910, in St Ebbes, membership came predominantly from the lower-middle and upper working classes. As the pressure increased all round to adopt the normalized bourgeois model, working-class youth tended to split into two mutually antagonistic groups: the lower-working-class ones reacting against the pressures to conform, producing their own model namely the 'corner-boy' with a distinctive mode of dress (wide leather belt and bell-bottomed trousers) and the more respectable, conforming youth, clean-cut, belonging to an organization and likely to be keen on sport. After 1912 youth workers concentrated on that section which could be controlled more easily and left the rest to their own devices and to the police.

The extreme concern over how young working-class males spent their free time was due to a combination of factors. The traditional integrative influence of the family was being strongly counteracted by changes in the economy, as the structure of the typical unit of production and the division of labour therein were now less likely to coincide with that of the working-class family and to reproduce its pattern of power and authority over the young.[19] There was a fear of industrial revolt and that army recruits were not sufficiently fit physically for military service. Lower-working-class youth was much less amenable to control than upper-working-class youth, and the controlling personnel were disinclined and/or culturally ill-equipped to bridge the gap successfully – hence the resort to other agencies of control for this group, such as the police and the schools. In terms of the technology and economy of control, it was more productive to concentrate on young, upper-working-class males. The daunting scale of the overall problem of control meant it had to be dealt with increasingly at the level of the state apparatus.

The gravitation towards an entertainment model of organization, albeit in the interests of discipline, continued in these normalizing institutions, but there was still a good deal of suspicion of what were seen as the counter-productive aspects of commercial influences. In the 1890s, for example, the boys' clubs promoted active participation in sport and physical fitness as the antidote to 'spectatorism' and gambling on sports events among the working class. This antipathy to commercial influence passed on into the ethos of physical training in the state schools.

Whether intended or not, the effect of the 'philanthropic strategy', as Donzelot calls it,[20] was to successfully deploy athleticist technology on lower-middle-class, upper-working-class and respectable working-class males. With the rest of the working class it largely failed. Unlike charity, a philanthropic strategy is designed to obtain a return. In return for the opportunity to enjoy sport and physical recreation facilities and services and the surrounding paraphernalia, the clientele was required to submit to supervision with the object of normalization. The variations on the athleticist register, which pervaded the practice and discourse of the whole range of philanthropic institutions and activities concerned with the use of free time, signified a model of a compliant, respectable, aspiring, working class. What was offered was not simply facilities and enjoyment plus ideology. Participation was an aid to stabilizing a section of the working class, which was offered a chance of social advance (or at least some stability) by conferring a badge of respectability on its behaviour and introducing some order into its members' lives.

Athleticist technology was deployed on men rather than women because sport was not part of the latter's culture, nor did women constitute a problem of control of the same dimensions, and in so far as they did so, the family was the primary instrument for integrating them. The cultivation of 'manliness' in sporting activity for the working class was linked to a deployment of sexuality at the time, which had the specific objective of extending control over the lower orders by focusing attention on the production of 'normal families' through public health measures. Hygienism not only operated through legislation permitting surveillance of the population to eliminate diseases like tuberculosis, but also campaigned increasingly with the aid of legislation allowing intervention in the working-class family against 'social diseases' like venereal diseases, prostitution and incest.[21] While athleticist technology promoted a specifically male identity around notions and practices to do with sport, which included notions of physical fitness and clean living, and thereby promoted a rigid division between the sexes, medical science and medico-therapeutic technology did likewise by authorizing a categorization of females as physically less suited to sports. But hygienism promoted by the medical authorities went further in function than this. It facilitated an alliance between working-class women and the medical authorities, which in turn facilitated state regulation of working-class families. By voluntarily submitting their children to regular health checks which, incidentally, extended the gaze of the 'dispensary' into the home, working-class women achieved some extra protection and security for themselves and their children through this method of stabilizing the family. Simultaneously, by co-operating in this way in the production of hygienized, normalized families, they functioned as a relay within the working-class family for an extended form of control over men and children.

A distinct tendency to deploy not so much athleticist, as physical-exercise/therapeutic technology, can be detected, which resulted from a shift in the climate of opinion in ruling circles, where worries about national efficiency and racial degeneration had been provoked in particular by Britain's inept military performance in the Boer War and by the revelations about the poor physical condition of army recruits. Kipling's 'flanneled fool at the wicket' jibe voiced increasing scepticism in the imperialist camp about the efficacy of athleticism and the danger of substituting sport for more serious pursuits. *The Times* spoke for those who wanted more efficient scientific body management when it pointed to the threat of Germany and advocated more vigorous physical training on Prussian and Swedish lines, and appealed for sports to be embraced less passionately.[22] It does not seem accidental that Swedish drill and therapeutic gymnastics started to be promoted more seriously in the state schools at about this time. The Scout movement above all embodied this kind of thinking. From 1908 to 1911 its membership and its personnel grew to over 100,000, organized in 4,000 troops, led by 4,000 scoutmasters and 3,000 assistants. Overseas, the movement had a remarkable success with 250,000 members before the First World War.[23] The lengths to which this kind of deployment could go can be seen in the activities of Lord Meath. A strong believer in training the body as a prerequisite for indoctrinating the mind, the founder of Empire Day, the Duty and Discipline Movement and the Lad's Drill Association, he was prominent in almost every military–imperialist organization of any note. He agitated for military training in schools, universal physical training for boys up to the age of eighteen, and he was instrumental in getting the Board of Education to institute compulsory drill for school teachers.[24]

From Reconstructed to Mass Sport: Class Differentiation and Accommodation

Two other analytically distinct, yet empirically related processes under the control of dominant groups overlaid the deployment of athleticist technology described so far: the expansion of the voluntary sports apparatus and the increasing commercialization of sports. These developments embodied quite different objectives, but they nevertheless exerted pertinent effects on the way working-class people became involved in sports and on the overall character of the sports network, of significance for the achievement of hegemony. The voluntary sports network's expansion continued unabated from the 1870s to the 1900s. Sports clubs of every description continued to proliferate and many national bodies were formed for newer, as well as for more minor forms of sport.[25] This process was interlaced with and existed in some tension with an accelerating tendency to commercialize sporting activity in response to the evident popular demand. By the last two decades of the century the outlines of the modern pattern of sport are clearly visible.

In view of its centrality in working-class culture the magnitude of the

expansion of football is particularly noteworthy. Competitive, commercialized League Football, professional football as a presitigious occupation
to which many young working-class men aspire, and a large proportion
of the Football League's major clubs – all originate in this period.[26]
Within a relatively short space of time League games and the Football
Association (FA) Cup Competition attracted enormous audiences. The gate
for the latter more than doubled between 1884 and 1888 (rising from 12,500
to 27,000). Four years later it had grown to 45,000 and thereafter the
average attendance from 1893–1903 was 80,000, until in 1913, 120,000
people jammed Wembley Stadium to capacity. Near the end of the period
12,000 clubs with a membership of 300,000 were registered with the
FA.[27] Although not quite on the same scale or of the same significance
in relation to working-class culture, other major sports experienced the
same kind of development. Gate-money had been charged regularly in
cricket and horse-racing before the 1880s. With W. G. Grace at his zenith
from 1876–86, crowds flocked to watch him and county matches could
attract large audiences comparable with football. In 1892 for example, over
63,000 attended the match between Surrey and Nottinghamshire at the
Oval.[28] Now the pattern was becoming more common in other sports, like
rugby and athletics, particularly in the more working-class industrial north
and midlands, where local business interests were patronizing and promoting
sport more energetically.[29]

Britain's premier position in international trade and her status as the
leading imperial power continued to ensure the export of amateur-dominated
sports and the growth of sporting links of this kind with many parts of
the world. More commercialized sports with a traditionally plebian and
aristocratic following, such as horse-racing and boxing, also expanded
internationally.[30] Crowds could now enjoy contests between individuals
and teams from other countries, and the stage was set for sporting events
to symbolize contests between nations. In this connection the British amateur
athleticist tradition had a formative influence on emergent international
sporting institutions. Notably, de Coubertin founded the modern Olympic
movement on the British public-school amateur–gentleman ideal.[31] The
foundations of an international structure for competitive sport on a regular
basis began to be laid in this period.

The role of the mass-circulation press in encouraging the development
of mass sport merits particular attention. Hitherto, specialist sporting
journals with sizeable circulations catered largely for the upper- and middle-
class enthusiast. As sports acquired a bigger following among working-
class people, sporting papers for the working-class reader sprang up. By
the 1890s there were three dailies and twelve weeklies for horse-racing
alone, and by 1900 twenty-five sporting papers were being published in
London.[32] It is understandable then, that so popular an item as this should

be incorporated into, and occupy so prominent a place within, that miscellany of items which was to constitute the mass-circulation daily newspaper, and which emerged also at this time.[33] The sports pages were absolutely vital from the beginning, both in the successful selling of this form of popular press to working-class people and in the place sport achieved in working-class culture.

The fact that working-class people were establishing a presence within this domain was an integral part of the remaking of the working class in this period, whereby the class was to become a more homogeneous, organized, independent force and a more active agent in the social formation at every level. The new independence of working class people was manifested in their sporting activities and, in general, in the organizations around which they took place. Dominant groups' patronage and control over the Working Men's Club and Institute Union was rejected and a democratically elected representative body took its place.[34] The newly formed northern bike clubs provided access to the countryside and made possible different points of reference for working-class people.[35] League football clubs like Tottenham Hotspur and Aston Villa dissociated themselves from their original socio-religious sponsors. Certain reconstructed sports were colonized and changes forced on them by the working-class presence. Working-class people stamped sports like association football and rugby league with their own character and transformed them in some ways into a means of expression for values opposed to the bourgeois athleticist tradition: vociferous partisanship, a premium on victory, a suspicion of and often a disdain for, constituted authority, a lack of veneration for official rules, mutual solidarity as the basis of team-work, a preference for tangible monetary rewards for effort and a hedonistic 'vulgar' festive element, were all brought to sports. Disorder around football, later to be labelled 'football hooliganism' was also not unknown at this time.[36]

In this remaking process sports exerted two kinds of effects. They served to differentiate the two major class groupings, the working class and the bourgeoisie, so that different, in some ways opposed, class identities and conceptions of society were formed around sporting activity. And secondly, sports in complex ways reproduced internal divisions within these groups, which mitigated opposition between the classes. For the dominant groups the development of sport over the last three decades of the century helped to resolve two related problems: how the ruling elite was to demarcate itself as such, and how the middle classes were to differentiate themselves from the working class and identify with the elite. The failure of existing cultural tradition to perform this function adequately due to the rapidity of social change, brought forth newly 'invented' traditions like the sports cult, which came to perform it instead.[37] The strategy of promoting amateur athleticism, maintaining control over the major sporting institutions and creating socially exclusive sports, achieved the objective. The key discourse/practice through which differentiation was accomplished and through which power relations exerted their effect was the amateur–professional couplet and the key ideological figure was that of the 'gentleman'.

In some quarters the cult of athleticism was voiced more vociferously than ever, as the incursion of the working class, commercialism and professionalism challenged amateur–gentleman hegemony. The formal barriers, as such, to working-class entry and participation, however, came down relatively easily after some initial resistance: but the informal ones were rather more resilient and certainly more significant. Inside the governing bodies of sport reactions varied. The Bicycle Union dropped its 'mechanics clause' in 1878 when it came to be realized that: 'The lout was in fact turning out to be less of a threat to the new sporting ethics than had at first been feared.'[38] Under pressure from the Northern Counties Athletic Association, the Amateur Athletic Club was replaced by the Amateur Athletic Association and its 'mechanics clause' deleted in 1880. The amateur–gentleman character of athletics was retained simply by redefining manual-worker athletes as amateurs and having as little truck as possible with the practices of the more working-class sport of 'pedestrianism'. In fact, despite strenuous efforts to eradicate professionalism, it was perpetuated in covert form in this period, again especially in the north.[39]

Football preserved its amateur–athleticist ethos relatively easily until the FA Cup competition from 1871 opened up the game. An increasing number of northern clubs with working-class players entered the competition and a form of professionalism crept in with the payment of expenses for time off work. In 1883 Blackburn Olympic broke the southern amateur–gentlemen clubs' monopoly over the Cup, which the latter never won thereafter. In apparent consternation the FA passed a rule which effectively banned the incipient professional players from taking part, and the northern clubs, heavily reliant on them and on working-class supporters for their existence, formed their own association in response. Faced by a crisis, the FA wisely conceded in a way that accommodated and incorporated professionalism and the working-class element within a structure in which, at the same time, conflicting elements within the dominant class were accommodated. Professionalism was accepted, the northern clubs came back into the fold, the national apparatus of the game continued to be controlled by those more committed to the amateur–gentleman philosophy; while at local level, business elements which supported professionalism and facilitated entry of the working class, moved increasingly into the administration of the game. With the formation of the Football League in 1885 coming under the overall authority of the FA, and with the introduction of a separate cup competition for amateurs in 1892, the professionalized, commercialized, more working-class side of the game was insulated from the amateur side, competition between them minimized, and thus the risk of defeat at the hands of working-class players and the consequent humiliation and loss of prestige it might have entailed, was avoided.[40]

But contrary to received opinion, such evidence as there is at hand points to the limited extent to which the working class made this 'their game', in the sense of achieving control over it. It suggests instead that a three-way accommodation between classes took place in which the working class element was subordinated. The established, more gentleman–amateur oriented, bourgeois element retaining the formal positions of authority, remaining in overall charge of the FA apparatus and dominating the game normatively, working-class pressure to participate was conceded, but was confined largely to playing, supporting and spectating; and economic and financial control over the League clubs passed to local business interests. Also, working-class advance in society was not paralleled by similar advances in the industrial relations side of the game, which were remarkably backward by almost any standard.[41] With the exception of the level of wages, which were slightly above those of skilled workers, when compared with other employees the 6,000 or so professional footballers were in a quasi-feudal market and work situation. Footballers were subject to a cartel of employers which imposed wage and mobility restrictions and disciplinary procedures, to which no other category of labour, barring military personnel, were subject. They were not allowed to sell their skills to the highest bidder, and changes of employer could only be made with the consent of the current employer and in return for a transfer fee. But employers could also penalize a player for refusing a transfer initiated by the employer by witholding his wages. In 1912 the legality of the 'retain and transfer system' was upheld in the High Court in a case brought by the players union against the FA. Unionization was weak and kept so successfully by the FA and the Football League. In 1909 when the union took the FA to court under the law on workmen's compensation and when it sought to affiliate to the General Federation of Trade Unions (GFTU), the FA withdrew recognition, ordered all players to resign from the union and promise to obey FA rules on pain of suspension and suspended the union's officials. To the threat of a strike the authorities responded by preparing blackleg teams of amateurs. The outcome was a humiliating defeat for the union: it was forced to disaffiliate from the GFTU, in effect to give up the right to strike and to agree to bring disputes to the FA to adjudicate before taking legal action. From early on professional players were excluded from any decision-making processes by the FA and the League (in 1898 they were debarred from sitting on any FA committee). Players were forbidden to talk to the press, to criticize aspects of the game publicly and disallowed from reporting on matches in which they had taken part. No legal representation was allowed before FA disciplinary hearings.

No matter what the origin of the League clubs – religious, work organization, or whatever – their subsequent development was dominated by business organization. West Ham Football Club, for example, one of the few clubs of which there is a detailed scholarly study of its origins, was founded by a muscular-Christian ironworks owner, Arnold Hill.[42] In 1895 he created a series of clubs in the interests of good business and improving industrial relations – in fact, the football team was started immediately following a serious strike at the ironworks. Professional players from outside the community were employed from the beginning. In 1900 the club became a limited liability company controlled exclusively by its shareholders, all of whom by 1902 were self-employed or professional men. A business-model merger with a nearby club followed shortly, the club was transferred to the latter's ground, Hill's personal control passed to a self-perpetuating Board of Directors and local politicians were recruited as vice-presidents to establish the club's credentials with the local community. In 1905, just ten years after its creation, almost all the players were professionals from outside the community and the local working class's participation was limited to paying at the gate and supporting.

In contrast to the previous generation of philanthropic patrons the new men tended to take a more hard-nosed proprietorial attitude to the clubs and ran them like business enterprises in order to attract the maximum support and ensure financial viability. The limited liability road was being taken by business in general and the clubs were no exception. Starting in 1887 with Birmingham City, by 1900 all but one of the League clubs were limited companies and the process of shifting control away from vice-presidential patrons or members into the hands of non-working-class shareholders and specialist managers had begun. Under the impetus of commercialization the professional game developed rapidly: in 1888 there were twelve League clubs, all from the North and Midlands; by 1909 there were 6,000 professional players in 400 clubs and by the First World War there were 40 clubs in the English League. Despite the takeover of the clubs by local business interests and the more commercialized form of organization, the motivation of those in control cannot be said to be primarily an economic one. The clubs were not run like ordinary businesses, for the football authorities expressly restricted dividends and payments to directors and many clubs were run at a loss.

In an almost exactly similar crisis in rugby in the 1890s, centering on the Northern Rugby Union, the conflict between amateur and professional interests proved insoluble.[43] The former cut themselves completely adrift, with the result that two separate associations emerged to administer each side of the game. The mass following for Rugby League, that is for the professionalized version of the game, was confined to the northern working class. It has been suggested that the level of status anxiety among Rugby Union officials was higher than among their counterparts in association football, due to the fact that the former tended to come from lower down the social ladder than the latter and consequently felt more threatened by change. In South Wales, where working-class people were absorbed into the game unproblematically, it seems class antagonism did not find such expression, possibly because the region was more culturally homogeneous, the English could be defined as the outsiders and the game became a rallying point for the articulation of 'Welshness' instead of class feeling.

In cricket the working-class presence continued to be relatively unobtrusive.[44] Although highly competitive professional cricket leagues came into existence in the North at this time, they were a relatively minor part of the total cricket scene compared to the County Championship. Professionals of working-class origin continued to be essential, increasingly demonstrating their technical superiority by beating the gentlemen in matches between the two, but cricket did not hold the loyalty of, and have the same significance for, the urban masses as football did. Its ethos continued to be pervaded by the quintessential Victorian bourgeois values, reflected in the tendency for controllers with roots in land rather than in commerce or industry to be its patrons, although it did attract the support of some industrial capitalists in the North. The intrinsic nature of the game contributed here: it precluded violent bodily contact, the pace was more leisurely and thus it was more conducive to the display of standards of 'gentlemanly conduct'. Professional players of lower social origins could be accommodated precisely because those in control were relatively confident of their status and of their ability to remain in charge. Cricket, indeed, may have compensated to a degree for any status anxiety those with a claim to be gentlemen were possibly feeling as a result of social change in general. Consequently, professionals continued to be accorded a quasi-servant status: they tended to be used more for fielding and bowling in practices and in matches; they were referred to by their surnames only and not by initials; they were obliged to use separate entrances to the pavilion and were segregated from amateurs in hotel accommodation.[45] There were some disruptions to the cricket idyll when in 1891 and 1896 there were strikes over pay, but such incidents were exceptional and so cricket continued to symbolize a world of social harmony in which everyone knew their ascribed place, rather than functioning to accommodate working-class elements and achieve hegemony over them.

It is significant that the challenge to amateur–gentleman hegemony across sport was strongest in the North where industrial capital was stronger, class divisions sharper and the working-class presence more manifest. But it was neither simply a matter of northern versus southern interests (professionalism and commercialism in sport affected both regions), nor amateur–gentlemen versus the working class and industrial capitalists (public-school educated athleticist businessmen could be found on either side of the fence on the question of professionalism). These forces overlay each other and their effects were limited by the character of the individual sports in question. Also, the reaction of the oligarchies in control of the individual major games we have considered does seem to have been determined to some extent by the general state of class conflict pertaining in society and the relative strength of the working-class presence in each game. Cricket in the relatively calm 1870s was almost completely dominated by those committed to the amateur–gentleman ideal and continued to be so in the absence of a strong working-class challenge. As the working class grew more assertive in the 1880s concessions and compromises were made in association football by those in control; and with further increases in class tension in the 1890s, the rugby amateur–gentlemen felt more threatened, yet strong enough to cut off completely and to ostracize that side of the game in which the working class had established a foothold (Rugby League).

The fact that local capital moved into sports, especially into League football, the game that was most successfully capturing the loyalty of the working class, complicated the problem which dominant groups had encountered, of differentiating themselves from the working class. In fact, one of its effects was to produce a division within dominant groups in the form of the amateur–professional dichotomy. As we have seen already, capital had never been averse to cashing in on the popularity of sports for commercial ends, but football, and to a lesser degree other sports, was sponsored by local employers and business interests, not only out of genuine interest, but also as a way of acquiring prestige and of consolidating their power *vis-á-vis* both older ruling groups and the working class in the local community. Thus by identifying with and promoting the football culture, local capital allied itself with the working class and, indeed, achieved leadership in this area, in the sense that it also captured control over a key institution within working-class culture, the League clubs.

Division and Accommodation among 'Ladies' and 'Gentlemen'

The other major division within the dominant groups which was reproduced through sporting activity was that between bourgeois men and women, that is, between 'ladies' and 'gentlemen'. Bourgeois women's growing access to sports helped significantly to redefine the nature of this division without, however, fundamentally challenging bourgeois men's hegemony. The girls' public schools played a crucial role here in prising open this hitherto exclusively male preserve, and in thereby initiating changes in the image and identity of bourgeois women. For it was in these schools that modern physical education was pioneered, specifically as a strategy for advancing the educational opportunities of this group, the prerequisite for which was to combat the prevailing medically authorized ideology that academic education was inimical to a 'lady's' health.[46] The possibilities of athleticist technology, appropriated from the boys' public schools and hygienist medical–therapeutic technology were brilliantly exploited and brought to bear on the problem. Together with a rigorous academic programme, games and physical exercises were made a fundamental part of the curriculum and regular opportunities were provided for riding, swimming, gymnastics, and for games like tennis, cricket, and hockey, at the leading schools from the 1880s onwards. At Roedean two to three hours a day were spent on games and exercises.[47] These measures were combined with a new, carefully administered 'scientific' regimen of the body. Qualified medical staff made frequent, regular health inspections, involving checks on height, weight and posture; diet and sleep patterns were closely supervised; and remedial and therapeutic work was carried out. The disciplinary normalization of women through athletico-medical work on their bodies was thus initiated by bourgeois women and tested out on their girls in class-exclusive institutions, which at the same time of course, powerfully reproduced, if not widened, the division between bourgeois and working-class women.

Anticipating resistance, the strategy's protagonists were careful not to challenge prevailing conceptions of the position of women too radically. Their basic problem was to achieve a significant degree of change in the role of women without jeopardizing or interrupting the role that sports played in reproducing the bourgeois male's identity as a 'gentleman'. The unequivocal objective of physical education in these schools was, therefore, to produce 'ladies'. In an era when the gymn-slip and the new games-skirt, or the sight of a lady's ankles could still scandalize opinion, careful attention had to be paid to 'ladylike' appearance, demeanour and behaviour, manifested in style of dress, posture and movement and general adherence to the 'proprieties'. Physical education for bourgeois girls was consequently segregated rigidly and this segregation between the sexes, as far as the disciplinary, normalizing function of sport was concerned, was extended into adulthood. Separate organizations were formed for the major competitive sports played by both sexes, such as cricket, hockey, tennis, athletics, swimming, etc. This gave bourgeois women the autonomy to demonstrate achievement in this sphere without being inhibited by invidious comparisons with, or running the risk of being ridiculed by men while leaving the male sports sphere intact as a male preserve.

Why some sports were successfully prised open in this fashion, while others were not, must remain a matter for speculation in the absence of more detailed research. Entry to the more violent male-imprinted physical-contact sports, like football and boxing, was not, of course, on the agenda, due to the widespread consensus across the sex divide of their unsuitability for women. Violence as such, however, was not the determining factor, since hockey and lacrosse, which women did take up, could be so, and non-violent games like billiards excluded 'ladies'. It was rather that the likelihood of provoking male reaction by female incursions into heavily defended male sporting territory was probably anticipated as being counter-productive to the cause. The intrusion of women into sports, one suspects, was tacitly accepted by men, rather than positively welcomed, and there remained a deeply imbedded tendency for men to compare women's with men's sporting activity invidiously, and to look askance at the enthusiastic, competent sportswomen as somewhat abnormal and lacking in femininity.

Accommodation between the sexes within the dominant groups also took place through a more widespread mixing in sport and physical recreation on a 'social' basis. The croquet and the tennis party, the horse-ride and the bicycle-ride were recreative, rather than competitive and achievement-oriented, and therefore male identity through sporting achievement as such, was not at stake here. Rather, competence at sports, while confirming male/female identities, facilitated socializing and role complementarity on a more equal basis. A greater degree of mixing was also to be observed in the increasing propensity of women to attend sports events in men's company. Socializing through sport, in fact, formed part of an emergent restructuring of relationships between the sexes at this level, which was taking place outside the work sphere, in the home and at play, whereby ladies were being treated less as an appendage of or an ornament to, gentlemen, and more as a partner and companion whose wishes had to be taken into account.

The application of athletico-medical technology to bourgeois women and its interplay with the way they spent their free time, as well as having a normalizing, restrictive function thus also had an expansive aspect. Bourgeois men achieved hegemony here on a basis which allowed women to make certain gains. Playing and exercising in the new types of clothing designed for sports, which were less voluminous, lighter and less restrict-ing, and also healthier, was experienced as liberating;[48] and sports exerted a great influence on the development of women's, as well as men's dress, style and fashion. Successful achievement in sports provided tangible proof that, given the opportunity, bourgeois women were physically and mentally suited to higher-status occupational roles. Such women probably gained a greater confidence to challenge their subordinate position in the occupa-tional sphere (while no doubt enhancing their formidableness *vis-à-vis* subordinate groups) and in this sense contributed indirectly to opening up the occupational structure for them later. Playing sport on a competitive basis and indulging in vigorous physical exercise, not only improved their health but also, being able to socialize more freely with their own and with the opposite sex through sports, widened bourgeois women's social horizons and thus gave them a significantly greater degree of independence and freedom. To put such gains into perspective, however, it is worth noting the reaction to bourgeois women's attempts to become enfranchised. Although it was not long before this was conceded, it was initially met with repression rather than accommodation.[49]

Sports did, however, unite dominant groups and mark them off from the working class in a further way: they came to represent the quintessential bourgeois English qualities that were felt to make the English superior to foreigners. The link between athleticism, chauvinism and imperialism was forged at its strongest at this time. In the public schools especially, the celebration of athleticism with its chauvinist overtones reached hysteric proportions:

> Tis right as England beats the rest
> Of Europe and the world at all things
> That so her sports should be the best
> And England first in great and small things
> No German, Frenchman, or Fijee can ever master cricket, sir,
> Because they havn't got the pluck to stand before the wicket, sir.[50]

Such sentiments and a propensity to identify with the nation through international sport (which was, on the whole, dominated by amateurism) seems to have been confined to the middle and upper classes, and only manifested itself among the masses after this period.

Sport, Working-class Culture and the Achievement of Hegemony

Paradoxically, the dramatic moment in which the working class was remade involved both class advancement and the development of deeply conservative, 'corporatist' tendencies, which manifested themselves in the class's mode of involvement in sports.[51] Obviously, they did not prevent advance, as such, but there are indications that they formed part of a complex process by which the class ultimately became locked within an overall pattern of bourgeois hegemony. Certainly the new-found independence and militancy achieved only limited expression as far as sporting activity is concerned. Not only was the control working-class people exerted over the sporting institutions they had colonized limited, but there was a concomitant

inability, indeed unwillingness to create sufficiently differentiated, independent sporting activity, around which a more radical sense of class identity
could be constructed and maintained. The mode of involvement was more
assertive, but at the same time it was overwhelmingly accommodative.

Effectively, the options available to working-class people for organizing
their free time were limited. Three types of organizations and corresponding
modes of orientation can be distinguished: first, those that were run on
a philanthropic, patronage basis controlled by dominant groups, to which
the orientation of working-class people tended to be instrumental; secondly,
where control and leadership at the centre was in the hands of dominant
groups, but the sub-units were relatively autonomous and the orientation
tended to be more participatory (commercialized sports like football
approximated to this type); and thirdly, those directly under the control
of working-class people, for example, the trade unions and the working
men's clubs in the Club and Institute Union (CIU) after it gained its
independence from dominant group patronage where the orientation tended
to be participatory.[52] Each type presented problems in its own way in
terms of satisfying working-class needs. The presence of this particular
pattern of organizational possibilities and the manner of their operation
was a function of the interplay between working-class respectability on
the one hand, and the demand for amusement on the other; the urban gentry's
attempt to control working class people's leisure; the profit motive and
prestige-seeking among commercial and industrial interests; and the political
elite's appropriation of popular sports.

Some historians prefer the notion of respectability to the notion of class
in seeking to explain the nature of major social divisions and the mode of
social integration in late nineteenth-century Britain.[53] However, respectability and class are not mutually exclusive categories, rather they are
empirically related phenomena: the practice of respectability is both determined by, and itself helps to, constitute class relations. Others have rejected
the notion of respectability altogether on the grounds that it is conceptually
linked to spurious theories of the role of the 'labour aristocracy' and of
'embourgeoisement' in the integration of the working class.[54] Use of the
concept need not entail such theories, indeed, on the contrary, it can point
up the inadequacy of theories which underplay the contribution of cultural
factors to integration. Respectable styles of life embraced a good proportion of the eocnomically privileged strata within the class, as well as a
proportion of the not-so-privileged, the conservative element and the radical
one; and they were generated autonomously, rather than the outcome of
brainwashing from above. What working-class respectability does seem
to have done is to inhibit the degree of radical response to their cultural
subordination, and secondly, to continue to insulate the respectable elements
in much of their everyday lives, especially their leisure time, from the rest

of the class. Now, there is something to the argument that working-class respectability may not be all it seems, in the sense that the role could be manipulated instrumentally where non-conformity to dominant group norms would otherwise incur penalties.[55] However, there are limits to instrumental behaviour: it is difficult to see how people could be totally instrumental in their dealings with the powerful, unless one assumes an ability to compartmentalize their existence, which would seem to be incompatible with an ability to sustain normal everyday life. The only feasible way it would have been possible was if people were sustained by a culture constituting an alternative practice and vision of society, and there is little evidence that the majority were so sustained. Neither can it be assumed that working-class norms of respectability, whatever their limitations, functioned invariably in the interests of collective advance. Quite often respectability enabled individual escape from subordination. There is evidence of the existence of a syndrome of respectability among working-class people, and it is this, together with no doubt, at least some degree of instrumental manipulation of this role, which provided an important way for them to accommodate to the structure of power.

Sports functioned to disproportionately attach the respectable elements among young working-class males to a variety of organizations, which aimed at integrating working-class people by engrossing their free time. It has been estimated that 40 per cent of the young men born between 1901 and 1920 belonged to one or other of the two main youth organizations, the Boys' Brigade and the Boy Scouts.[56] If the thousands touched by the Volunteers, the missions and settlements, the institutes and clubs, the YMCA, the Sunday schools, the temperance bodies, and extra-curricular state school activities, throughout the whole of this period are added, the proportion of the nation's youth – let alone the adults netted by these organizations – must have been considerable. If we take the football culture, the case of West Ham for example, a club founded in a predominantly skilled workers' environment, shows that the commercialized sector's policy was to attract a diversified rather than a solidly working-class clientele. While football audiences became definitely more working class in their composition and in their behaviour, they were nevertheless diverse, attracting lower-middle-class and upper-working-class people disproportionately, reflecting the relatively better living standards of these groups in the 1880s and the concomitant demand for commercialized mass culture. The founder of the Football League not only noted in 1907 at Aston Villa's ground that the number of ladies in the stands equalled the number of men, but that on the whole the lower working class was not interested in football. The occupations of the victims in the Ibrox Stadium disaster of 1902 suggests a preponderance of skilled workers among the spectators.[57] Photographic evidence, together with the increasing orderliness of the crowds, points again to the conclusion that it was the more respectable working-class people who were more attracted to the game.[58] Skilled workers also seem to have been more involved in playing the game: they showed more initiative in forming teams and they were more likely to have obtained sponsorship to do so. Mason shows that the biggest group among professional players were skilled workers and that clerks, especially railway clerks, were active in starting teams which entered the League. Also, the evidence such as it is, suggests that it was the skilled worker or artisan that was attracted into joining local sports clubs catering mostly for the middle classes and which comprised the bulk of the voluntary sector.[59]

Respectable influences can also be seen at work inside organizations under the direct control of working-class people, around which sport was organized. Although the working class as a whole seems to have been well represented in the membership of the working men's clubs, which were important centres of sporting activity, there are some indications that the more respectable upper working class played a disproportionate part in running them.[60] The accent on respectability and order in the clubs can be attributed to the upper-working-class penchant for decorum, discipline and constitutionalism.[61] In Newcastle, for example, a working men's club committee employed a kind of policeman to keep order, prevent swearing and unseemly conduct.[62] It is little wonder that dominant groups were prepared to let these institutions alone to their beer, sports and amusements when they policed themselves so well, functioning ultimately like other respectable voluntary associations to accommodate their members to the existing order.

In terms of their integrative function the strong, ostensibly opposing desires within the class for respectability and for amusement were, in effect, complementary. Harmless amusement, which was increasingly the norm, was not incompatible with respectability; and once institutionalized, both orientations encouraged in their different ways, corporatist tendencies in the class. For those who, for whatever reason, were able to maintain respectable standards, membership of the football or cricket team was all of a piece with the Sunday suit, clean children, and a well-kept house, in conferring a sense of self-respect and dignity. But they also fitted in well with bourgeois visions of a well-ordered working class, and the petty invidious distinctions within the class that such values engendered, in turn produced a sense of indignity, resentment and inferiority among those who could not, or would not, live up to them, making for deep and lasting divisions within the working class.[68] Similarly, being able to indulge in amusing sports and pastimes was a source of strength and dignity, in that it enabled one to shrug off and laugh at adversity. But both types of responses taken beyond a certain point, and to the exclusion of a critical penetration of their situation, constituted modes of withdrawal into independent, yet self-contained, self-confirming and reassuring worlds. Sporting activities, together with other aspects of working-class culture, came to serve a double sealing-off function: they demarcated 'respectables' from 'roughs', but they also in certain respects became the focus of strong feelings of local patriotism and of community identity. League Football is the outstanding example of a sport performing this latter function. A loyalty to local community or region was fostered, which could provide a source of pride and strength at times for working-class people, but which could also easily breed a parochial, inward-looking suspicion of, and hostility towards 'outsiders' from similar types of communities elsewhere, so dividing them off from each other.

Sports radically sectionalized the class in another way, by providing a particularly potent basis for the reproduction of sexual divisions. The crystallization of sport as part of working-class culture came precisely at the time when the dominant position of the working-class male was being undermined by changes in occupational structure and in work organiza-tion,[69] and by the suffragette movement (in so far as the latter affected the working class). Working-class males' participation in sports enforced segregation on women far more radically than that of their bourgeois counterparts. Women's almost total exclusion, in all but the most passive and subordinate capacity as helpers and spectators, from a valued, deeply meaningful part of working-class men's lives, signalled their inferiority; and it strongly reinforced all those other forces, cultural, economic, and political, which restricted their horizons and induced passivity. Working-class males' hegemony over women of their own class, which was repro-duced in sports, helped to retard the latter's development, and in doing so indirectly and inadvertently contributed to the corporatist, segmented nature of working-class life. In terms of how this ultimately aided bourgeois hegemony, the crystallization of sports as a part of working-class culture and as a primary source therein for the construction of male chauvinist identities, can be seen as a way working-class males compensated for the loss of autonomy in other spheres, notably in work, and thus as a way they were integrated at the cultural level. The potentially disintegrative and radicalizing effects of the loosening of economic and political bonds were counteracted by the creation of a haven into which working-class men could withdraw with an enhanced sense of their own dignity and identity – but it was at the expense of working-class women.

A few individual working-class leaders were aware of the danger of allowing dominant groups to pre-empt independent working-class organiza-tion of free time, but they acted more or less *ad hoc*, in isolation, so there was little fresh initiative exercised in formulating specifically working-class alternatives to the business model or the vice-presidential, club models of organization.[65] Each initiative that was taken tended to either recreate the improving, earnest, respectable ethos of the voluntary associations and was consequently rejected by a lot of working-class people, or unrealistic solutions were proposed and energies wasted, or what resulted were safe, harmless amusements compatible with dominant groups' values and interests. The labour leadership in Reading, for example, in rejecting the business model for the Reading Football Club in favour of a participatory, democratic model, fell into the trap of being pulled into an alliance with the amateur–gentlemen of the club, with the result that the working class was excluded altogether from the ensuing organization by the level of subscription demanded. Valiant efforts were made to offer a kind of alternative working-class model with grass-roots participation: 500 people were involved in a 'special efforts' committee, the town was divided into districts, each with its group of football-club supporters, who organized exhibitions of industry and agriculture and a card collection in each large industrial establishment; a Saturday football festival was put on with a band and parades and a smoking concert.[66] In other places – Bristol at the turn of the century for example – the Co-operative and Trades Council organized labour festivals and fêtes with a wide range of entertainments, including games.[67]

On the whole socialist groups seem to have paid little attention to sport. In 1896 Social Democratic Federation members in some places formed football teams which competed successfully in local leagues, but little attention was paid apart from that.[68] Robert Blatchford's Clarion Clubs exhibited a more lively interest: his journal ran a sporting gossip column, devoted considerable attention to sport and cycling in particular, was promoted by the clubs. However, the anti-urban, romantic, back-to-nature outlook seems to have appealed more to middle-class socialists than working-class people.[69] Some socialists recommended taking an interest in football, as the working class was so involved, and the *Fabian News* advocated trade-union sports clubs along the lines of the Social Democratic Party (SDP) in Germany, pointing out that: 'capturing the social life of the workers is one of the most potent weapons of the servile state...the fellowship of cricket and football field will bear precious fruit in sterner fields of industrial warfare'.[70] Shortly after 1900 it seems that some workers' sports organizations existed in England and in 1913 English representatives attended an international congress of workers' sports organizations under the aegis of the Bureau of the Socialist International.[71]

Enterprising as some of the practical efforts were, they were not to be sustained long within the system of financial and cultural constraints and few schemes were even put into practice. This reveals not only the enormity of the task of building a specifically socialist alternative leisure culture, but also the limited horizons of labour and socialist groups in this respect. Little seems to have been attempted or proposed that was qualitatively different from the sort of thing approved by dominant groups. The same, indeed, could be said of much of what is now currently recognized as authentic working-class culture – brass bands, choral societies, miners' galas, music-hall, the pub, etc. – customarily lionized by members of dominant groups, who seem to have recognized there was little here to challenge their cultural hegemony. Also, the socialist groups, like the working class, were split in their attitudes towards sports. One of the most important groups, the Independent Labour Party (ILP), thought the British working class wasted time and energy in sports instead of politics, and adopted the same censorious attitude towards mass sport as the middle- and upper-class critics, making the same hackneyed comparison of football to Roman gladiatorial combat.[72] The absence of a socialist alternative, the lack of imagination, was due at least in part to the low priority that leaders of the working-class movement gave to cultural matters in the broad sense. Much cultural terrain was ceded without ever really giving battle and was left instead to voluntary organizations which split off the respectable elements and encouraged them to be upwardly aspiring: 'They fragmented their clientele into innumerable specialised groupings – by age, sex, status and class. By such divisions they vitiated any notion of community and anticipated or reflected the way the subsequent competitors in the mass leisure market would behave.'[73] What strikes one about the sporting activity and the leisure and cultural aspirations in general of the respectable working class, especially among the more economically privileged sectors of labour and among working-class leaders, is that it seems to have aimed at, and tended to be satisfied with, a recognized place within an already constituted cultural system, which it showed a limited inclination to change fundamentally.

It is no more easy to explain the trades unions' and socialists' lack of interest in, and in a lot of cases antipathy towards, popular sports, than it is to explain the relative absence of a radical or revolutionary socialist vision in Britain. The problems are connected. Partly it was due to the, by then long- and deeply ingrained attitude to work in the national culture, so heavily influenced by and expressed in Nonconformism and, in particular, in Methodism, that defined leisure and amusement as 'unserious', poten- tially anti-improving, vaguely threatening and decadent. Methodism did exert a significant influence on the working-class movement and on British socialism. The concentration on limited economic advance and on reform within the existing political system on the part of labour's leadership similarly gave primacy to the sphere of work, which seemed to assume in a determinist manner that cultural improvement would somehow auto- matically follow advance in the economic sphere. The reformism of the majority of British socialists at this time expressed an acceptance of a narrowed-down definition of politics, which equated it with activity within the established parliamentary political system and which downgraded the importance of the cultural dimension of political change. Thus among socialists an essentially elitist, conservative perspective on popular amusements was commonly accepted, namely that they expressed the least important side of life and tended to encourage the more backward instincts of the mob, performing a bread-and-circuses function. The failure of revolutionary socialist ideas to exert more than a marginal influence on political culture in Britain was a consequence of the specificity of British conditions and it was a vital missing ingredient responsible for the limited appreciation among socialists – to which William Morris was a rare exception – of the importance of cultural as well as economic and political challenges.

The fact that the working class's cultural fortifications do not seem to have been as sound as those constructed on the economic and political level, is important. Contrary to those who contend that struggles over cultural activities such as sports were of minor consequence and simply flowed from what occurred at the level of the mode of production, the class accommodation that was achieved over the uses of ostensibly non-political free-time activities like sports, fed into and helped reproduce the British working-class movement's celebrated propensity to settle for 'economism' and 'labourism'.[74] It enabled dominant groups to pre-empt alternative uses of free time and thus to circumscribe the opportunities for constructing a more cohesive, outward-looking, critical working-class culture, one which more radically synthesized economic, political and cultural life – which, as Gramsci pointed out, is essential if the working class is to challenge the power structure effectively and radically.

When compared with the limited capacity of independent working-class organizations and bourgeois-controlled voluntary bodies to satisfy working-class expressed needs, the commercial organization of free time possessed the advantage of anonymity, flexibility, and efficiency in producing the services required, that is, it apparently offered a wide freedom of choice without constraint. Support was attracted and costs met by charging for the facility on demand, that is, reliance was placed on the intermittent expenditure of small sums of money by large numbers of consumers, rather than on larger subscriptions and regular, but smaller numbers of attenders. Like their contemporaries, the press barons, who were cashing in on the popular demand for sport, the new football barons too were happy to more or less abandon the dominating, moralizing style of the voluntary organizations and to adopt a populist tone instead. Typically, the commercial development of sport was ratified in terms of 'giving the masses what they want', a formula which conceals the way the market context can itself constrain and shape demand. What a lot of working-class people evidently wanted was more harmless amusement and commerce tapped this strong demand very successfully.[75] In terms of the achievement of hegemony over the working class, the function of participation in the mass market and in mass politics was similar: both responded relatively flexibly to demands and achieved a high degree of legitimacy and popular appeal, while at the same time constraining and shaping that demand. A direct descendant of plebian cultural tradition, the demand for amusement which characterized much of late nineteenth-century working-class culture could be indulged more now that working-class people had more of the wherewithal to fulfil that urge, and 'having a good time' took on a new lease of life. This development signified also a degree of depoliticization within the working class which commercial interests were quick to exploit.[76] Although it is possible to exaggerate their centrality, football and popular sports, together with the pub, music-hall and the popular press, became in some ways a more integral part of working-class culture than socialist politics. The trend can be seen in the direction independence took in the working men's clubs. All commentators agree that these clubs, after being closely involved in radical politics in the 1870s and 1880s, although they by no means switched their allegiance to conservatism, turned apolitical in the 1890s when the formula became harmless amusement in the form of beer, sports and entertainment.[77] Their apparently greater degree of independence than the football clubs did not insulate them from commercial pressures and in their subsequent development they became closely reliant for their financial survival on the brewing and entertainment industries.

The political elite's response to working-class people's interest *en masse* in sports was rather mixed at first: suspicion and hostility on the part of some sections was on the whole eventually outweighed by a guarded acceptance and an increasing propensity to appropriate sporting symbols for their own purposes. Blackburn Rovers' supporters, up in London for the FA Cup in 1884 were likened in the pages of the *Pall Mall Gazette* to: 'A northern horde of uncouth garb and strange oaths – like a tribe of Sudanese Arabs let loose'.[78] Twelve years later the *Spectator* was drawing parallels between professional football and the excesses of the gladatorial games of imperial Rome, castigating it for encouraging spendthrifts, loafing, drinking, betting and neglect of family responsibilities.[79]

Perhaps with more than a little tongue in cheek then, the Establishment and local politicians learned to take advantage of the opportunities that mass-spectator sports afforded to exercise influence and increase their popularity. Joyce maintains that the latter did so quite consciously. Charles Box, a cricket writer and popular philosopher of the time, articulated this tendency when he wrote that sport was: 'the bulwark of the constitution...it has no sympathy with nihilism, communism, nor any other ism that points to national disorder'.[80] By 1892 it was common for MPs, mayors, titled people and notables in general to start matches, entertain teams and be photographed with them. Clubs like Manchester United were liberally sprinkled with MPs, JPs (justices of the peace), local councillors and aldermen and other dignitaries. The *Spectator*, commenting in 1892 on Joseph Chamberlain's expression of sympathy with the love and devotion cf his Birmingham audience for outdoor sports, noted that the mixing of the classes gave to games 'a peculiar social significance'.[81] In 1899 the English FA Cup Final was attended by the Prime Minister (Lord Salisbury), Lord Roseberry, Cecil Rhodes, and the majors of the two towns in question, Sheffield and Derby. Presenting the Cup to Bury United in 1900 Lord Roseberry said candidly: 'This is the second year running you have had a distinguished Cabinet Minister amongst you to preside over this sport. It is good for football, and it is not bad for the Cabinet Minister.'[82] By 1901 Edward VII had become the patron of the FA and in 1914 the Cup Final was graced with the presence of royalty, a timely move in view of the need for national unity after the industrial and political unrest of the previous years and with war in the offing. Football culture above all provided at this time not so much a focus for nationalism as such, but 'a concrete demonstration of the links which bound all inhabitants of the nation-state together'.[83]

In view of the powerful way the game could symbolize the values underpinning social relations it seems significant that players could be, and often were, punished severely in full public view for rule infractions, which included word as well as deed. For example, sending players off as a punishment, almost like naughty children, was far more frequent in football, where it was likely to apply to working-class players and be witnessed by working-class audiences, than it was in rugby, where it was relatively rare. Professional football, a commercialized entertainment whose rationale was ostensibly profit and enjoyment and not social control, was made to function as a symbol of the necessity for tight discipline and control over working-class people. What had become a major working-class institution, watching football on the terraces on a Saturday afternoon, had also in a sense become the occasion for weekly sermons on knowing one's place in society. Some indication of the efficacy of ruling-class influence in football can be gauged from the way football authorities and the War Office joined together in the recruiting campaign for the First World War. Football grounds were put at the disposal of the War Office as drill grounds and for making patriotic public addresses by well-known figures. By the end of 1914 half a million men had enlisted via football organizations, almost 50 per cent of the total number of volunteers in that year: 'Football and its machinery offered the state a swift and acceptable entry into working-class communities which might otherwise have proved difficult to penetrate.'[84] The sports stadium had merged in function with other more easily recognizable formal ritual spaces specifically designed for performances of the theatre of the great, like the Mall, Whitehall and the Cenotaph, and Horse Guards Parade.

The dominant classes' control and influence over working-class people's free time which was manifested in sports, was effective not because there was a ruling-class master plan, which was inexorably put into practice, but precisely because dominant groups' responses were not monolithic, because the working class was internally divided and, in different ways, was willing to tune into the wavelengths upon which dominant groups were broadcasting. There was sufficient plurality of response and counter-response for strategies to be elaborated when programmes failed and resistance was encountered, for dominant groups to ally on some issues with key working-class groups without threatening, indeed while enhancing the structure of bourgeois hegemony ultimately. Thus, while failing to normalize the working class as a whole, the urban gentry's philanthropic strategy succeeded in detaching skilled workers and respectable working-class people for much of their free time; and its ability also to form alliances with subaltern intellectuals from the upper working and lower middle classes, and with working-class women, helped substantially to achieve the ultimate effect. Sectors of local industrial and commercial capital, recognizing the potential benefit to themselves from supporting and promoting a more commercialized pattern of sport as an attractive alternative to the patronage model promoted by voluntary organizations, allied themselves with the working class's demand for amusement against the protagonists of amateur domination and rational recreation – an alliance which allowed working-class people to gain greater access to sporting leisure. The political elite in turn capitalized on these developments, progressively tried on and successfully appropriated the key symbols of sports in a conscious attempt to consolidate its power at local and national levels. Working-class people made important gains in this sphere and were often able to resist and thwart attempts at control. However, the cultural fragmentation of the class, the absence of a socialist alternative capable of critically penetrating this domain and of mobilizing a more coherent, organized challenge, and the class's consequent retreat under pressure into corporatism, ensured that the challenge to bourgeois hegemony at this level neither synchronized with, nor matched in strength, the challenge the class mounted at the economic and political levels. In contrast, dominant groups, although divided in certain respects, were ultimately unified in a hegemonic bloc. A consensus was reached among them that sports constituted a primary disciplinary technique for producing normal younger working-class males, for constructing normal 'ladies' and 'gentlemen', and constituted a source of harmless amusement for the adult working class, that is, that sports contributed to social order. Thus the older established disciplinary technology of athleticism was supplemented increasingly by, indeed, began to fuse with, a qualitatively different, newer developing technology for producing the normal individual. The transformation of sports into items of consumption was introducing a more subtle, expanded form of surveillance as part of this normalization process.

Consolidating Hegemony: the Inter-War Period

We do not arrive at another turning-point until after the Second World War. The inter-war period, nevertheless, is important, but curiously we know rather less about the pattern of leisure in this period than we do about the preceding era and the period since.[85] The received interpretation of its general character which depicts it as bleak, depressed and at a standstill, has taken a knock in the last few years, and it is quite possible that the period is more important than is generally supposed as far as developments in leisure and the sport–power relation is concerned. In general terms it appears that the way sport related to the pattern of hegemony which had been achieved prior to the First World War, is maintained, and that at the same time changes occur which constitute a working out of established tendencies, that is, the existing pattern is extended and elaborated. This consolidation process is still confined largely to the sphere of civil society: the state's role – apart from significant developments in education, which will be analysed in detail in chapter 8 – remains minimal until the Second World War. Subordinate groups are enabled to make certain significant advances, but they are contained firmly within the overall pattern.

Spectator sports expanded, taking their place alongside radio, the cinema, and the dance-hall as a main component of a more commercialized, popular mass-entertainment industry. This was the golden age of football and cricket attendances: professional football had ceased to be so strongly associated with the North and spread southwards in popularity; County Cricket became a truly more popular game; the Amateur Athletic Association Championships enjoyed a boom in attendances.[86] New highly commercialized sports appeared in the 1920s, for example greyhound-racing, speedway, and Tourist Trophy (TT) motor-cycle racing, which gained rapidly in popularity with working-class people.[87] Some sports became a firm part of the working class man's cultural and sporting repertoire for the first time. For example, large numbers of people started to play snooker, both on a casual basis and also in highly organized local leagues; and as a professional game it attracted a very large following. Gambling on sports, always a prominent feature of working-class attachment, developed apace with the expansion. Introduced under the Betting Act of 1928 to regulate on-course betting, the totalizator was attracting £230 m of small-punters' money in a year – and this did not include, of course, the millions of pounds laid with bookeepers and in illegal, off-course betting.[88] The 1930s saw a massive growth in expenditure on the football pools, generating literally one of the largest industries in the country and employing thousands of workers.[89]

The role of the press and radio in the growing popularity of spectator sports was absolutely crucial. Newspapers, for example, found horse-race tipping to be one of the most important ways of maintaining and expanding circulation against competitors. From the late 1920s commentaries on the major sporting events became a staple part of radio broadcasting. Perhaps even more than the popular press, radio brought these great national occasions into millions of households and for the first time it was as they were actually happening. Under the impact of the mass media the sports-star/national hero/celebrity really took off as a feature of sports culture.

Many sports, though, remained essentially participant sports, and so differences remained between sports and other forms of mass entertainment, like the cinema. Take League football for example, which rivalled the cinema in the size of its audiences, and which adopted a commercial form of organization to maintain its financial viability rather than to profit from it. Here there existed a degree of active involvement in and control over the game at the grass roots, and a voluntary element in its administration at the top, for which there was no equivalent in the way people related to the cinema and other forms of mass entertainment.

One of the most significant departures of the inter-war period was the emergence and growth of the movement for more participatory, non-competitive, self-organized and healthy outdoor physical recreation, indicated by the boom in cycling, camping, hiking and rambling. Working-class people in particular, took up cycling, both as a recreative and as a competitive sport. The number of bikes sold annually in the mid-1930s was well over a million and a half and by 1938 there were 3,500 clubs catering for 60,000 members.[90] By the late 1930s there were about half a million regular walkers and the Youth Hostels Association's membership alone was 83,000 in 1939, compared with 6,000 five years earlier. A variety of streams flowed in the open-air and fitness movement, from the Nonconformist and philanthropically inclined Holiday Fellowship, Co-operative Holidays Association, and the Youth Hostels Association, with their antecedents in the rational recreation tradition, to the Women's League of Health and Beauty, nudism and the more overtly politically inclined bodies, like the Ramblers' Association, the Independent Labour Party Guild of Youth, the Woodcraft Folk and the Communist Party-inspired British Workers' Sports Federation.

It is not clear yet to what extent the working-class adherents were typical of their class, many of whom were after all unemployed. One suspects that open-air, healthy activity appealed more to the respectable, aspiring working class and the lower middle class, and that as far as the majority was concerned such activity did not compete seriously with the seaside trip or holiday, the cinema and the dance-hall.

The advances that women made in this domain were among the most significant developments in the period. The watershed in the long process of women's emancipation, and with it a rupture in their previous relationship to sport, came after the First World War in the 1920s. The shorter games-skirt, the briefer bathing-suit, wearing shorts and trousers and shorter hair-styles, and, indeed, the fact that more of women's bodies were revealed in public, signified a profound change in mores governing the position of women – and sports helped to bring it about. Sportswomen, like Suzanne Lenglen, the Wimbledon Ladies Singles Champion for several years in the 1920s, became popular idols for the first time. Independent organizations catering for women's growing interest in sport, physical recreation and fitness came into being. The Women's Amateur Athletic Association for example was founded in 1922, and for the first time, in 1928, women entered the Olympic Games. The Keep Fit Movement and the Women's League of Health and Beauty, launched in the early 1930s, attracted large followings, the latter organization having 120,000 members by 1937. Also, large numbers of women took up sports like rowing, cycling, swimming and running, independently. In terms of professional development and anticipation of future patterns, women's physical education was far in advance of men's.

Yet advance, once again, tended to be uneven: bourgeois women gained far more from it and, if anything, it widened the divisions between them and working-class women. Probably the biggest mass advance among women then, was made among the lower middle class. And despite advance, this was still decidedly a man's world: men controlled the leading organizations and women were still restricted to a narrower range of sporting activities which men considered suitable for them. In the Olympic Games for example, they were prevented from organizing events in excess of 800 metres on the grounds that the greater distances were too strenuous and distressing for them.

The significance of the period in terms of the gains made by subordinate groups appears to be two-fold. Firstly, this is the period when organized sports and physical recreation can genuinely be said to have reached all layers of the working class, although significant differences remained in the mode of attachment to sports between different strata. Secondly, this is the period when sports can be said to have achieved the status of one of the main components of a nationally extensive popular culture, that is a culture extending to the majority of the population.

However, the forces maintaining the sport–power relation remained intact. The philanthropic strategy waxed rather strongly. The organizations employing sports and physical exercise in the interests of discipline, like the Boys Scouts, Boys' Brigade, YMCA, Girl Guides, etc., continued to consolidate their positions, although they do not seem to have been any more successful in penetrating previously untapped layers of the working class. Such organizations were now up against even stiffer competition to engross working-class people's free time from the commercial, mass-entertainment sector. In the course of elaborating its efforts philanthropy made some important initiatives which fostered active involvement in sport and exercise. Apart from the formation of the King George V Jubilee Trust in 1935 and the National Playing Fields Association (NPFA) in 1925 the most important of these was the formation of the Central Council for Physical Recreation (CCPR). Created on the independent initiative of key figures in the physical education profession with Establishment connections, it was to become the most important factor in state intervention from the centre at a later stage.[91] Their proposal to form an umbrella organization for all the voluntary bodies and agencies concerned with sport and physical recreation immediately received a sympathetic response among dominant groups and was taken up by the Board of Education. From the beginning the membership of the Council read like a roll-call of the Establishment, attracting the active participation of figures like Lord Aberdare, Lord Hampton and its President Lord Astor, as well as generous royal patronage. The initial finance was provided by the main professional body concerned (the Ling Association, later to become the Physical Education Association), the NPFA and the King George V Jubilee Trust and by individual wealthy patrons. The fact that it rapidly attached a large proportion of the voluntary organizations in the field (82 national bodies in the first year) stimulated the Board of Education to provide it with the first injection of statutory aid in 1937. However, relations with the Board of Education were already sufficiently close in 1936 for the Council to be asked to submit the memorandum on post-school physical recreation, which on the approval of the Cabinet led directly to the establishment of the National Fitness Council.

The CCPR's stated aim was: 'To help improve the physical and mental health of the community through physical recreation, by developing existing facilities for recreative activity of all kinds and also by making provision for thousands not yet associated with any organisation.'[92] Such aims resonated strongly with received notions among dominant groups concerning the value of physical recreation and sports as a form of social control. The working class, which formed the majority of the population, perforce constituted the main target. The 'unattached' were to be integrated and their energies mobilized to serve the national interest through sport and physical recreation; and the appropriate task of the CCPR was seen as providing the leadership required to achieve these objectives. The idea, harking back to the rational recreation tradition, that sport and physical recreation performs a harmonizing social function, improves national efficiency and that leadership can be given through these activities, orchestrates all future state intervention in this sphere.

In fact, the state does enter the picture more in this period, but as yet largely in an uncoordinated variety of ways: through local authority initiatives, the development of physical education in schools, the public health services, the aforesaid CCPR, and the ritual practices of the political elite. It was the local authorities who were, in the main, responsible for the modest expansion of publicly provided sport and recreation facilities and services that took place in the period. Central governments followed a policy of financial stringency in the inter-war period, which limited the scale of public provision quite drastically. Nevertheless, we owe many of the public swimming-pools, playing-fields, open spaces, bowling-greens, tennis-courts, etc. in existence today to this period. Provision was very uneven: some of the more responsive authorities, like the London County Council had a relatively good record compared with some who did the minimum.

In 1920 the Report of the Consultative Committee on Medical and Allied Services (The Dawson Report) had strongly recommended the integration of 'physical culture' into the health services: 'Physical culture is thus concerned with education, with the maintainance of health and the recreation of the people and with the curing of disease and disability, and there is no sharp dividing line of demarcation between these functions.'[93] 'Physical culture' in this view enables bodies to be observed legitimately and publicly: they were to be freed in physical activity the better to increase the power of the observing eye and extend surveillance over subjects. An alliance was formally proposed and worked at in the inter-war period between the 'educational' movement of bodies and a regime of hygiene which progressively linked up with such self-organized activities as walking, camping, hiking, cycling and nudism.

Concretely, until 1937 centrally co-ordinated state intervention in the post-school adult population's sporting and recreational activities did not extend beyond insisting that young men receiving the dole should attend Junior Instruction Centres in makeshift premises to receive physical training, handicrafts instruction and some games. The Commissioner for the Special Areas noted the low medical standards of boys and young men and as apprehension grew about the war with Germany: 'comparisons were drawn between the apparent listlessness and lack of patriotic idealism which were thought to mark so large a proportion of British boys. . . and the well-drilled Hitler Youth.'[94] The first major intervention took the form of a Physical Training and Recreation Act (1937), under which a National Fitness Council was created and empowered to grant financial aid to voluntary organizations promoting physical fitness and recreation. In 1939, under the Social and Physical Training Grant Regulations, capital grants were also made available to national voluntary organizations and local authorities for recreation provision.[95]

Sports and recreation continued to differentiate dominant from subordinate groups in major ways. Although voluntary organization was put more on a commercial basis, the amateur–gentlemen retained their hegemony. Most of the controlling bodies were run by amateur, part-time administrators; the international bodies were dominated by the amateurs; many major sports, like tennis and Rugby Union, rigidly enforced amateurism as a condition for participating; and the invidious distinction between amateur and professional players remained in major sports. Working-class people were still unable to participate on an equal footing with others in a whole range of sports which went on expanding between the wars, due to the costs of participation and low public provision – sports like rowing, skiing, climbing, sailing, motor-racing, tennis, and golf. And some sports, which had expanded greatly among the suburban middle class, like tennis and golf, were deliberately kept exclusive. The association football/rugby union divide across the length and breadth of England starkly symbolized the class divide and showed how it could be replicated in sports. In the absence of any strong evidence to the contrary it must be assumed that the significant division within the working class between the regularly employed, better-paid, skilled and respectable strata – with their traditionally greater propensity to participate in organized sporting activity hegemonized by dominant groups – and the rest of the class, continued to be reproduced around sports.

With better communications and the establishment of international sports bodies like the International Olympic Committee and International Federation of Football Associations (FIFA), the nation came more to the forefront of sport. Despite appearances to the contrary, such as the 'bodyline' controversy when the England Test Team's tactics in Australia in the early 1930s soured relations between the two countries, it appears that relatively little of the nation's identity was invested in sport when compared for example, with the nationalist fervour in Germany surrounding the Nazi Olympics and Italy's success in the World Cup at the time. It is likely however, that the increasing popularity of sports indicated an emergent identification of sports with the national way of life for many people.

By now sporting symbols were a standard prop in the theatre of the great's repertoire. One of the leading players was, of course, the Monarchy, especially noteworthy for its patronage of sport and recreation bodies (NPFA, etc.), its ritualized appearances at the major sporting occasions (the Derby, Cup Final, etc.), and its penchant for indulging in more exclusive, 'aristocratic' sports, such as riding, hunting, shooting, etc.

Commercial influences, the media, the schools, the sports bodies, philanthropy, the medical authorities, the local and the national state, as well as pressure from bourgeois women and working-class people, combined in their influence to ensure that much sport and physical recreation was hegemonized by dominant groups. Sports culture became more firmly perceived in common-sense terms as a unifying activity to which all sections of society could relate, and as nothing to do with power and conflict. Seen in this light football matches between police and strikers during the General Strike of 1926 were no aberration. Sport more than any other aspect of popular culture, and possibly even of the national culture, had come to serve as a common reference point for different social classes and other social categories, which on other grounds were opposed.

Pressure for change from subordinate groups took a more consciously political form only in a relatively minor way. The most celebrated example perhaps is the ramblers' direct action against land-owners and their armed retainers in the form of a mass trespass on Kinder Scout in the Peak District, as part of a campaign to regain access to the countryside for ordinary people.[96] Set aside exclusively for the rich to shoot grouse, the area strongly symbolized the relationship between leisure, sport and privileged power. The composition of the access movement is not entirely clear – in particular, the extent to which working-class people, as opposed to middle-class radicals, were behind it. Apparently, the movement was weakened by internal political divisions, and although the Kinder Scout episode seems to have scored a resounding propaganda success, the extent to which the movement was successful in getting access to the countryside is open to question. Between 1929 and 1935 the Communist Party, which was behind the British Sports Workers Federation and was a prime instigator of the Kinder Scout trespass, was pursuing an ultra-militant policy. The *Daily Worker* was rejecting 'capitalist sport', refused to report on football or to publish racing tips. Other groups, such as the Youth Hostels Association (YHA) were more concerned with social control; and some viewed healthy walking and practice in map-reading as industrially and militarily useful.[97] Although thousands of ramblers were attracted to the rallies, and the Rights of Way Act (1932) and the Access to Mountains Act (1935) were passed, access to the countryside was still highly circumscribed and inadequate. The Communist Party abandoned its stand in accordance with Popular Front policy and the *Daily Worker* then covered sports in terms not dissimilar to the popular press.

The working-class movement does not seem to have taken this issue or sports as a whole very seriously. In fact, in marked contrast to what was taking place in Europe at the time, where the Workers' Sports Movement was an integral part of the politics of the Left, whether social democrat or communist,[98] the British working-class movement, and the Left as a whole continued to ignore the growing significance of sport in working-class people's lives, tacitly allowing this terrain to be hegemonized by forces unsympathetic to the Left. Of course, in Britain sports culture was not appropriated directly and politicized overtly by the government or by the Right. The Foreign Office's attempt to use the England Football Team as an instrument of the government's policy by determining whom they should play, and culminating in the notorious occasion when the team gave the Nazi salute at the opening ceremony of the England–Germany match, was the exception rather than the rule. But given the balance of political forces in Britain, a balance which favoured the Right, the strong influence dominant groups exerted over sports, and the Left's neglect, the sports culture understandably tended to have greater affinities with rightist thought, feelings and practices.

5

Sport and the Recomposition of the Working Class in Modern Britain

Introduction

By the 1950s the most recent turning-point had been reached. A whole series of changes were transforming the British working class: the 'second Industrial Revolution', changes in occupational structure, full employment, the consumer boom, more free time, the erosion and breakdown of traditional working-class communities, the growth of a more privatized existence, state intervention in the economy and welfare on an unprecedented scale, rising expectations and increased assertiveness and industrial militancy. In addition, after the 1950s, ethnic, gender and generational differences began to cut more radically across working-class culture.

Despite the differences in the degree to which different social groupings are involved in sport, the importance of sport in the national popular culture is incontrovertible. The precise pattern of involvement in sociological terms is, however, not easy to establish, given the imprecision of the official statistics and the paucity of sociological studies focused on the problem. Quantitative estimates of involvement can be especially misleading if certain distinctions are not borne in mind: between recreational pursuits with a physical component like walking, gardening, camping and caravanning, dancing etc. and sporting activity proper; between physically taxing sports and other sports like darts, snooker, angling etc.; between achievement-oriented sport and recreational forms of sport (playing in the local football league as opposed to the street or park kick-about); and between active involvement as a participant or as an official and passive involvement as a spectator, through gambling and media sport.[1] The point of making these distinctions is not to enter the value-loaded controversy about the merits and demerits of the different modes of involvement in sports, but in order to be able to analyse the different ways in which sports are plugged into the power network.

The scale of involvement is enormous. In terms of active involvement for example, a million people belong to football clubs, 36,000 of which were affiliated to the Football Association in the early 1970s.[2] By the late 1970s the English Golf Union had 450,000 members and 1,231,000 fishing licences were being issued annually.[3] Although attendances at events have fallen, when gambling on sports and media sport are taken into account again involvement is massive. In the early 1970s the BBC's 'Match of the Day' programme, with an audience of nine and a half million for a single broadcast, was watched by more people in a month than attended Football League games in the whole season.[4] Over a third of the ten most popular sports for active participation are activities in which a relatively low output of physical energy is required: darts is equal first with indoor swimming; billiards/snooker is second; watching football is fourth, and fishing is fifth. Three of the five most popular sporting activities – darts, billiards/snooker, and watching football – are very closely associated with commercial activity and with gambling. A surprisingly small proportion of people actually participate actively in any one individual sport, including the major sports like football, cricket and athletics, in which the proportion watching is greater than the proportion participating actively.[5] Gambling is a frequent *raison d'être* for involvement: seventeen million people do the football pools, and approximately 10 per cent of the population gamble on horse- and dog-racing.[6] The bare fact that the majority of the adult population do not participate actively at any one time, or over a short period, tends to conceal the probability that most people have participated in some form of sport at some time in their lives, perhaps on a regular basis. The General Household Survey (GHS) confirms that active participation as well as spectating, drops off with increasing age, indicating a declining interest or inability to participate, among older people.[7] In the nature of the case, many sports make demands on participants in terms of time, resources, skill, training, fitness and access to facilities, which entail an entirely different sort of commitment than other kinds of leisure activities like using TV and radio, reading, eating and drinking in pubs and restaurants or visiting friends, which go into the official statistics on leisure, and the latter take no account of this. Seen in this light, although the 38–47 per cent of the population who are reported to participate actively in sports includes walkers and so on, it probably represents a more sociologically significant compo- nent in the pattern of leisure than the figures at first might suggest. Also, the level of active participation which the surveys reveal is a function of the notorious lack of appropriate provision in this country and so they take no account of potentially interested participants.[8] There is not much doubt then, that with the exception of falling attendances in some sports, involve- ment in, and thus the popularity of, sports has increased. But to put the expansion of and involvement in sports in proper perspective, it should be noted that outdoor recreation and recreational forms of sport have probably increased most of all in popularity, and that the expansion of this sector of leisure is part of a global expansion of leisure activity. The relation between the commercial aspects of the expansion of sports and working-class culture will be explored in detail in the next chapter.

Class Divisions

The propensity to participate actively in sports varies with social-class membership – the higher the class, the greater the rate of participation (see table 5.1).

Table 5.1   Class differentiation in sport and recreation

Socio-economic group	% Outdoor	% Indoor	% Watching	% Total pop.
Professional and managerial	52 (15)*	25 (13)	16 (16)	11
Other non-manual	43 (35)	21 (30)	11 (30)	31
Skilled manual	40 (23)	28 (30)	13 (26)	23
Semi- and unskilled manual	27 (21)	14 (19)	9 (23)	29

Note: * The figures in parentheses represent the weight, in percentage terms, of each social-class grouping in the populations participating in each of the three categories of sport.
Source: A. J. Veal, *Sport and Recreation in England and Wales* (Univ. of Birmingham, Centre for Urban Studies, 1979), p. 18, table 4.

Now, measuring class differentials in involvement in sport simply in terms of occupation is unsatisfactory in certain important respects. First, it reduces class to one dimension, the nature of work, whereas classes are constructed politically and culturally as well. The class position of women, for example, is difficult to characterize in terms of occupation since a large proportion of women's work is either tangential to or not encompassed by the labour-market.[9] Most occupational classifications are based in any case upon conventional conceptions of what constitutes men's and women's work and what constitutes skill – conceptions which discriminate against women; and they take no account of the resulting economic differences between men and women, such as the level of income, fringe benefits and qualifications. Even as a measure of men's economic class such categorizations are unsatisfactory, since they take no account of the significance of the relationship between occupation and ownership and control over the means of production.[10] One important consequence is that correspondences between the position of routine non-manual workers – a large proportion of whom are women – and many manual workers are overlooked. We will consider the problematic relation between gender and class further in a moment.

Bearing these drawbacks in mind, when used carefully this kind of data is, nevertheless, better than no data at all. The professional and managerial group is the most involved in sport: in 19 out of 31 activities listed in the GHS this group has a greater proportion of its members involved than any other. Other non-manual workers are the second most active group overall, particularly in more individualistic sporting activities like cycling, horse-riding, climbing, tennis, keep fit and yoga. Skilled manual workers are almost equally active overall, and most active in playing and watching football, fishing, ten-pin bowling, billiards, darts, and watching motor sports. Semi- and unskilled workers are easily the least active of all.[11] It should be noted that high rates of participation in the above sense do not necessarily make a group the biggest group in sports overall or in an individual sport, since this depends on the relative size of class groupings in the total population. In fact, other non-manual workers form the biggest group numerically, usually constituting around 30 per cent of participants. Skilled manual workers form the biggest group playing and watching football, fishing, ten-pin bowling, billiards, darts, watching motor sports, field sports, cricket and bowls. Note particularly that skilled workers are the biggest group of participants in the traditionally important major games in Britain – cricket and football.[12] Surveys of the users of local sports centres strongly confirm the pattern of participation shown in national surveys: statistically non-manual workers are over-represented, skilled workers adequately represented, and semi- and unskilled workers grossly underepresented.[13]

Commitment to sport then, in terms of active participation, is higher among non-manual workers as a whole than among manual workers, that is to say in these terms the middle and upper classes are still more involved in sport than the working classes. But put like this the unique level of involvement of the upper working class, in particular of skilled manual workers, is concealed. The significant division is between the latter group and the semi- and unskilled working class. Thus sports continue to mark a cultural boundary among working-class people. In simple numerical terms active participation in sports is dominated by lower non-manual and skilled manual workers, that is, by the lower middle and upper working class. As we know, a significant proportion of lower non-manual workers are working class in terms of their material position and their self-identification, which means the degree of upper-working-class involvement in sports is greater, and consequently, the class as a whole is more sharply divided at the cultural level than appears to be the case at first glance.[14] Since lower-class groups are more involved in gambling and they also rely more on television for their entertainment, it can be assumed that they are relatively more involved in sport through watching and gambling.[15] A BBC survey of the early 1970s for example, found that adults in the lowest social grade spent 45 per cent more time watching TV than adults in higher grades. The mass media take up to two-thirds or more of the total disposable time of this group of heavy users.[16] On these grounds it would seem reasonable to conclude that a greater number and proportion of semi- and unskilled workers are involved in sport than is indicated so far, but in a more passive way than other groups.

Unfortunately, evidence of this kind cannot reveal the concrete pattern of class relations in sport. It is tempting to assume that people with a common cultural interest, whatever their class background, tend to be integrated or pulled together in this respect. Empirical studies of local communities, of working-class culture and of membership of clubs and voluntary associations on the whole, do not bear out this expectation. There is little class mixing between manual and non-manual workers and their families. Working-class people either tend not to join formal organizations, or if they do, they belong to a very limited number of organizations of very much the same type, that is ones with small committees and a large membership, both drawn from the same class, of which the classic example is the working men's club.[17] They are either locked into a relatively dense social network at the local level consisting of family, neighbourhood friends and workmates, which precludes the need for, and reliance on, formally constructed voluntary associations. Or, as seems to be increasingly the pattern as these more traditional arrangements decompose, they are privatized in their non-work lives, having fewer social links outside the immediate family. But in either case the result is segregation of working-class people from other groups.[18]

On the other hand, middle- and upper-class individuals belong to a multiplicity of voluntary associations, and processes of dissociation and social closure largely ensure the class homogeneity of these institutions. On the whole, working-class people tend not to aspire to join anyway, and the middle- and upper-class groupings consciously or unconsciously exclude them. If this is the general pattern of class interaction it should not come as much surprise to learn that the limited sociological evidence available on the conduct of sport at the local level confirms it is no exception in segregating the classes. Some community studies rather unconvincingly suggest that a degree of class mixing takes place in sport, which encourages a shared sense of community. These are mostly studies of more rural-based communities, where traditional patterns of social intercourse and accompanying deferential attitudes are likely to have outlasted those elsewhere.[19] In a more urbanized setting social classes seem not to mix in sporting activity and community sentiment has a different basis. For example, Stacey's early study of Banbury examined the class composition of various types of voluntary associations, including sports organizations – bowls, cricket, football, tennis, cycling, golf, sailing, squash and table tennis – and it shows a fairly clear line of division between classes defined in terms of 'occupational status'. The clubs for squash, rugby, tennis, and bowls were overwhelmingly middle and upper class in social composition, the working-class groupings belonged to a far narrower range of sporting organizations, and where the same game was played by people from different social classes it was organized in separate clubs. Although club committee members as a whole came from higher-status groups, the committees of the different clubs catering for the same sport, but for different social classes, were also different in class composition. Sport, in fact, was a central feature of two separate social networks dividing the upper from the lower groups. It served as an important means of integrating higher-status groups, but was much less important in this respect for the lower. And no one sport represented the unity of the community.[20] The process of social closure through sports is illustrated graphically in Willmott and Young's study of a London suburb, Woodford, in the late 1950s, where they were informed by one of their middle-class respondents:

> Supposing a plasterer or someone like that applied to join...we want something a bit higher social standard than that...[another informant confided]...We welcome anyone who likes a good game. We wouldn't turn a man down for class prejudice, you understand. But we can't let our status down either. He must be able to mix, a good fellow socially. A new member has to be proposed and seconded and no member would introduce a friend he didn't think acceptable. [About other clubs his would not play against]...they play well, but socially they are not the same. We gave one of them a game not so long ago – it stood out a mile they were of a different standing. I don't mean to be snobbish, but there it is.[22]

The rather convoluted apologetics here underlines the important demarcating role that sport still played in 'affluent' Britain at the borderline between the middle and working classes. Elaborate procedures of affiliation and the level of subscriptions achieve the effect.

Studies of traditional working-class communities, such as Jackson's account of Huddersfield and Dennis et al.'s study of 'Ashton', a coal-mining town in the West Riding of Yorkshire, show how sports reproduced traditional working-class identity and culture in the 1950s and 1960s.[23] Crown-green bowling, Jackson claims, was Huddersfield's most popular sport, engaging as many as 5,000 players in 33 main clubs, centred on local greens, working men's clubs, local Liberal and Conservative associations, and factories and mills. The game is peculiar to, and the property of, the northern working class and serves to knit the class together at the local level. Rugby League football has a similar character and function in Ashton, where, apart from the working men's clubs, the pubs and the cinema, it was the only institution bringing large numbers of people together. The most important social activity, in fact, was supporting the town's team against its rivals among other northern towns. The game's importance at the time and the active nature of support is indicated by the fact that in a town where the male population over the age of eighteen in 1953 was 4,800, attendance at local matches never fell below 3,200 and reached as many as 10,000. In such cases sport reproduces a corporate consciousness among working-class people, the main features of which are a generalized sense of belonging to 'us' against 'them', a pride in manual work and in strength and skill, a desire for active, collective and independent participation in social life and a rigid gender division. But it is doubtful whether such active involvement in, and commitment to, sport at the local level is typical of the class as a whole nowadays, for such communities are either smaller scale and well bounded, or are located in older, declining industrial areas where the sport concerned has a strong regional flavour. Ashton, for example, is neither a typical working-class community, nor even a typical Rugby League town, but a relatively small mining town or industrial village, where most of the team were local miners. In larger-scale, more modern urban settings, although working-class people are involved in sport in ways that largely segregate them from contact with other classes, the contribution that sport makes to a sense of working-class community and class solidarity is likely to be more limited compared with this, and with the contribution sport makes to the cohesion of bourgeois groupings. The reasons for this are highly complex and in order to understand them we must analyse the forces producing internal divisions within the working class, and the non-class forces cutting across working-class solidarity and the way these are reproduced through sporting activity.

Intra-Working-Class Divisions

Given the decomposition/recomposition of the working class that has taken place over the last three decades, it would perhaps be more appropriate to talk of 'working-class cultures' than 'working-class culture' in the singular.[23] The consequent divisions between respectable and 'rough', skilled and unskilled, traditional and privatized or dislocated sections of the class, are reproduced in sports. The traditional, more organized and respectable working class, of which a major part is made up of skilled workers in the older trades, has declined in importance with the demise of older industries and working-class communities. As we have seen, sporting activity for this group tends to form part of a local network of working-class institutions, more or less insulating people from dominant group influences, and when these influences are encountered in sporting activity around bureaucratically ordered leisure and sporting institutions, in either the private or the public sector, they can be shrugged off and reinterpreted in terms of traditional working-class norms of respectability. The traditional and 'rough' working class which tends to be made up of mostly semi- and unskilled manual workers has been decomposing at a rapid rate as well.

The new working class consists of a privatized and a dislocated element, neither of which possess, or have access to, their own network of social institutions and concomitant cultural resources which were a source of strength for the traditional working class. The privatized new working class is expanding, and consists of the more prosperous, mobile manual workers – skilled and otherwise – in the newer or more modern sector of industry, together with a growing proportion of non-manual workers. No doubt there is among this group a proportion of upwardly aspiring individuals. This stratum's active involvement in sport is likely to be conducted in an instrumental manner, that is to say, individuals possess the credentials to participate according to the middle-class norms and values of those in charge of sporting institutions but without necessarily having any positive commitment to them. There is little reason to believe that the respectable working-class user, whether 'traditional' or 'privatized', mixes socially or forms relationships with participants from non-working-class groups.[24] The contacts are too fleeting, the environment too impersonal – and crucially, activity around such institutions is mediated by existing class relations and group organization. The relative ease with which class segregation may be maintained, despite the fact that people from different class groupings mix together in the same physical space, is amply illustrated by the fate of the comprehensive school.[25] Both traditional–respectable and privatized–respectable elements share with non-working-class groups a relatively high involvement in sport, but without any significant degree of assimilation to the bourgeoisie taking place.

The dislocated working class with a preponderance of semi- and unskilled manual workers, the unemployed and the unemployable, and an increasing proportion of people in ethnic minorities, has a relatively low involvement in the more organized, institutionalized forms of sporting activity, due to the relative weakness of the social network, the low accessibility and availability of alternatives and inability or unwillingness to comply with middle-class norms. Sporting activity tends to occur more on an irregular, casual basis and to be more confined to a limited range of mostly commercially organized activities. Part of the reason seems to be that the structure of public provision and the manner in which facilities are run, reflects more the needs, demands, values and norms of middle-class users and those who conform to them, rather than those of lower-working-class users. The result is a form of closure in the public as well as the voluntary sector, as far as this group is concerned. A study of the use of a sports centre in Moss Side in the later 1970s, one of the poorest parts of Manchester, where a large proportion of the population are lower working class, and where semi- and unskilled workers predominate, showed it to be substantially under-used. It has a swimming-pool, a learners' pool, a large sports hall with seven badminton courts, a projectile range, weight-training room, three squash courts, sauna, sun-ray and private baths. But the only catering facility is a small vending area and the billiard room has been closed because of 'thefts and vandalism'. The study ascribes the relatively low rate of use to 'the notoriety of the area' and notes that the squash courts in particular are under-used, have a higher cost, and are inappropriate for the area.[26] In another documented case, this time in north London, where more plush facilities succeeded in attracting the local population, soon after it opened it became, in the words of one critical commentary, 'a hotly contested space'. A battle developed between two radically different sorts of users, with the sports centre's authorities backing one against the other, to one side's exclusion: 'On the one hand there was supervised club use. On the other, casual use of the ice rink and the coffee bar. On the one side, a mainstream of users in correct kit and carrying shower towels. On the other, dodging past the booking counter, gangs of lads in platform heels and tapered shirts.'[27] The result was vandalism and violence, with the authorities eventually employing local heavies as bouncers to get rid of the disruptive, non-conforming elements. In such examples the local community's needs are being defined in terms of middle-class norms and values and what is really at issue here is what constitutes 'the community'. The plethora of regulations – conditions of membership, the booking system, admission charges, management of space, etc., signal a bourgeois-club model of organization and express the values of rational recreation, which go directly against lower-working-class cultural traditions and thus alienate this stratum. Although policy-makers and leisure-facility managers in the public sector are becoming more sensitive to the issue, they have yet to address seriously this kind of problem, which is inherent in the clash between different cultural traditions that goes on around public provision.[28]

Where a policy of closure along these lines is implemented and built into provision, apart from favouring the middle-class user, the other main category of user to whom access will be available actually, as opposed to formally, is the respectable working-class user. But the lower the income, the greater the reliance on public provision. Paradoxically, the poorest areas, that is the areas where the lower working class tend to be concentrated, are also usually served worst in terms of public services in general and sports and recreation facilities in particular. In such areas, where the network of working-class institutions has been severely weakened, the informal organization around which sporting and recreative activity traditionally took place is now less and less available precisely where it is most needed. Deprived in terms of the availability of public provision, and experiencing differential access to it even when it is available, the lower working class is thrown back on and is uniquely reliant on commercial provision. The low incomes of people in this group and the fact that business operates for profit, necessarily restricts what the commercial sector can provide to a relatively narrow range of cheaper activities, in effect patronized almost exclusively by lower-working-class people. Thus, once more, contact between the classes is minimized. The figures for sports in which semi- and unskilled-worker participants are more strongly represented – and these occupational categories embrace a relatively high proportion of lower, more dislocated working-class elements – bear this out. All the sports in which levels of participation are high for this group tend to be less associated with public-sector provision, they can be indulged in on a more casual 'drop-in' basis, that is without having to satisfy rigid organizational norms and they are relatively cheap. Prominent among them are sports heavily associated with commercialized recreation – notably, with drinking –darts, billiards/snooker, ten-pin bowling and fishing.

Gender Divisions

Given the historical importance of sports in the formation of male identities, it is somewhat surprising to find so little attention being devoted to their contemporary role in the construction of gender relations.[29] Women's involvement in sports differs radically from that of men. Although few sports are exclusively male, and as much as a third of women participate actively in some form of sport, in statistical terms they are grossly underrepresented in most of the better-known sports. The sports in which women are mainly involved are ones in which the majority of participants are male (cycling, golf, bowls, sailing, swimming, table tennis, squash/fives, ten-pin bowling, darts, watching motor sports, and watching rugby and cricket); and on the whole they do not participate in a range of sports that are more or less exclusively male (athletics, football, rugby, cricket, fishing, billiards/snooker, watching football and field sports).[30] Sport then, is still an area of cultural life which is dominated by the presence of men. Again, if more passive forms of involvement, like televized sport and gambling are taken into account, women come into the picture on a more equal footing with men.

How working-class involvement in sport reproduces gender divisions is a function of the combined effect of gender and class. However, studies of working-class culture, like much of the sociological analysis of class, are by and large concerned with male working-class culture. Much of the feminist-influenced literature has over-reacted to this kind of gender-blindness by mistakenly opposing gender to class, treating class simply as an economic phenomenon and in many cases giving primacy to gender over class,[31] whereas these divisions can only be understood adequately if we treat them as being constructed together. Working-class culture is constructed as much through gender as gender is constructed through class. The experience and the meaning of being a working-class man is qualitatively different from that of being a working-class woman, while at the same time both partake of a culture which is radically different from that shared by bourgeois men and women. Thus the greater leisure opportunities enjoyed by bourgeois women are gained to a significant extent at the expense of working-class women (and men) who forego their leisure by having to sell their labour. For example, the former benefit from their ability to employ working-class women as cleaners and home-helps to relieve them of domestic labour, and from working-class women's employment in low-paid service industries that they use, like hairdressing, fashion, and catering and retailing.

Historically, working-class culture has been built around men's experience of industrial work, the family and local community activities, of which sport and recreation is a major component. Traditionally, gender, age and ethnic divisions within the working class have been subsumed within an English working-class male hegemony. One of the most salient features of this working-class culture is the subordinate position of women, which is legitimized by a pervasive sexist ideology. Involvement in sports has been one of the major ways this gender division has been reproduced. To explain such divisions exclusively in terms of men's capacity to control women's leisure however, is simplistic. For a start, it does not explain the enormous differences between working-class and bourgeois women's involvement in sport, nor the multitudinous other uses to which women put their leisure. The claim that married women with children and employed women, have virtually no leisure and that the leisure women do have is mostly controlled by men – a claim which has achieved the status of holy writ in some quarters – is crudely deterministic, exaggerates the degree of women's subordination, and takes no account of men's experience.[32] Such claims, when made about working-class women, and indeed most accounts of the position of working-class women, are based on an ahistorical notion of gender relations derived from post-war studies of traditional working-class culture. As we have seen in this culture male identities cohere around a notion of toughness associated with the qualities deemed necessary to master heavy industrial work. Women's proper place is considered to be in the home, where they are needed to support the breadwinner in his struggle to gain a livelihood for the family through physically exhausting labour, to bring up the children, and to keep a respectable home.[33] Gender roles in leisure follow this rigid division between paid labour and domestic labour. Most studies of clubs and voluntary organizations for example, reveal that it is men rather than women who belong. In the early 1950s Bottomore's study of an Oxfordshire locality showed that two-thirds of voluntary association members were men. There was a clear difference between working- and middle-class women in this respect, with the former having a much higher propensity to join. Stacey in 1967 found that a third of men, but just over half the women studied in Banbury belonged to no association at all. Hutson's study of Bonymaen, a traditional Welsh working-class community, in the lower Swansea Valley, found that the largest group of people who did not attend or do anything outside the family, were women.[34] In the 1950s traditional working-class communities like 'Ashton' were characterized by an extreme subordination of women, whereby the principal leisure institutions were dominated by men, women were consciously excluded, or only allowed to participate as long as they did not challenge men's hegemony. They were excluded almost totally from the world of men's sports and from the principal source of community pride, the town's Rugby League team. Studies in the 1960s, such as Littlejohn's study of Westrigg, a village in the Cheviot Hills of North-East England, show the pattern being perpetuated. Here 'sports talk' was one of the main constituents of working-class men's casual conversation and as such an important form of social intercourse, from which women were excluded as incompetents and unequals through the device of ridicule.[35] Even non-physically demanding sports today are used in some instances to enforce a rigid gender division: in working men's clubs it is still not uncommon to find women barred from playing snooker because it is deemed to spoil the atmosphere of a man's game. Where they are permitted to enter this world, the roles accorded to them tend to parallel their dependent subordinate familial roles – turning out to cheer the local football team, making the tea for the players, etc.

But as we have observed previously, traditional working-class culture has undergone fairly rapid decomposition over the last 30 years or so, so that the rigid divisions depicted in the studies only apply at best to a shrinking proportion of the working class nowadays. If the crisis of male hegemony has not been as acute among working-class men as it has among their bourgeois counterparts, working-class male hegemony has not escaped challenge and change, both at work and in leisure. There are now women's football and rugby teams and an organization that challenges the sexism of the snooker room in places like working men's clubs.[36] Accommodation between the sexes has occurred so that divisions between working-class men and women, especially among those born since 1950, are less rigid than they were. The steady growth of home-centredness, due to a great extent to pressure from women for a more equally shared partnership, and epitomized above all by the phenomenon of the do-it-yourself enthusiast 'captive husband', is evidence of a significant change. Similarly, among the new working class, gender divisions in leisure no doubt still exist, but they are being challenged and broken down, under pressure from women, in conjunction with forces generated within consumer culture, to promote family-centred leisure and particularly family-centred sporting activity. We will discuss the ramifications of commercial pressure and state intervention in this connection in later chapters.

As the traditional networks of working-class life based on locality are eroded, and increasing reliance is placed on leisure activity around bureaucratically ordered institutions run either by the local state, commercial enterprises or the voluntary sector, sporting activity takes its place alongside, and is integrated into, a more individualized, consumption-oriented mode of existence, constituting a constant pressure to atomize the class into a series of separate consumption units. Thus we see the changing role of women in relation to leisure as part of a redeployment of sexuality, whereby they function as relays in a process promoting the growth of family-centred leisure and family-centred sport, that is as a crucial part of the elaboration of the power network through which the traditional working class is deconstructed and the new working class is made. At the same time sporting activity is the focus of a countervailing, conservatizing tendency. With the steady decline in the ability of work to provide working-class men with a sense of identity, and with their hegemony being challenged within the family so that it no longer represents so safe an enclave compensating them for their relative powerlessness in work, society and politics, involvement in sports becomes one of the few remaining ways working-class men's identity can be reaffirmed and their hegemony shored up. In this way the interaction between gender and class, as far as contemporary working-class culture is concerned, exhibits profound contradictory tendencies. If it is not so already, it certainly constitutes a potential battleground for the construction of gender and class in the future.

Localism, Chauvinism and Racism

One of the most striking aspects of this conservative tendency manifests itself in the way working-class youth relates to football. Football culture, both traditionally and in its latter-day version, is stridently male chauvinist, sporadically violent and is the focus of fierce local patriotism. Now it has acquired in addition a racist, white-nationalist dimension. The 'normal' young working-class football supporter denigrates women, despises effiminacy in men, and fights other young males and the authorities to demonstrate his manhood. And young working-class women expect them to be so: they acquiesce in, and concur with, these norms and values and they thus connive at their own subordination.[37]

Localism (which is constructed around football in particular) equates class solidarity with loyalty to one's mates and to the local community. Thus working-class people from other localities and other subordinate groups are identified as rivals, as 'outsiders' and even as enemies. So, groups of similarly placed, deprived and exploited working-class youths from different localities strive to defend the communities symbolized by the teams they support. In doing so they come into violent conflict, not only with each other, but crucially also with the adult working class, to whom they increasingly appear as a threat. The conflict thus generated within the class between locally based working-class youth groupings and between different generations, can be exploited politically.

From the later 1970s the Right has responded to the older generation's and the respectable working class's fear of disorder and violence by singling out 'unruly and undisciplined youth' as a cause. In much the same terms as other perceived problematic elements – blacks, strikers, political demonstrators, etc. – football hooliganism has been identified as a species of problem requiring repressive measures.[38] The vehement denunciations of football hooliganism by politicians, heavier policing, bigger fines and longer terms of imprisonment for offenders, has become an integral part of an approach to law and order designed to deal with a range of challenges at the economic and political level and to mobilize working-class people behind conservative forces. We will discuss the politicization of football and its effects further in chapter 9.

Localist sentiment clearly flourishes in urban settings especially around the Football League clubs, but the sense of shared community that is fostered in sports varies according to social class and social category. Local teams and individuals participating in international competitions like the European Cup, can come to represent the nation as well as the locality. The question of how the nation is constructed through sports will be discussed at greater length in chapters 7 and 9, but it is necessary to establish how nationalism and working-class culture are broadly related at this point. Feelings of national superiority and a suspicion of foreigners and things foreign have rarely been far from the surface of British working-class culture, and the consequent chauvinism and transient xenophobia receive expression in sports. The growth of international competition, particularly since the 1950s, provides regular opportunities now for the expression of varying shades of nationalist sentiment, from the patriotism of the respectable, law-abiding

English working class, to Scottish, Irish and Welsh nationalism and to the xenophobia of the football hooligan. Localism and nationalism possess in common the strong capacity to counteract working-class solidarity and solidarity between subordinate groups as a whole, a capacity which, in practice, is ultimately supportive of the social order despite the apparent opposition to it that is often graphically present in football hooliganism.

The nationalism, racism and general ethnocentricity of the English working-class football hooligan is a case in point. To him, Englishness, manliness and belonging to one's local community are all of a piece and when the chips are down the essence of these qualities is the willingness and ability to fight for them. Asians are despised and attacked because they are perceived as weak and passive. Blacks are respected for their fighting ability, but as they are perceived as immigrants who are taking over the country, including 'our game', black players are vilified with racist abuse, especially when (final insult) they are selected to play for England; hence also the inroads the National Front and the British Movement have been able to make into football supporters.[39] Apparently, the English rioters who attacked Juventus supporters at the Heysal Stadium in Brussels in 1985, with such tragic consequences, looked upon themselves as fighting for England, and they found it difficult to understand the degree of opprobrium their action incurred at all levels, and particularly the idea fostered by dominant groups that they had shamed their country into the bargain. Dominant groups in turn find it difficult to understand that such sentiments are not just those of a tiny minority of criminally inclined elements, but a constituent element in a culture. How close such apparently different versions of nationalism are to each other, and how easy it is for a link to be forged between them so that working-class people are pulled in behind dominant groups within the greater unity of the nation at a time of crisis, may be gauged from the fact that during the Falklands War, Tottenham Hotspur's two Argentinian players were subjected to jingoistic, racist abuse by their supporters, and had to be withdrawn from the team.

The tendency for sporting activity to become more ethnically based and in the process to become an additional factor cutting across working-class culture, is in part at least, a response on the part of ethnic minorities to the closed, corporatist nature of working-class culture towards those defined as outsiders and to the incipient racism therein. Ethnic sport is growing in importance as ethnic minorities attempt to assert their independence and to establish their own cultural identities in a largely hostile society. Not a great deal is known about the meaning, the importance and the social function of sport for the different ethnic groups in this country. There are indications that the black community, in particular, has become increasingly organized on an autonomous basis in this respect. For example, the West Indian Organizations Co-ordinating Committee in the Manchester area runs a thriving centre catering for a wide range of social, cultural and recreational interests, among which sports are prominent.[40] In the Manchester Sunday Football League there are not only many black players but there are also entirely black teams. Work on black youth culture suggests that black sports clubs and black sports celebrities are an important source of identity and pride for black youth.[41] In London the Muhammed Ali Sports Development Association in Lambeth is thus designed to develop the talents and aspirations and confidence of young blacks. Ninety per cent of street hockey players are black; and due to their enthusiasm for this tough, macho game there is now a national league and international competitions.[42]

Working-Class Involvement in Sport and the Restructuring of Hegemony

Having examined the relation between class, gender and ethnic divisions in sport with reference to working-class culture, we are now in a position to assess more precisely how all this relates to the power network and to bourgeois hegemony. It is clear that sports in modern Britain, despite the transformation that has taken place since the Second World War, continue to mark off and unify dominant groups and the middle classes *vis-à-vis* the working class and other subordinate groups.

It has been argued by some that sports support the structure of hegemony by contributing to the reproduction of labour power.[43] This would certainly seem to be the case as far as the sexual division of labour is concerned, since there is a strong homologous relationship between sexual divisions in sport and the sexual division of labour. The next most obvious link would appear to be the demands of heavy industrial work, such as coal-mining, etc., and the involvement of working-class men in sports demanding a high degree of strength and physical exertion, such as Rugby League, boxing, etc. Yet, as we have seen, so far as it is possible to judge, only a fraction of working-class men are actually involved actively to any great extent in such sports. It is true that the upper working class are more actively involved, but it is also true that a decreasing proportion of these workers, and indeed of the labour force as a whole, is to be found in heavy industry and so the more obvious connections between the nature of work and indulging in certain kinds of sports are becoming increasingly tenuous.

More plausibly perhaps, it could be argued that what is important in the reproduction of labour power as far as sport is concerned, is not so much the physical correspondence between types of work and sports, but that they are structurally and culturally homologous spheres or levels. That is to say, orientation to the task, attitudes towards discipline and authority, the experience of competition, etc., are similar in both these worlds, so that they are mutually sustaining. But even if working-class participation in sport does involve acceptance of discipline, obedience to rules and a competitive ethos, it is by no means clear that the norms and values structuring such features coincide with bourgeois notions. For example, what has been distinctive of traditional working-class styles of involvement in some team sports, notably football, is the primacy which is given to a type of team-work and discipline which expresses the solidarity of the group and victory in the collective interest, as opposed to individual ambition and achievement. Rather than conforming labour to capital's requirements, it is precisely this type of solidarity that historically, has formed the basis for trenchant opposition to employers. However, a collectivist mode of involvement is not universal among working-class people: a good many are involved in sports that are more individualistic, like boxing, cycling, snooker, darts, etc., and in addition, among the new, more privatized working class, this kind of collectivist ethic is less likely to be expressed in sporting activity. There may accordingly be a more homologous relationship between these categories' more individualized leisure patterns and their work. The tendency of the skilled group and of routine non-manual workers to be more involved in organized, more physically demanding, fitness and achievement-oriented sports – in particular, the major games, in which norms governing management of the body have traditionally transmitted a rational-recreation, work and discipline ethic – is probably significant here. While possibly contributing in a diffuse manner to the reproduction of these categories of labour power, there is no indication, on the other hand, that occupational solidarity among such workers is reduced by it, indeed if trade union membership is taken as an indication of solidarity it is, if anything, greater among them.

Equally pertinent is the fact that a great deal of working-class involvement in sports is not homologous to the character of work, indeed, it often takes on exactly the opposite features. Sporting forms popular among working-class people like the kick-about, fishing, cycling, ten-pin bowling, snooker and billiards, darts, swimming in natural surroundings, etc., offer relaxation and relief rather than a training in work discipline and they are often surrounded by an air of conviviality rather than competitive striving. It is precisely because popular culture and its sporting forms provide workers with rewarding involvement in a multiplicity of activities that provide a contrast to work, that facilitates the process of accommodation to the latter as a part of their lives which is widely perceived among them as unfulfilling. The fact is that work is not a central life interest among subordinate groups.[44] In the trade-off the gravitation towards a pattern of family-oriented leisure and sporting activity, in which women play a greater role, is a highly significant factor in the recomposition of the working class along privatized lines and the restructuring of hegemony. On the other hand, sport is plainly dysfunctional from the point of view of integrating those alienated groups who are put off by the association between sports and rational recreation, and conforming them to the Protestant ethic. The more reflective youth and community workers and policy-makers in this area appear to have read the lesson, and in some instances have responded by making leisure activity more oriented to commercial entertainment. Here nightly live music or discos, drinking within certain limits, and the presence of the opposite sex, is spiced with creative activities like dance and drama workshops; and sport is demoted as being rather square.

We can dismiss the idea that sports nowadays embourgeoisify the working class. As we have been at some pains to demonstrate, involvement in sport, whatever section of the class we consider, does not induce an identification with, or facilitate mixing with bourgeois elements, or lead to the adoption of a bourgeois life-style. The structure and the meaning of involvement for the different groupings we have examined is specific to each of them, and the divisions between them are reproduced autonomously rather than as a result of control and influence from above. The effects of social mobility through sport, achieved in successful pursuit of a sporting career, will be dealt with in the next chapter, but one aspect is relevant here. We know the middle and upper classes effectively place obstacles in the way of the lower classes mixing with them in sporting activity; and we know also that working-class people on the whole do not aspire to join them. But social mobility through sport can exert an effect and make an input to hegemony by functioning as a myth about, and as a symbol of, the openness of the society. One of the most common ambitions among young white working-class men and young black working class men alike is to become a professional sportsman (among the former the ambition is usually to become a professional footballer). Necessarily, the chances of doing so in view of the limited number of openings available in relation to number of aspirants, are pretty slim. But such is the power of the myth, supported by the effect of the success of the few, that aspirants will go to extraordinary lengths to succeed. There is a more diffuse effect as well, in that it also provides dramatic symbolic support for the pervasive myth that social inequality coincides with degrees of merit. By definition, high-performance sports are meritocratic: the whole rationale is selection and reward according to demonstrated superiority of performance. What point would there be in giving the accolades to the failures? Consequently, in practice, sport approximates more to the ideal of a meritocratic social order than any other sphere of social life. Sport as a social institution therefore gives convincing substance to the ideology that the ambitious, hard working, talented individual, no matter what his social origin, may achieve high status and rewards, and so it reproduces the belief among subordinate groups – some individuals from which are actually successful in sports – that the social formation is more open and amenable to change than it really is.

The sectionalization or fragmentation of subordinate groups is a pre-condition for maintaining hegemony, and sports are a constituent part of a process generated within such groups which results in fragmentation among them at the cultural level. Differential involvement in sports continues to reflect and reproduce the division between routine non-manual and skilled workers on the one hand, and semi- and unskilled workers on the other; between the more and the less respectable working-class elements, and between the upper and lower working class. Furthermore, sports help reproduce a more complex cross-cutting modern pattern of vertical and lateral divisions – between traditional and privatized/dislocated elements, between whites and non-whites and between working-class men and women. This complex pattern of fragmentation means that fractions of the working class and other subordinate groups are placed in somewhat different rela-tionships to the social formation as well as to each other, and crucially, they are each fixed in a different relationship with dominant groups. The differences in the way working-class fractions and subordinate groups as a whole are involved in sports then, tend to deconstruct the working class and pre-empt the possibility of subordinate groups achieving a cohesive unity at the cultural level. For the more traditional working class experienc-ing fragmentation, class cohesion takes a corporatist form, epitomized above all, in the localist sentiments expressed in sports. A way of life is encouraged which, while insulating working-class people from direct cultural and ideological domination from above, at the same time constitutes a withdrawal into a restricted, socially and culturally conservative, in some respects apolitical retreat, which is ultimately accommodative to the global structure. From within this culture society tends to be perceived and treated as a relatively fixed set of parameters which, while not necessarily accorded legitimacy, is accommodated to perforce.

The divisions and forms of accommodation we have discussed are to a large extent self-imposed. They arise in the course of subordinate groups' attempts to cope with and control the conditions of existence they encounter. As such, they are example of how a class adjusts and at the same time is adjusted, of how it renders itself subordinate and is at the same time conformed to a wider structure of hegemony by relatively autonomous processes. Hegemony is never merely a matter of self-imposition: the processes, if not directed entirely from above, are certainly not without aid from that direction. For example, economically based differentiation within the working class – the division of labour, disparities in income and work conditions, authority at work – are plainly determined to a large extent by the economic power of owners and controllers and they have important cultural consequences. The capacity of dominant groups to exert limits and pressures on cultural space so as to determine the availability and accessibility of sporting activity, cannot be dissociated from their economic and political power. Hegemony therefore, depends not just on consent to rule and self-imposed limits, it depends also on the differential capacity of the hegemonic class, when compared with subordinate groups, to shape the context of class relations. Where sport is concerned, although dominant groups cannot determine the content of working-class involvement and turn it to their own advantage at will, they can nevertheless, strategically delimit the boundaries of cultural space so that in the sphere of sport, relations between classes and between different elements within the working class can, to a significant extent, be affected.

Cultural life is never entirely uncontested either. Even the areas of 'mass' culture most apparently lost to working-class control, i.e. those aspects defined as 'merely leisure' by their participants (the Hollywood musical, dance-band music, and popular songs of the 1930s and 1940s, for example), had to be negotiated,[45] although it is difficult to realize that now. The fact that control may be successful does not mean it does not go uncontested. It has to be said though, that working-class resistance to bourgeois hegemony over leisure, sport, and recreation is still signally weak. Witness the character of the apparent 'resistance' expressed in football hooliganism, riddled as it is with sexism, jingoism, racism and nationalism, but ultimately supportive of the social order. Where sport has become politicized it is dominant groups and middle-class radical groups who have made the running, while the working-class responses have been in support of the more conservative forces. The classic example is the utter indifference among working-class people on the whole, to the Anti-Apartheid Movement's attempts to cut Britain's sporting links with South Africa, and the open hostility of supporters towards anti-apartheid demonstrations at sporting events. We will take up this question in chapter 9 and in the concluding chapter.

The absence of the working class as a coherent, mobilized force contesting the sporting terrain is significant because it is an important component not only of working-class, but also of the national popular culture. Hegemony reduces contestation to a large extent by removing issues from the political agenda. So, getting what is done with free time on this agenda can be seen to be not without importance to the outcome of struggle at the political and economic levels.

6

The Commercialization Process

In this chapter we will be dealing with those economic processes with pertinent effects on the relation between sport and power which are generated within civil society. The effects of the state as an economic actor on involvement in sports have specific features which are best treated separately later. We shall be concerned with the significance of spectator sport involving large numbers of people as audiences at the events themselves or via the media. To some extent also we shall be concerned with the significance of the production and consumption of sports goods and services on a capitalist basis. At the outset, it must be emphasized that to attribute the character of mass sport in Britain today solely to the nature of modern capitalism, is to indulge in economic reductionism. In developed non-capitalist countries such as the USSR, the character of mass sport is, in some key respects, similar (mass enthusiasm and the figure of the privileged sports star are common to both) but the means by which it is produced differ fundamentally.

Market pressure imposes an instrumental rationality on sporting institutions, just as it tends to do so on the institutions that comprise civil society as a whole, but this does not necessarily transform them into capitalist enterprises. It is important then, to distinguish the different ways sport can be related to capital. Some sporting activity is organized as a profit-maximizing business enterprise in which investment functions to accumulate capital, and where capitalists and/or their agents own, control and organize. Professional boxing and many aspects of horse-racing and motor sport are prime examples. A good proportion of organized sport is highly commercialized but does not operate on this basis: its objective is rather to break even, or to operate at least cost in order to remain financially viable. Thirdly, sporting activity can stimulate the accumulation of capital indirectly by providing a market for goods and services associated with it (sports-clothing and equipment, gambling, etc). Fourthly, sport may aid capital accumulation indirectly, by making an accommodation with capital such that the former functions as a sales adjunct to the latter through the medium of sponsorship and advertising. It is important to understand that business interests also invest in sport for non-economic reasons: to gain prestige from being associated with a popular cultural activity, individual businessmen's commitment to a life-style and to exert social and cultural influence. It is often difficult in practice to differentiate economic and non-economic objectives: both may be pursued at the same time, in that prestige and influence is pursued at least cost and investment for profit may incidentally enhance the image of the investor.

Financial Crisis and Change in Sports

Since the late 1950s crisis has reigned over, or has never been very far away from, most popular sports. Most of the English Football League clubs are either unprofitable and making losses, or are deeply in debt to banks or individual financial backers.[1] In football, the watershed was the abolition of the players' maximum wage as a result of the Eastham case in 1961, when the Professional Footballers' Association (PFA) took the employers, the Football League, to court and won. Higher wages and players' transfer fees thereafter became the crucial cost factor. Over the last fifteen years the game has gone up-market: admission prices were raised seven- to eightfold to offset falling attendances; the capacity of grounds has been reduced by converting terraces into seated accommodation; expensive and exclusive 'executive' boxes have been introduced and the game has been increasingly promoted as a 'family entertainment' (as opposed to a working-class man's entertainment). Sponsorship, advertising and TV money have become an increasingly important source of revenue (sponsorship alone brought in £8m. in 1982/3). The last contract for the TV rights to League Football brought in £10m. from the BBC and ITV over four years (1981–5). The League is polarized between a few rich, secure, successful clubs, like Arsenal, Liverpool, and Manchester United, and the majority of clubs, some of which are just hanging on. There is now strong pressure for the bigger, richer clubs to form a 'super league'. A few years ago athletics had to be hauled out of deep financial trouble and the British Amateur Athletic Board (BAAB) was losing money up to the end of the 1970s. In a relatively short space of time an alliance of commercially minded administrators, athletes eager to exploit their latent market potential, and an influx of corporate sponsors, has transformed the sport at the top level from an amateur-dominated to a professional sport in all but name.[2] The governing body of Rugby Union football in this country, one of the staunchest defenders of amateurism, has been forced to resort to sponsors and advertisers to get itself out of financial difficulties.[3] By the end of the 1950s cricket was sliding into bankruptcy; in the mid-1960s it was in deficit;

and in the 1970s, when most of the first-class county clubs were losing £175,000 a year, the game was hit by the 'Packer affair'.[4] Kerry Packer, by creating World Series Cricket (WSC) as a direct competitor to official Test Cricket, and by conducting a successful fight in the English High Court against the cricket authorities' ban on playing for WSC, broke their control over the development of the game and ensured that the only way cricket could survive in the future is by attracting a sufficient level of business sponsorship. In the 1980s, the county clubs, especially the smaller ones, are still in trouble. Horse-racing in the 1960s experienced a decline in popularity and had to be bailed out by the Horse Race Betting Levy Board, a state body financed mainly through the tax on betting.[5] Other sports like motor-cycle racing went through periods of depression at the end of the 1950s and in the 1960s and continue to suffer today.[6]

In simple accounting terms the perennial crisis is caused by the fact that costs continually tend to outstrip revenue, but behind this lie important social changes. First, changes in occupation, income and life-style have made the sporting clientele's loyalty much more volatile, a fact reflected in fluctuating and, over the long term, declining attendances. The figures for four major selected sports give some idea of how serious the decline has been. Cricket attendances fell from 2,126,000 in 1949 to 1,408,000 in 1954, picked up slightly to 1,640,000 in 1956, and plummeted to 750,000 in 1960. From 1949–66 cricket lost 75 per cent of its audience, and in 1970 the average daily attendance at county matches was a mere 581. Attendances in 1952 at Rugby League matches were approximately 4,000,000 but by 1972–3 they were down to a third of that figure, at 1,365,700. The average daily attendance at horse-racing in 1953 was 11,194 and by 1967 it was down to 7,530.[8] There were almost 40 million attendances at English Football League games in 1950–1. In the 1960s this had fallen to between 28 and 29 million; in 1980–1 they were down to 22 million, and to less than 18 million in 1983–4.[9] Undoubtedly the most potent combination of factors in reducing attendances is the drift to family centred-ness, the availability of alternative activities and in particular the spread of TV viewing over the past 25 years as a result of increased income and leisure time. Secondly, patronage from ruling groups, long enjoyed by many sports, failed to keep pace with inflation, or dried up altogether with their declining economic and social influence. Thirdly, sports tended to be administered on a voluntary basis by amateur officials unschooled in modern business-management techniques. Consequently the sports organizations were, and still are to a great extent, relatively inefficient at using their resources, and at seizing existing opportunities to obtain revenue from alternative sources. British sport has not been run on capitalist lines to anything like the same extent as, for example, North American sport. Football and cricket are not run as profit-maximizing enterprises: the English

Football League for example, still forbids payment for directors' services, there is a limitation on payments of dividends to shareholders and all but one club are private, limited liability companies, with restrictions on transferability of shares.

In this situation costs have risen steadily. Wages of playing and other staff, travel expenses, the cost of coaching and training schemes, the maintenance and replacement of equipment and facilities, the costs of development, have all risen. The traditional ways in which sports bodies cope with financial problems – sweeps and lotteries, selling debentures, socials, tapping the occasional philanthropist, levies, raising the price of entry – have proved insufficient. State aid, in the form of Sports Council grants and sponsorship by local state, is helpful in individual cases, but in relation to the global problem it is not enough. Little aid has been forthcoming from the state via fiscal policy. Tax exemptions for sponsorship, charitable status for sports bodies, more generous transfers to sport via the betting tax and a levy on the football pools, have all been called for and resisted. These circumstances have rendered sports vulnerable to market forces and subject increasingly to a capitalist pattern of rationalization.

Relations have been transformed in the process: owners and controllers of sports organizations and the sports elite tend to treat the audience increasingly as consumers and to see their task as one in which sales have to be maximized; modern business methods and management techniques are being introduced; and as more professional expertise is employed at all levels, power and control is passing out of the hands of the traditionalist amateur interests and into those of an efficiency and publicity-conscious, more business-oriented group of sports administrators. In the ensuing struggles for control the larger and/or better-organized interests clash with the smaller weaker ones, amateurism is jettisoned or drastically modified, and with the accompanying further professionalization and specialization of the sportsman's role, greater inequalities and conflicts of interest are generated within the ranks of the performers. It is important to bear in mind that the commercialization of sports develops unevenly: it is dependent upon the existing structure of control, the allegiance of the relevant public, the objectives of interest groups and the nature of individual sports traditions. Horse-racing, association football, Rugby League, professional boxing and motor sport are already substantially commercialized; some older sports, like cricket and tennis are somewhat less so; some sports, like snooker, have experienced a commercial explosion over a very short time; others, like athletics and perhaps some of the lesser-known, minority sports, are poised on the brink of radical commercialization, or are in a transitional stage, where the pressures to do so are still somewhat contained and their ultimate effects uncertain; and lastly, some sectors of sport, like Rugby Union, still remain rather more closely bound by tradition and are still relatively unattractive for commercial exploitation. A sharpening of economic crises tends to accelerate the whole process of commercial rationalization across the board and although the evidence is incomplete, it is likely that most sports in which working-class people are involved have been affected significantly.

The Sponsorship/Advertising/Media Axis

The sponsorship/advertising/media axis is the key factor in the current redevelopment of sport. Business sponsorship establishes a closer relationship between corporate capital and sport than is the case in straight advertising. The former uses sport to secure what it considers an appropriate image of the sponsor, or to achieve a specific marketing objective – 'Englishness' in the case of Gillette's support for cricket; 'public spiritedness' in the case of NatWest's (National Westminster Bank) support for rowing; 'fun, liveliness and youth' in the case of Coca Cola's support for a range of energetic sports and for school sport; to achieve 'product normality' in the case of Durex's support for motor-racing; to associate beer with playing darts in the case of Watney's support for the latter sport; and in the case of the tobacco companies, to evade the voluntary agreement between the tobacco industry and the Department of Health and Social Security (DHSS) not to associate smoking with sports heroes, success and healthiness.[10]

TV coverage, from the sponsors' and advertisers' view, is virtually obligatory nowadays because it puts them in contact with such a massive potential audience and the amounts needed to finance sports are so large. Sponsoring televized events and advertising at events covered by the media is an extremely cheap and efficient form of advertising. The time given to clear display of advertisements during one Test Match on BBC TV has been estimated as taking up eight minutes during an hour's coverage, and this did not include peripheral messages shown as the camera followed the ball when it was hit to the boundary. Every time the score is shown during the Cornhill Test, the sponsoring company's name comes into full view at the top of the score-board. On the other hand, the rival channel, ITV, is statutorily forbidden to show more than six minutes of commercials in any one hour, and one minute of prime time on ITV costs advertisers £51,000, plus the cost of making the advertisement.[11] The names of sponsors and references to them are scattered throughout the media's coverage of sport. For the amount that sponsors put into sport, it is extremely doubtful whether the equivalent amount of exposure could be procured elsewhere. Corporate sponsors also gain exposure by running their own sports teams, motor sport and cycling being prime examples. The cycle firm Raleigh, a subsidiary of the conglomerate Tube Investments, broke into the lucrative continental cycle market, by entering their own team for several successive years in the Tour de France, thereby receiving over 100 hours of TV coverage on the continent each year.[12]

Linking the sponsors, the media and the sports apparatus are the agencies specializing in sports promotion and consultancy, like West Nally, the Mark McCormack International Management Organization and Alan Pascoe Associates, which put advertisers and sponsors in contact with sports bodies and individual sports stars. They act as consultants to both kinds of parties, and even sometimes become directly involved by setting up, organizing and presenting sports events themselves. These institutions are a vital ingredient in the process of fusing sport with business interests, and their spokesmen are among the most vigorous and vociferous proponents of commercializing sport.[13]

The Sports Council also encourages sponsorship by acting as a clearing-house through which potential sponsors can be put in touch with sports bodies requiring investment, and also by ceaselessly propagandizing in favour of sponsorship as a major solution to the financial problems of sport.[14]

The way the sponsorship/advertising/media axis works tends to encourage uneven development across sports. Those sports and sports events which attract large media audiences tend to attract sponsors and are relatively advantaged – sports like cricket, snooker and tennis, for example, are ideal for TV – tennis in particular, is never short of sponsors.[15] On the other hand, lack of a sponsor caused the cancellation of the World Squash Championships in 1978 when TV coverage could not be guaranteed.[16] The diversion of sponsorship money away from sports that are already being squeezed by the market, or can only muster a minority following, and the further development of other sports or forms of an individual sport in competition with them, may accelerate their decline. Paradoxically, sponsorship may cause uneven development between different levels within a sport. The flood of sponsorship money into tennis for example, has revolutionized the sport at the elite level, but it has done little to halt the withering away of the game at its grass roots.[17] Indeed, it is conceivable that sponsorship may exacerbate the problems of division between top and bottom levels, for there is no guarantee that the additional resources will percolate down to lower levels. Also, the process of decline, in a sense, may be amplified by sponsorship. Cases in point are the transformation of horse-racing and football into TV spectacles. This coincides with the decline in attendance at the gate, and this in turn has stimulated further demand for sponsorship money to offset the loss of revenue, which is followed by a further drop in attendance and so on in a vicious downward spiral. Sponsorship in this sense may not be much of a solution as far as the spectator at the event is concerned.

If a sport wants to attract investment from the sponsor/TV nexus, it has to adapt itself to its specific requirements and it is in this way that the character of some existing sports has already been altered. Probably the best known case is cricket, in which for example, the one-day game has increased the pace and placed a premium on certain skills. Rothmans the cigarette manufacturer encouraged attacking batting skills and defensive bowling by paying more for when the ball was driven to the boundary, so that the advertisements on the periphery of the ground would appear more frequently on camera.[18] The introduction of the tie-break in tennis and in squash, changes in the colour and size of the ball and in the design of the court, are further examples. Dates, times, and venues of events are now arranged to suit TV programming. Between them the sponsors, promotion agencies and TV also develop sports in new ways by running their own competitions around existing sports – examples are Packer's World Series Cricket, Mark McCormack's 'Love Doubles' tennis matches, pro–celebrity golf, the BBC FLoodlight Trophy and the Pot Black snooker competition – or entirely new events may be created specially for TV, like the TV Superstars, 'The Strongest Man in the World' and 'The Crypton Factor'.

Just as money flows into sport in accordance with sponsors' objectives, it may flow out when these are achieved or where there is no longer a perceived gain. Colgate withdrew its £1m. from tennis and golf because it no longer suited their rationalization plans; Gillette pulled out of cricket because it discovered it was no longer associated in people's minds with their product (apparently, Gillette was thought to be an old England cricketer!).[19] Football's violent image in the aftermath of the Heysal Stadium disaster has reduced its attraction for sponsors and the media: already the League's major sponsor has withdrawn and another sponsor is considering doing so.[20] Sports have thus entered a world in which they can never be secure: the more reliant on it they become, the greater the opportunity for the corporate sponsor to enforce conditions; and fear of withdrawal by sponsors is a powerful inducement to compliance. Their power, it must be emphasized, is not absolute. Some sports are adept at exploiting the market and at playing off one potential sponsor against another. Some now have specialized departments or officials skilled at building sponsorship portfolios and at spreading the risk of losing sponsors. Obviously, sports which are not well organized are in a weak position to defend themselves against encroachment by commercial interests or to take advantage of opportunities. But nevertheless the power of sponsors is formidable and economic insecurity makes sports more vulnerable to the pressures which they may put on them. Athletics' dependency on sponsorship highlights the problem. When the International Athletes Club opposed sponsorship of athletics by British and American Tobacco on health grounds, no support was forthcoming from the athletics authorities, the Minister for Sport, the Sports Council, or the Central Council for Physical Recreation (CCPR), all of whom are aware that the tobacco industry is the biggest single sponsor of sport and that it would suffer financially if the industry withdrew its support.[21]

Sports have helped to strengthen capital also in that they have become a major factor in breaching the remaining barriers to the commercial penetration of public broadcasting.[22] Under its charter the BBC is not allowed to accept advertising, but every time it covers a major sports event, strictly speaking it breaks its charter by transmitting the advertising surrounding sports events. There is a standard agreement with sponsors of events allowing them two banners in camera-shot, two mentions of the sponsor's name every half an hour and full credits in the *Radio Times*.[23] The BBC does attempt to restrict blatant breaches, but given its strong commitment to cover sports as they are structured, it is now an integral part of the sponsorship/advertising/media axis. If one considers that according to one estimate the BBC screened 1,500 hours of sport in 1982, one can get some idea of the amount of advertising being obtained by the private sector at public expense. Breaches of IBA (Independent Broadcasting Authority) regulations also occur, for example when an advertisement featuring a sports star is shown during coverage of the event in which he appears as a performer, or within half an hour following the transmission.[24] In contrast, there is a sensitivity about political advertising. Thames TV blacked out coverage of the 1985 Edinburgh Games, when the organizers, Edinburgh Council, refused to remove an anti-apartheid banner out of camera sight; and the Greater London Council (GLC) also came into conflict with TV over slogans displayed at venues under their control.

In order to serve the interests of capital it is not necessary for sports to be under the direct control of capitalists, or to function themselves as profit-maximizing enterprises: all that is necessary is for a given sport to enter into the kind of accommodation to capital outlined here. With the increasing penetration of capital in the form of advertising and sponsorship then, sports are becoming increasingly dependent on the movement of capital. Dependency is such that sport cannot afford to ignore the wishes of advertisers and sponsors, or potential advertisers and sponsors, indeed they must learn to anticipate their wishes. The relation between individual sponsor and sponsored is one of reciprocity, but the relation between capital as such and sport as a whole is not symmetrical. It would seem that particularly as a result of sponsorship, corporate capital uses sport increasingly as an adjunct to capital accumulation, and in doing so pulls sport more into its orbit.

The Social Position of Sports Workers

The volumes of trivia written about sports workers contrasts with how sparse our knowledge is of them as a social group and how they relate to the power structure. Sports workers are a relatively small, select occupational group, the majority of which are men since opportunities are still relatively restricted for women. If we take the major sports in Britain for example, we find there are roughly 2,800 professional footballers plus perhaps 900 apprentices; 2,500 professional golfers plus 1,000 trainees; 450 licensed jockeys plus 450 apprentices; 475 professional boxers and 230 first-class county plus other cricketers.[25] Their heterogeneity makes them difficult to conceptualize as a group: work tasks, conditions of work, pay, social origin of entrants, the social milieu of individual sports, and the status of different sports, vary tremendously. Compare the snooker player and the marathon runner, the professional golfer and the footballer, the show-jumper and the darts player, the boxer and the tennis player. Yet a few useful generalizations can be made about sports workers as a group.

Almost by definition, like manual work sports-work involves physical labour, in many cases extremely hard physical labour. Some sports demand such physical fitness and ability that careers may be considerably shorter than the average industrial worker's. Competitive sports are highly specialized and in team sports the division of labour may be very elaborate. As in industry the sports worker's performance is analysed and developed with the aid of time-and-motion techniques; and in this respect the scientific programming of labour power in sport has advanced beyond that in industry. Just as the division between mental and manual labour in industry entails the growth of an elaborate technical and administrative structure to control and support the labour process, so sports work too has developed an elaborate hierarchy of specialists and officials: managers, coaches, trainers, medical experts, sports psychologists, etc. The parallel with manual work is also close when hazards and safety standards are considered. In many sports, injuries are a normal occurrence as part of the job and individual sports have their own typical injuries and ailments; in extreme cases injury may result in permanent disablement or even death. Sweated labour and unhealthy and dangerous conditions of work can be found in sport: stable lads' scandals, the lack of adequate medical safeguards in boxing and the use of drugs in many sports show that. However, the parallels with industrial work already need qualification, begin to run out and to be replaced by contrasts. It is probably safe to say that the physical health of sports workers, despite the hazards in some sports, is better than the average industrial worker's health, simply because it is attended to more systematically by the individual and by the relevant authorities, as a condition of efficient performance in the job. Many sports require little physical energy output anyway, being in the main tests of skill (darts, golf, bowls, snooker, etc.) and are not especially hazardous or physically stressful. Almost without question the mental strain of sports work is more severe.

Even if we accept without question the thesis that manual work in industry has been deskilled down to the semi- and unskilled levels, is less satisfying consequently and that knowledge of the labour process now tends to be monopolized by technical specialists and by management, the same cannot be said of sports work.[26] Certainly, narrow specialization has long been the case in many sports, and there is a tendency in the more developed ones for knowledge and planning to be monopolized by specialists and administrators. However, in sports work, on the contrary, the evidence suggests that on the whole there is far more opportunity to exhibit and develop skill, and that professional sport is one of the few types of work with a high physical component where the 'instinct of craftsmanship' can still be satisfied to a significant extent. Where there is a deterioration in the general skill level in certain sports, it is more likely to be caused by a decline in their popularity. It is difficult to see how sports work could be deskilled and standardized as in industry, because the very point of the sports spectacle, *qua* entertainment, is the display of talent. All work to some extent can be routinized, but the more creative it is, the more difficult it is to routinize, and entertainment work requires the retention of a relatively high level of skill and a concomitant freshness and creativity if it is to work as entertainment. This type of work has inbuilt limits beyond which it can not be readily deskilled or its productivity rationalized. The retention of skill gives sports workers more control over their work tasks and they are, therefore, not only in a better position in relation to the exercise of authority than at first appears to be the case, but work satisfaction is also likely to be greater.

There is little in the way of systematic, hard evidence on the nature of the satisfaction that sports workers in Britain derive from their work compared with the wealth of material on the industrial worker and other work groups,[27] but there would seem to be a *prima facie* case for concluding that sports workers enjoy greater satisfaction from their jobs than the average industrial worker. Few occupations open to working-class people possess such prestige; few provide the equivalent opportunity for acquiring and exercising valued skills and abilities; few jobs can be 'played at' for a living – a feature that sports workers readily recognize when talking about their work.[28]

Brookes' study of cricketers' attitudes towards their work and Wagg's study of footballers indicates greater overall satisfaction and a greater degree of commitment to their work than the average industrial worker.[29] Only further empirical work will tell whether these groups are typical, but at the moment the balance of the evidence suggests they are. True, attitudes to work are somewhat ambivalent: players are torn between what they see as the traditional professional standards of their craft and those they feel are prescribed for them by a sensation-seeking, ignorant audience. They commonly feel that the drive for success has also driven the pleasure and the play element out of sport and the younger players in both games have a more achievement-oriented, instrumental attitude to their work. Despite their complaints about nervous tension and feelings of insecurity about future prospects when playing careers are over, players derive much satisfaction from playing itself, and from the companionship the sport provides, and almost all respondents perceive sport as having a relatively high status, or at least as not having a low one – all of which is in marked contrast to how industrial workers perceive their position.

This may go some way to explaining the lack of strong reaction to the unusually tight pattern of control over the labour process. Sports workers seem to be the only category of worker to be routinely admonished publicly for rule infringements and whose punishment is also part of the spectacle. Dismissal from the scene as a punishment is also not unusual; and the status of the individual seems to make little difference. Suspension and banning from sports as a punishment, either for a prescribed period or even permanently, with consequent loss of earnings or of livelihood in some cases, as well as fines for misconduct, are common.

The system of rules under which the governing bodies of sports commonly operate often involves reliance on procedures which scarcely conform to the principles of natural justice: disciplinary tribunals tend to function as prosecution, judge and jury. Vaguely worded charges such as 'bringing the game into disrepute' and 'dissent' are difficult to refute; defendants are often not informed of when the proceedings take place or allowed to attend; and if they are allowed to attend, often no representation is allowed. The extension of paternalistic control into sports workers' lives outside the immediate context of their sport is fairly common, and they may be severely disciplined for conduct that takes place well outside the context of their work. Top stars have been thrown out of international teams for relatively minor transgressions, such as a punch-up in a night-club, shoplifting and so on. Authority does not go totally unchallenged of course, but the fact that such impositions are so prevalent, and that they are, to a surprising extent, tolerated by sports workers, calls for some further explanation. Sports workers, it seems, largely concur with the authorities that since sport is a public spectacle, it can be affected adversely by misconduct and by observable rule infringements, and that an extreme sensitivity on the part of the authorities, in order to promote a good image of sport, is justified. Secondly, control over sports workers lives beyond the work sphere is motivated by the knowledge that the sports spectacle, like all entertainment, depends for its success on the performance of the stars. In contrast, in industry and other occupations, a relatively poor performance by an individual worker, or even the absence of the individual altogether for short periods, makes little difference to the quality of the product. But in sport the performing personnel are the most important input, and anything that interferes with this factor's performance makes all the difference.

The market situation of sports workers is again quite different from that of most working-class people: it gives rise to sharper divisions than exist within the working-class, the most significant of which is the division between the elite and the rest.

Labour-markets in sports are in certain respects distinguished from most other markets for labour by the special restrictions imposed on the sale of labour power. Amateurism as an obstacle to the sale of labour power is commonly evaded by 'shamateurism', but the latter is still a restriction which distorts the price labour would receive if the market were more open, or 'perfect'. Entry to, and participation in many sports and events are governed by birth and residence and sex qualifications. Recent advances in commercialization have rendered such restrictions less important. There are also specific restrictions on labour mobility, which inhibit the freedom of labour to chose its own employer and which increase dependence on owners and controllers of sports.[30] County cricketers for example, have to obtain permission from the relevant authority to register with another county. In some of the more commercialized sports, career opportunities depend on entering into complex and legally binding contracts, which effectively shackle the individual to a particular employer or financial interest. Boxing and motor sport have long been notorious for this kind of practice. The transfer system which pertains in certain sports, like League Football, Rugby League and speedway, means that players can be bought and sold by their employers, and it is therefore, the employer who chooses the employer. In League football the system no longer operates so rigidly against the player as it did until recently, when players could be transferred or retained at will. Players now sign fixed-term contracts, the clubs do not have the automatic right to retain a player's services, players' permission must be obtained for a transfer and they now receive a percentage of the fee. Nevertheless, pressure can still be brought to bear by employers eager to make a deal with another club and refusal to comply can jeopardize a player's chances of selection.

One of the distinguishing features of a commercialized sports culture is its elaborate mythology about the size of monetary and other rewards for success. Obviously, secrecy surrounding 'shamateurism' breeds rumour and distortion, as it does about professionals' contracts, which are mostly negotiated on a private basis. Available figures for basic wages tend to be meaningless, since there are many possible additional sources of income for individuals – bonuses, prize-money, endorsements, 'benefits', media work, etc. The media mostly exaggerate the sums involved, by (among other things), failing to give the necessary deductions, not the least of which is the manager's and/or agent's percentage. Where details are given accurately, the celebrated high earnings of sports workers need to be put in the perspective of the worker's total career pattern: injury or loss of form may reduce earnings drastically or end a career prematurely; earnings tend to fluctuate with ups and downs in careers, with the rhythms of the sports season in many cases, and with age of peak performance; and full careers are relatively short – between ten and fifteen years for footballers and cricketers, shorter in athletics events and somewhat longer in golf. The chances of maintaining or improving the level of income after retirement from a sport are very uncertain (in the 1960s former England team footballers were going back to jobs like the local milk-round).

From the information that is available it is fairly clear that earnings as well as conditions vary greatly from sport to sport and within individual sports. Differences in income, security, length of career and future prospects produce substantial economic inequalities between sport workers, at least as great as those generated outside sport across the occupational structure. Some are at the level of semi-skilled workers, others command the equivalent of better-paid skilled workers, professional people, managers and small businessmen; and the earnings of the superstar–elite vie with those of top company executives and employers. Among the elite, women are a small minority, earning considerably less than their male counterparts. The largest group of full-time sports workers, the professional footballers, provides a good illustration of the spread of differentials. As a result of the abolition of the maximum wage at the beginning of the 1960s, differentials widened progressively. From the early 1970s to the beginning of the 1980s, players in Divisions III and IV and at the lower end of the scale were earning the equivalent of semi-skilled workers.[31] In the English League the really big gap in earnings is between Division I players and the rest, and within this division between the stars and the rest. Top earners in the later 1970s and into the 1980s, like Kevin Keegan and others, could make as much as £200,000 a year from salaries, advertising endorsements, consultancy, bonuses, media work, appearances, business interests, and so on. Clive Allen, a nineteen-year-old, who was transferred twice within a period of 63 days, emerged with £100,000 as his percentage of the deals. Most of the indications suggest that average earnings in Division I are pretty high. It is reasonably clear then, that a minority earn a great deal, the majority earn far less, and among the latter group a proportion are comfortably off at a solid middle-class standard, while the rest are on the level of the average industrial worker. Cricketers were rather poorly paid by almost any standard up to the mid 1970s. The top earners now are the

230 or so first-class county players, whose earnings can be topped up after ten to fifteen years in cricket by as much as £25,000 or even £50,000 from benefit matches. Selection for tests, inclusion in overseas parties in the winter, writing articles, doing advertisements, can bring incomes for individuals in this group as high as £30,000 a year. Minor county and league players, who form the majority, receive considerably less. In athletics now, a star like Steve Jones, the 10,000 metres and marathon runner, can receive £79,000 for winning just one race (the Chicago Marathon).[32] In other commercialized sports – motor racing, boxing, tennis, etc., the pattern seems to be the same – a small minority at the top securing vast amounts a year, some being quite well off, and quite a few struggling.

Given this pattern, to what extent do sports function as avenues of mobility for working-class people and how do sportsworkers relate to the class and power structure? Some sports have traditionally constituted such an avenue for young white working-class males: football is the obvious case, and boxing, Rugby League, jockeying and speedway are others. Today, boxing, athletics and football seem to perform the same function for young black working-class males as well. With the exception of footballers and cricketers and to some extent boxers, there is little sociological evidence concerning the social origins and perceptions of sports workers. Recruits to football are still almost exclusively working class, despite the picture of the game becoming classless, with graduates, teachers and grammar-school boys supposedly flooding in. There is an increased proportion of the latter, though they are still a small minority. Significantly, in view of the close association of skilled manual workers with football historically, and the propensity of this group to respectability, over half the entrants' fathers are skilled manual workers.[33] It would seem therefore, that as usual the socially mobile element of the working class tends to come from its upper reaches, but what has changed drastically is the reward structure and the cultural ethos of the Football League clubs.

Very few other sports seem to function to any great degree as avenues of social mobility for working-class people. The other major team game, cricket, although it has experienced a loss of social status in recent years shows a tendency to recruit now from declining social groups, predominantly from the middle classes.[34] Previously, in the days of amateurs and professionals, it seems the latter tended to come more from working-class backgrounds.

The market and work situation of sports workers as a whole places them in somewhat contradictory class locations. In common with working-class people they are employees selling their labour, experiencing insecurity and are subject to the authority of employers and officials. But in terms of levels of earnings, work satisfaction, autonomy in the work task and future prospects, most are clearly closer to the middle and upper levels of society.

As we might expect from this, footballers for example, have considerable difficulty in locating themselves in the class structure, and this may indicate a more general pattern applying especially to sports workers who originate in the working class. They do not see themselves as working class, nor as part of any clearly defined grouping: instead, they see themselves, in the main, as part of a large, amorphous middle grouping encompassing most of the population. This perception is, of course, open to interpretation as being no different from the way in which a sizeable proportion of working-class people perceive class, but if we combine it with other indicators, such as the character of their trade unionism and their political and social outlooks, their marginality is confirmed. Cricketers, on the other hand, identify themselves firmly as middle class and regard themselves as socially superior to footballers.[35]

Footballers are not unequivocally absorbed into the middle classes and they remain, by and large, relatively well-paid skilled workers – and skilled work is what all sports workers have in common. However, sports work is skilled work with a difference. Success in the sports worker's career is achieved on the basis of individual aspiration and action – it does not depend primarily, as it does for other skilled workers, on collective bargaining and a strong trade union. The isolated position of the sports worker from the working class, the differential reward structure, the power of owners and controllers and the individualist ethos, mutually reinforce each other to produce a group, which as a whole is scarcely trade-union conscious, let alone class conscious in any real sense. It is no accident that throughout the history and contemporary functioning of sports, trade unionism has been either absent, or where it appeared, it is usually rather weak and/or limited in function. The existence of a number of organizations representing the interests of sports workers – the Professional Footballers' Association (PFA), the Cricketers' Association, the Professional Golfers' Association, the Association of Lawn Tennis Professionals, the Jockeys' Association of Great Britain, the International Athletes Club, the International Motor Cycle Riders' Association, etc. – indicates that sports workers are aware that some form of collective organization is necessary to protect their interests *vis-à-vis* owners and controllers. At times there have been quite sharp clashes over particular issues – the abolition of the maximum wage in football very nearly became a strike issue; cricketers have become roused over salaries and tour fees; motor-cyclists over prize-money and safety. But these organizations rarely function like normal trade unions, and the scope of the issues are rarely, if ever broadened to take in social and political implications. Intuitively one might expect that the PFA, with its relatively great numerical strength and its strong links with the working class through its members' social origins, would be potentially a strong union, yet it is, instead, a classic example of weak, business unionism.[36] It has very close links with, and is extremely accommodating to management; there have been very few disputes in which it has been active; and it does not negotiate over wages any more, or help players negotiate their contracts with the clubs. In fact, it has encouraged the development of gross inequalities among footballers and done little to represent the interests of those at the bottom on semi-skilled workers' wages and in insecure positions. Every one of its former secretaries, with one exception, has gone over to management and joined the ranks of the employers. The union was thrown out of the Trades Unions Congress (TUC) in the early 1970s for registering under the anti-union Conservative government's legislation. On the other hand, footballers and sports workers in general, are not professionals in the conventional sense either, since they exercise virtually no control over entry to the occupation (in contrast to skilled workers) – quite the contrary, sports are wide open. Sports workers have no monopoly over the relevant bodies of knowledge; they cannot lay down standards of work, or control the labour process, as established professionals do. In this respect the market for sports labour corresponds with the capitalist ideal of a free market.

The superstar elite who go on to become managers and administrators, media personalities and businessmen, and who move in the world of the new bourgeoisie which has formed around the leisure, entertainment and public-relations industries, are clearly differentiated from the rest – marginal they are not. Individuals in this group, whether professional or 'shamateur', have distinct interests conferred on them by their market value. Closely allied to the sponsor/advertiser/media axis, which could not have succeeded in hegemonizing sport without their active assistance, this elite constitutes a subaltern group forming a bridge between subordinate groups, sports workers and dominant groups. As exemplars of successful achievement and the extraordinary rewards that go with it, they give the lead and set the tone for the non-elite. In the superstar elite we can see the present character of sports work writ large. The elite has been progressively won over into performing the role of sales staff, not only for particular products and organizations, but for a way of life as such. When stars' performances and appearances endorse products and business organizations they simultaneously endorse the system of production and consumption and the ideals associated with it – the alleged classless and meritocratic order of Britain today, competitive individualism, the privatization of existence, etc. Whereas the non-elite relates ambivalently to working-class culture, especially in the case of the footballers, the elite is unequivocally distanced from it, relating to it in a purely ritualistic manner – the mayor's reception at the town hall on the return of the victorious team or individual, the victory lap of the track and the wave to the crowd, the speech at the Sports writers' dinner, the media appearances, etc. In no way is the integration of this elite into the power network revealed more clearly than in its conventionality concerning political and social issues. On the one political issue which has intruded into sport continuously over the years, apartheid in South Africa, the elite's silence and its tacit acceptance of the propensity of some of its members to support South Africa by continuing to play with its representatives, proclaims the political slogan 'sport has nothing to do with politics'. Racist abuse of black players by sections of the crowd at various Football League club grounds, is largely accepted in silence – with some notable exceptions (such as the stand against it made by Chelsea player Pat Nevin). The contrast with the response of many pop stars in the music world, who have involved themselves in a whole range of issues, is instructive. When footballers for example, (including black players) take a stand on issues, it is entirely within the current conventions about what constitutes a social or political problem – hence for example, condemnations of football violence *ad nauseam* from all and sundry, and exhortations to youth from the Liverpool and Everton captains to avoid taking drugs. Without organic connections with the working class, without commitment in any shape or form to the working-class movement, sections of this elite do nevertheless, function as working-class heroes and as role models, especially the footballers – models and heroes whose silence speaks volumes.

Sports as Consumer Culture

The commercialization of sports that we have been examining is an aspect of a more general process, the expansion in the circulation of commodities that marked the consolidation of 'consumer capitalism' and the emergence of a comprehensive consumer culture by the later 1950s, reached its apogee in the 1960s to mid-1970s, and which has faltered and become increasingly uneven since then. These developments made one of the most crucial contributions to the strategic elaboration of the power network in the post-war period.[37] Clearly, it constituted part of a selective, uneven response on the part of dominant groups to pressure for change from subordinate groups. One of the highest priorities was to defuse and displace the incipient conflict between capital and labour, a project which required the willing co-operation of the working class in its own recomposition. The active role of culture in this transformation has been grossly underrated.

We will postpone the more detailed analysis of the mechanisms whereby working-class people are affected by commodified sport as an aspect of consumer culture until the final chapter, that is until we have examined the way the media, the schools and the state apparatus other than the schools, relate to sport. For now, we want to draw attention to the general character of the link that has been forged between sports and consumer culture through the commercialization of sport, that is, to the points of articulation, the correspondences (and the discrepancies as well), and to look at some of the outcomes which have a bearing on the way working-class culture relates to commodified sport.

We can start by getting some idea of sport's weight and importance to people in general, as far as their expenditure is concerned. Expenditure on spectator sport is a relatively minor proportion of the total spent on sport, as table 6.1 shows.[38]

Table 6.1 Annual expenditure on sport, 1978

Items of expenditure	£ m.
Spectator sport	73
Equipment	120
Clothing	197
Boating	141
Subscriptions, admissions and equipment hire	203

Source: W. H. Martin and S. Mason, 'Broad Patterns of Leisure Expenditure' (SSRC/Sports Council *State of the Art Review*, 1979).

Although expenditure on sport and recreation constitutes only just over 4 per cent of total consumer expenditure, it displays the second fastest growth out of all the items in the table below over the period 1970–7, and it is expected to grow at roughly the same rate in the 1980s (see table 6.2).

Table 6.2 Annual consumer expenditure on selected items of leisure, 1977

Items	£ m.
Sport and active recreation	682
TV, radio and audio	1,855
Reading	1,220
Alcoholic drink	6,539
Hobbies and pastimes	1,327
Eating out	980
Gambling	712
Do-it-yourself and gardening	1,454
Holidays	2,039

Source: Martin and Mason, 'Broad Patterns of Leisure Expenditure', p. 30, table 3.2.

These figures actually underestimate the amount spent on sports, since some of this expenditure is also included in the amount spent on TV and gambling. Gambling is a major industry in this country. In the 1950s for example, the football pools constituted the seventh largest industry in Britain, employing 100,000 people.[39] Today, £233m. is staked annually. £3,447m., most of it in off-course betting, was staked on horse-racing alone in 1983–4.[40] By the later 1970s the total amount spent on all forms of gambling was a staggering £8.000 m.[41] Through gambling and sponsorship the giants of the leisure industry like Mecca, Coral Leisure, Grand Metropolitan and Ladbrokes, link sport to the structure of ownership and control in casinos, betting shops, bingo halls, bowling alleys, hotels, beauty contests and numerous other interests. Straightforward expenditure on sports, running into several hundred million pounds, is still not a particularly weighty component in total consumer expenditure; however when gambling on sports is added the picture changes radically. At a very conservative estimate the total of £1,360 m. can be seen to be a major component in consumer spending, roughly equal in magnitude to the other major items in table 6.2 with the exception of alcoholic drink and holidays.

Consumer culture is a highly complex construction. The way it is put together and its mode of operation are ill understood, and our understanding is hardly improved by the tendency among many commentators to moralize about it from an elitist perspective. The most misleading way of understanding the relationship of producers to consumers is to perceive it as a relationship over which the latter have no control. It cannot be stressed enough that involvement in commercialized sport is as the result of an active process of choice. It is not imposed, or passed on, from above and accepted passively below; choices are not made irrationally as if the consumer were addicted to a drug or had no knowledge of the product; and consumption is not a simple function of capital's need to reproduce itself. Nor, incidentally, do consumers 'maximize their utilities' like dessicated calculating machines. Consumption is a social act structured by frameworks of meaning with cognitive, emotional and aesthetic dimensions. Consequently, people are 'won' to consumer culture, rather than blinded and tricked to it. People also draw on it selectively, accepting some aspects and rejecting others according to their felt needs, that is there are other cultures on which they draw. And very importantly, consumer culture itself draws selectively on these different cultures – from working-class and popular culture, youth culture, etc., and from bourgeois culture as well. Although drawing on materials from a variety of cultural sources, consumer culture is autonomous: it possesses its own materials and mechanisms of production and its products cannot be reduced to the character of any other factor.

Consumer culture is that way of life in the modern era, which is organized around the consumption of goods and services for the mass market. It is not that commercialization of sport is new (it was highly developed in some sports as early as the eighteenth century), rather it is the particular pattern represented by consumer culture and the way sports are associated with it, that is new. The greater concentration of economic power among producers, the extended scale of operations, the growing remoteness of controllers and decision-makers, the packaging of sports as classless family entertainment, and the generally closer integration of sports with business culture, are certainly key aspects, but by themselves they do not explain the power-generating capacity of consumer culture. It is the way other discourses and practices are articulated on these features, and the way the whole complex is orchestrated by certain key themes, that gives it its coherence and power. The orchestrating themes of this culture are directed at selling a specifically modern, pagan version of the good life – the dominant discourse/practice is of youth, beauty, romance, sexual attraction, energy, fitness and health, movement, excitement, adventure, freedom, exotica, luxury, enjoyment, entertainment, fun. Above all, this culture valorizes 'self-expression'. A truly astonishing variety of goods and services – from washing-powder, cars and foreign holidays, to cosmetics, fashion-wear, eating and 'aerobics', circulate on this basis; and concomitantly, major segments of social life are organized around consumer culture. One has only to think of family life to appreciate this. We find some of the most prevalent themes in working-class culture represented in a certain way here, especially the more hedonistic ones – the love of entertainment, living for the moment, showing you have a bit of money in your pocket, going on a spree, being a real man or woman, pride in the wife and kids, etc. What we encounter especially is a meticulous attention to those aspects of their lives that are deeply personal to people. The close attention to what is personally important can be seen in the way, for example, one's appear-ance (how one dresses, what cosmetics to use, whether one is too fat, how good one's teeth are), how one feels (headache?, confident?, happy?) and even how one smells, are given priority. The discourse selects, from the range of experience, certain ways in which we are affected personally and offers personal solutions. Collective concerns and collective, as opposed to individual forms of consumption as a solution to problems, are largely absent from the discourse. The collective is displaced to the level of personal reality and the individual is made solely responsible for doing something about it. The priority given to individual autonomy and responsibility, and the ideal of a private existence shows consumer culture drawing strongly on bourgeois tradition. One of the strongest representations of this phenomenon in consumer culture is the depiction of family life. It is not that this kind of systematically produced imbalance displaces what is important with what is trivial; it is that this culture is hegemonized through the thematization of concerns which are, indeed, absolutely central to people's sense of identity on the one hand, and the suppression of the relationship between these, and other equally important public issues or collective concerns, on the other hand. For example, the discourse of diet gives priority to personal care of one's body, but diet is not unrelated to the problem of food production, world prices, and food shortages. Rather than express concern about the latter, consumer culture articulates diet with the issue of convenience-foods and family life, or *haute cuisine* and bourgeois sociability.

What links up consumer culture with sports culture so economically is their common concern with, and capacity to, accommodate the body as a means of expression.[42] The centrality of the body in consumer culture has gone largely unnoticed, but it is clearly the focus of a high proportion of consumer discourse and practice.[43] Cooking, dieting, fashion-wear and keeping fit and attractive are only the more obvious of many ways this is so. Indeed, a good deal of the strength of consumer culture resides in its ability to harness and channel bodily needs and desires – for health, longevity, sexual fulfillment and so on, to the production system. Sports culture's stress on play, contest, strength, energy, movement, speed and skill, etc., allows such themes to be given a particularly vivid, dramatic, aesthetically pleasing and emotionally gratifying expression. To be sportive is almost by definition to be desirable, fit, young and healthy. If consumer culture's overriding concern is with the personal, what could be more personal than one's body? – I am my body; my body is me; scarcely anything could be more revealing about me than my body. So, sportive expressionism thematizes the personal in an extraordinarily powerful way.

The significance of the progressive commodification of sports is that athleticist and physical recreationist discourse, practice, knowledge and technology, are now unified with a heterogeneous array of other elements in an emergent programme of discipline and surveillance in which consumer culture is at the heart. Control by meticulous, restrictive work on the body, characteristic of the moral economy and practice of the Protestant ethic and operationalized in the rise of what Bentham termed the Panopticon (a prison which maximized surveillance and discipline) is giving way to control through the stimulation of desire. In the emergence of the new disciplinary mode the redeployment of sexuality and of age are key elements in the way consumer culture and its sportive forms are articulated on the power network. The dominant icon of consumer culture is the youthful, sexually attractive, healthy, physically fit person; and the cultural imperative to all alike, irrespective of age, appearance and sex, is to look, act and feel as if we are so. The objective of repressive discipline and surveillance is to produce the 'normal individual', through the strategy of extending the gaze of authority so that the subject is perfectly visible to it, while authority itself remains invisible; and it is achieved through meticulous work on the subject's body, as directed by authority. The objective of expansive discipline, which is installed through consumer culture, is to produce the 'normal person' by making each as visible as possible to the other, and by meticulous work on persons' bodies – at the instigation of subjects themselves. The 'liberation' of the sexual and the youth apparatuses is a prerequisite for the successful achievement of this programme. Consumer culture literally abounds with the discourse and practice of youth and sex – with the slogan 'freedom from all inhibitions on their expression' – hence rights to sexual fulfillment as one wishes, earlier and extra-marital sex, contraception, counselling on 'sexual, personal and emotional problems', therapy, abortion, divorce, women's rights, youth opportunity, voice of women/youth, etc. Our increased visibility to each other in public space, in the street, work, office, school, college, the media, the swimming-pool, the beach, the health club, etc., constitutes a comprehensive system of mutual discipline and surveillance, which can be far more relentless than repressive discipline. Witness the disciplined enjoyment of freely chosen activities like jogging, dieting, dressing fashionably, keeping clean, applying unguents and cosmetics, playing sports, displaying at discos, etc.; and consider the volume of freely chosen goods and services that is consumed in the process of producing oneself as the youthful, authentic man or woman. The sale of youth and sex in consumer culture never closes: it fetishizes these attributes and puts in circulation a profoundly sexist and ageist discourse and practice. For example, the liberation of sex equalizes the sexes while simultaneously reproducing divisions and power relations between them. The image of the 'raunchy', economically independent, predatory female, so at home in consumer culture, is the equivalent of the image of the 'successful' macho male, although male hegemony is won in a myriad other ways, at this and at other levels. In the 1980s, especially in the form of the health and fitness boom, sport and physical recreation are now emerging in many ways as the focal point of a regimen for producing sexually attractive, youthful, healthy and fit persons, a regimen which combines or unifies several advanced technologies – athleticist-fitness, medical–pharmaceutical, nutritionist–culinary, and beautician-sartorial. The notion that to be doing something about one's body is to be doing something about one's self, is profoundly true. At the same time, it represents a response, which individualizes more than ever what is plainly a problematic social condition, at this particular conjuncture – a condition which requires collective as well as individual solutions.

Insightful as it is in many way, the danger of a Foucaultian analysis of consumer culture is the implication that control programmes actually achieve their desired effects. We can see, with reference to commodified sport, that such programming falters at several points and fails, more or less altogether, with large sections of the subordinate population. This aspect will be examined in more detail later, but some indication of contrary, opposing tendencies is necessary at this juncture. It is useful to bear in mind that we are discussing consumer culture as such, a culture hegemonized by bourgeois elements – not working-class culture, or popular culture, with which it overlaps and which in some ways act as repositories of materials for resisting and distancing subordinate groups from its influences.

Take the programme to sell sport as a classless form of family entertainment. The more commercialized, rationalized and competitive that sports become, the more they generate characteristics and produce outcomes which are antithetical not only to the amateur–gentleman and rational-recreation traditions as a whole, but to this particular remnant of the latter tradition in particular. Professional fouls, rows between players and officials, violence around football, power struggles and financial scandals in the boardrooms, revelations about breaches of amateur status, the growing problem of drug use in sports, the spatial representation of class divisions in seating arrangements at football grounds (executive boxes and seated accommodation in the stands, versus the uncovered caged terraces and the 'ends') are hardly compatible with, let alone capable of, sustaining such an image.

The characterization of people's involvement in sporting activity, simply in terms of commodity consumption, is not good enough: in terms of the kinds of expectations and typical experiences of sports audiences, involvement in sport is more akin to attending the theatre or participating in a festival, that is it is invested with a specific meaning and draws on a stock of knowledge quite different for example, from the act of shopping in the local high street. Football hooligans, in fact, care passionately about their teams, exercise their choices very carefully and are very knowledgeable about the game.[44] Selling sport as exciting entertainment tends to raise the level of consumers' expectations faster than they can be satisfied and this, together with the greater degree of impersonality between producers, performers and the audience, generates changes in people's perceptions and evaluations of sport: it creates tensions between producer and audience, which may at times erupt into violent confrontation. Indeed, the attempt to bourgeoisify football is salutary: the more up-market it has moved and the more it has been packaged as 'family entertainment', the greater the propensity for unruly crowd behaviour. The remoteness of the stars and those who control the game has reduced the effectiveness of traditional informal processes of maintaining order, so that other agencies, notably the police, have had to assume responsibility for it.

Football violence is by no means the only example, although it is the most notorious. The conduct of cricket and tennis audiences at the major championships for example, has changed noticeably over the last few years, from adherence to a more sedate bourgeois model of spectating to vociferous partisanship, barracking of officials and playes, chanting and singing and actions bordering on, or spilling over into, actual violence. However they are described, these kinds of audience responses can hardly be described as passive consumption.

It is thus that the commercialization of sport disturbs in some ways the utility of sport as a component in the kind of control programme to which some elements among dominant groups are strongly committed, and in doing so it creates dissension among them as well. The notion that sport and healthy physical recreation promotes discipline and order, and that sporting occasions observed by mass audiences should legitimize the existing order of things, dies hard among dominant groups, and its supporters are still influential, at the level of the state in particular.

Most evidently, the promise of 'healthy entertainment for all' that consumer culture holds out in the form of commercialized sport and physical recreation, has not been fulfilled. The reach of consumer culture has never been completely even, of course; and now, in the economically depressed 1980s, it is obviously not so. A lot of people among the poor and the unemployed have been virtually removed from its reach altogether, and many others among subordinate groups, notably working-class women, the old, and blacks are marginalized. If an increasing proportion of the population is uncoupled from consumer culture and its sportive forms, the capacity of the latter to make an input to the network of power is likely to be lessened accordingly. We will have more to say about this aspect in the final chapter.

7

Media Sport

Introduction

Of all the apparatuses involved in the achievement of hegemony none is more implicated in sports than the mass media. Of the media's different facets we need to concentrate on the press and broadcasting, since it is these institutions, rather than the cinema, book publishing, etc., that are in more or less instantaneous, continuous touch with the majority of the population. Most work on the media and power has concentrated on the character of news and current affairs, while the significance of other aspects of the the media's output in this respect has tended to be overlooked.[1] Media sport is ostensibly nothing to do whatever with power, politics and ideology, and is everything to do with skilled, exciting and above all entertaining leisure activity. The importance of testing this claim can be seen when we recall that more people are involved in sport through the press and broadcasting than in any other way.[2] Furthermore, the heavier reliance of working-class people on the media in their leisure-time activity makes it fairly safe to assume that media sport has gained the allegiance of a large proportion.

Today, the sports section of the mass-circulation newspaper is crucial in maintaining its market position. As Hall points out, the tabloid is a reversible newspaper: it can be opened and started at either end and even bigger headlines at the sports end stimulate the reader to start there.[3] We find the more working-class the readership (*Daily Star*, *The Sun*, *Mirror*) the greater the proportion of the paper devoted to sport, with the *Daily Star* giving 55 per cent more space to sport than the *Daily Mail*, the tabloid with the lowest working-class readership (see table 7.1).[4].

Although a fairly large number of different sports are covered, one of the most striking features is the virtual saturation of the available space by the coverage of football and horse-racing, two sports which have traditionally enjoyed a large working-class following. At times, horse-racing gets more actual space than football, but in terms of the main sports stories,

Table 7.1 Percentage of space devoted to sport
in tabloid newspapers

Newspaper	%
Daily Star	22.16
Sun	20.4
Mirror	17.36
Daily Express	16.45
Daily Mail	14.22

the vast majority concern football.[5] The policy is quite clearly to attract working-class readers with coverage of the sports to which they are most attached. The fact that sport is classified in the trade as a 'revenue goal', rather than an 'advertising goal', that is it increases circulation as opposed to attracting advertising directly, supports this interpretation.[6] It is not possible to ascertain the proportion of the readership which is motivated to buy papers because of their sporting content, but we know for example, that once purchased, more than half the men and a third of the women read the sports pages of the Sunday newspapers.[7]

The advent of televised sport from the 1950s onwards marked a crucial step in the development of a mass audience for sport. The ease of accessibility, its immediacy and apparent authenticity, made TV the major competitor of the popular press. It is possible to estimate the size of the audience for sports programmes, as well as the proportion of the total output devoted to sport. Near the end of the 1970s 12.2 per cent of BBC TV programme time was taken up with sport, putting it in fourth place behind current affairs/features/documentaries, the Open University and films, while BBC Radio devoted only 3.45 per cent to sport, which places it in sixth position out of twelve categories.[8] IBA (Independent Broadcasting Authority) figures for televised sport are roughly similar at about 11.5 per cent of viewing time.[9] Sport is probably more central than these figures suggest, since it is often programmed for prime-time transmission and because the categories with which it is compared cover, in some cases, a fairly heterogeneous output. In the 1970s the BBC sports programmes 'Grandstand' and 'Sportsnight' regularly attracted audiences of three million and seven million respectively; and particular sports events attracted even larger audiences – of the magnitude of ten million for the Commonwealth Games and professional boxing, thirteen million for the Wimbledon Final, fourteen million for the Grand National, and as many as twenty-nine million, or over half the population, for the World Cup Final.[10] Such figures compare very favourably with those for the most popular programmes in other categories on both public and independent channels.[11] It is plain that sports coverage is a major weapon in the ratings war between BBC and ITV, and the undoubtedly high ratings for sports include large numbers of working-class people. Sport not only attracts large audiences, it does so relatively cheaply. Expensive as it may be in terms of absolute costs (satellite charges, rights, etc.), the high unit costs per hour for the very high ratings gained, compare favourably with drama and light entertainment: in these terms an hour of drama is three times as expensive as an hour of the World Cup.[12]

The argument that the nature of the media's output is determined by market forces and the social background and experience of their personnel, and that the media ultimately serve the interests of dominant groups, does have merit.[13] It cannot be entirely insignificant that virtually all the top sports commentators, presenters and management in both commercial and public broadcasting graduated via the commercial press, many of them from Fleet Street itself.[14] Nor is the fact that the structure of ownership and control of the media as a whole, which is remarkably concentrated in Britain, gives owners in the private sector, and governments where public-sector broadcasting is concerned, the power to appoint and dismiss management.[15] The relationship between media sport professionals and the sports community off whom they live is structurally and culturally close: a considerable proportion of sports journalists and management are former outstanding sports performers, coaches, administrators or erstwhile sportsmen themselves. Jimmy Hill, former professional footballer and secretary of the Professional Footballers' Association, now chairman of Coventry City Football Club, and BBC sports presenter, epitomizes the phenomenon and there are plenty of others who do so, although perhaps not so spectacularly. Sports reporting and commentary, like critical appreciation of the arts in the media, tends to be merged with and positively oriented towards, the community upon which it reports and comments. Also, with regard to the evident success that media sport has registered with a working-class audience, it may be significant that football journalism and perhaps some other branches of sports journalism, attracts proportionally more recruits from a working-class background than any other field of journalism.[16] Their status as a group among their colleagues is low – with crime reporters, they are the lowest-paid journalists. As such, sports journalists are closer than others to working-class culture, a fact that is likely to enable them to trade off it in their work in a way that resonates with familiar modes of expression and structures of feeling, rendering it both more intelligible and more appealing to the working-class audience.

Constructing Media Sport

A perspective stressing the exogenous structural and cultural constraints on the media can be a useful corrective to attempts to tackle the problem of the media and power purely in terms of a content-analysis of news and current affairs. As Golding and Murdock point out, the determining pressures underlying the construction of what is finally presented to audiences cannot be simply read off the content.[17] But neither, on the other hand, is the character of media sport reducible to the economic and political context and the social background of the personnel. To treat it as such is to neglect what it is about the media themselves as institutions that enables media sport to involve a mass audience so successfully. Like all cultural production, media sport requires elucidation in terms of the specific character of the institutions concerned, the technology that is employed and, above all, the occupational culture of media-sport professionals. It is on this latter aspect we wish to concentrate from now on, in particular, on media-sport news values.

Media professionals claim to be reporting impartially on reality, or merely conveying to the audience 'what actually happened'; but this doctrine of epistemological naturalism will not hold up to an examination of how the media treat sport. Alternatively, it is now a commonplace in media sociology that news is constructed in terms of professionals' values and the routine practices to which they give rise.[18] Sporting events undergo a transformation when they are presented in the media: what appears on the screen and in the press and comes across on radio, is not what the spectator or performer at the event experiences. Media sport does not just present the world as it is, already constructed – it re-presents the world in terms of its own inferential framework and thus creates events with their own features – media events.[19] Sports journalists and editorial staff select from, rank, classify and elaborate the world of sport in terms of a 'stock of knowledge' as to what constitutes sports news. An interpretive framework is thus encoded in the flow of communication to the audience – in the items selected, the language, the visual imagery, the stylistics of the presentation, which constitutes an inducement to the audience to interpret the world reported on in preferred ways. It is as if when readers, listeners and viewers are presented with sport in the media, they are simultaneously issued with a set of instructions or maxims as to how the communication should be read, heard and seen. In order to accomplish this successfully, this inferential framework must be related to the culture of the majority of the audience. The transformation of sport into a media spectacle draws not only on professional values – through the latter it draws on the audience's knowledge, values and expectations, as well as the sports community's.

That media sport intervenes in what it reports on, rather than reporting it as it is, is already clear from the fact that sports have actually been changed to make them more amenable for media coverage. The process of constructing media sport that we are analyzing here, however, is of a different order altogether from this aspect.

At the simplest level what is selected for reporting and commentary is often a function of the distribution of information-gathering resources. For economic reasons these tend to be concentrated in areas previously defined by professionals as 'news-worthy', so sports-news gathering tends to be a self-fulfilling prophecy: we receive lots of news about sport in elite nations, and the media professional is constantly surprised by 'upsets' 'shock results', when 'unknowns', notably from Third World countries, defeat the elite. It is perhaps, in many cases, only surprising precisely because of the failure to attend to them earlier.

Media sport operates a preferred view of the social world by naturalizing it.[20] It is because sport is so 'obviously' physical, i.e. concerned with the body, governed by natural laws, which function irrespective of what the observer thinks or feels about them, that it can be claimed to have nothing to do with politics or society and that values can be encoded in reporting on sport. Yet sport is no more or no less 'natural' than any other activity in which we indulge collectively – it is socially structured. The main way that sport and social order are naturalized in media sport is through the fiction that sports constitute a separate reality. The separate reality of sport is signified by the routine practice of separating out sport from other news and confining it to a separate sector – the sports section of the newspaper, the sports programme, the sports news. The occasions when sport escapes from its status as separate reality are relatively rare, and they occur when there is an angle present that justifies redefining the item as falling outside this separate reality. In our analysis of a week's popular daily newspapers, out of several hundred sporting stories, on only fourteen occasions did a story involving sport appear outside the confines of the sports section, and in only two out of these was sport the real focus of attention. Half of them were in fact, related to sex, politics and crime, and the rest fell into the 'bizarre' and 'personality' categories. Only one of the fourteen managed to achieve front-page status and predictably this concerned the attempted suicide of a married woman with whom an England international footballer was alleged to be having an affair. In this particular week none of the international-status events managed to reach the front pages, although there were, in fact, three that were theoretically eligible, – a world boxing championship fight, the Wightman Cup and the Wales–All Blacks rugby match.

The most usual way sport breaks out to the front page, or becomes a major news item on radio or TV, is when Britain triumphs in an international event. During the Moscow Olympics in 1980, for example, the only time sporting events, as opposed to the boycott, broke through to the front page was when a British performer's fortunes were at stake and when Britain won medals.[21] Otherwise, sport achieves prominence in the main news when it gets pulled into issues over which political forces are mobilized already, such as South Africa and the Moscow Olympics boycott, or football violence and law and order. The institutionalized separation of sport from the rest of 'reality' in the media encodes that notion with which we are all familiar, and which begs the question of the relation between sport and power, namely, that sport has nothing to do with politics. Under the auspices of the 'no politics in sport' rule, media sport as we shall see, can accomplish much ideological work.

The claim to be merely reproducing reality is most tenaciously held and appears to be most persuasive where TV is concerned, which indeed shows the event 'as it is actually happening'. But even here the technology of TV and the preferred practices of the professionals construct sport differently from how the spectator sees it. For example, when football is televised, the positioning of the main camera at the half-way position, on one side of the ground, in the stand, gives a view of the game that is quite different from the view of it from behind the goal.[22] The former approximates more to the perspective of the middle-class spectator, with the cameras taking up an 'impartial' location, giving an equal view of both teams and with the commentator supporting neither team; whereas the latter corresponds to that of the working-class supporter, who has traditionally stood on the terraces in all weathers, behind his team, urging it on in a thoroughly partisan manner. The relatively poor picture quality of TV means the camera can only cover a maximum of an eighth of the pitch in long-shot, if the players are to be at all distinguishable. In face of this technological limitation, English professionals, when compared to others, such as the West Germans, have been found to prefer frequent alternate long-shots with close-ups of individual players, or small groups of players, and it has been calculated that the ratio of time spent on close-ups of this kind to time spent on long-shots, is much greater in British televised football.[23] The viewer's attention tends to be thereby directed away from team strategy, towards the game's more individualistic aspects. The greater proportion of the game that occurs off-camera then has to be filled in for the audience by the commentator, giving him more latitude to interpret the action.[24] What occurs on-camera is also interpreted for the viewer by the commentary ('that was a good goal' etc.) Unlike the spectator at the event the TV viewer's observation is interrupted by 'action replays', which again, typically, close in on the individual performer at what are interpreted as key dramatic, entertaining moments – the tackle and confrontation, the goal, the shot, the save, moments of successful achievement or failure, with individuals' facial expressions and gestures highlighted. More often than not nowadays, the average viewer sees a heavily edited recording of the highlights, a multiple construction of reality, a truncated, action-packed spectacle, injected with pace, with omits the build-ups and the 'dull patches'. The crucial point here is that British TV coverage plainly gives primacy to entertainment when compared with other styles of coverage. The BBC, for example, explicitly acknowledges that action replays are put in for the benefit of the 'mums and daughters' watching, rather than for the connoisseurs, a practice in keeping with TV producers' perceived need to hurry on the pace to keep the audience with the programme.[25] The concurrence of the British press in such practices provides additional evidence of their cultural specificity. West German TV coverage of the World Cup in 1974, which eschewed close-ups for a more 'neutral' coverage, focusing on team play in long-shots, was criticized by columnists like Brian Glanville of *The Sunday Times* and by Derek Dougan, for its 'lack of professional skills'(!).

Further confirmation that the media do not merely report on events or show them as they actually happen, is provided by the fact that a good deal of work beforehand is put into preparing their audiences for how they should be seen and interpreted, that is, in building up the event. For example, the TV and *Radio Times* and *TV Times Magazine*, with their enormous circulations, built up the 1974 World Cup by nominating several stars beforehand as representatives of their countries' playing styles and national characteristics.[26] The opening sequences of TV sports programmes set the scene immediately prior to the event to be shown. The graphics draw attention to selected aspects and themes, like the Scottish bagpiper symbol at the beginning of ITV's coverage of the 1978 World Cup in Argentina, which signalled the nation's importance *vis-à-vis* others in the competition. The montage of insets, packed with champions in action, at the beginning of BBC TV's 'Grandstand', prepares us for non-stop action and excitement. The use of 'atmospheric' music in the signature tunes (quasimilitary, or with an ethnic trace) connotes entertainment, excitement and visits to exotic places.

Impartiality and objectivity is signalled by the practice of analysing performances with the help of accredited experts. Structured access is a fundamental feature of the organization of the media, and the use of the accredited expert in broadcasting is now a time-worn device, which developed originally in BBC news and current affairs programmes as a solution to the problem of establishing objectivity and achieving 'balance' over politically controversial matters.[27] In the press the equivalent of the accredited expert enters through the use of the attributed quotation and the sports-personality-as-writer. Expertise, in signifying objective, factual treatment and knowledgeable opinion, functions to authorize preferred interpretations. Since experts are used as primary definers of reality in the media, who is defined as an expert, which experts are selected from those available, and what kind of questions are put to them by reporters, presenters and anchormen, is crucial in the definition of reality. 'Recognized experts', are selected by professionals, and they are almost invariably former sportsmen or practising performers, or coaches and officials – but these are not necessarily the most expert among those in the field. An additional qualification is that they should be celebrities or stars with entertaining personalities or 'characters' who are good on TV. Little-known or relatively unsuccessful figures, say, a Fourth Division footballer, never appear as experts; it is the elite who are so identified, that is, what is considered relevant is not only what is said, but also who is saying it. A framework of values necessarily underpins the selection and definition of issues in the ensuing analysis, and what the audience is presented with therefore, is a summing up reflecting the values of media professionals and their expert advisers. On this basis performances are assessed and achievement or failure is recorded, praise and blame are allocated, stars are nominated, the level of entertainment rated, whether the rules were adhered to and properly enforced is ascertained and whether nations and representatives conformed to the consensus stereotypes of them. The sports spectacle is thus used, not only to exemplify and judge technical skill, but to prescribe moral values and to comment prescriptively on social relationships.

We wish to focus from now on, on those aspects of media sports discourse and routine practice, which are most important in this respect and which articulate on key processes whereby hegemony is achieved. We will examine how order and control, competitive individualism and civil privatism, sex and gender, the primacy of the nation and ethnocentricity tinged with racism, are constructed in media sport. Before doing so, it should be clear that there are differences in the ways individual media sports are constructed and more work needs to be done on elucidating these differences. We do not claim there is a uniform input to the power network from media sport, but what we do claim is that it makes a significant input in certain identifiable ways.

Constructing Order and Control

Media sport often reads like a handbook of conventional wisdom on social order and control. There are homilies on good firm management, justice, the nature of law, duty and obligation, correct attitudes to authority, the handling of disputes, what constitutes reasonable and civilized behaviour, on law and order and on the state of society generally. Media sport encodes an ideology of order and control, in the way the conduct of participants in sports events and that of spectators is depicted.

The main news values that structure order and control as a theme are the notion that news should be placed within a familiar framework to make it intelligible to the audience (conventionality); that sport should be presented as dramatic, sensational and full of suspense; that sport is about structured competition and the orderly resolution of conflict; and that unpredictable, deviant, rare and violent aspects are newsworthy, since they threaten change and change for the worse. Consequently, routine practices draw our attention to whether participants are conducting themselves in the prescribed manner. The media-sports professional treats the rules and procedures governing the behaviour of participants as 'constitutional' or sacrosanct. Participants are, therefore, expected to abide by the rules, and crucially they are expected to submit without question, to decisions made by those in authority over the proceedings. One does not argue with the officials in charge – one gets on with the game and leaves the officiating to them. When rules are infringed, the guilty parties are expected, as a matter of course, to be punished by those in charge, and the officials, unless they are foreign, are seen as administering the rules impartially. When rules are broken persistently, the situation is presented as problematic, as a threat and a challenge to authority, which has to be dealt with firmly and the situation brought back under control. Instances of rule infringement and confrontations with figures of authority consequently figure among the most dramatic moments in media sport. It is this framework that determines the media's routine practice of focusing on whether 'what happened' was within the rules or not: was the ball in or out?, did the player foul the opponent?, was there dissent with an official? and so on, and crucially, whether the decision of the official in charge was correct, or in other words, was justice done? TV technology supports a very powerful claim to infallibility here, through the device of the slowed-down action replay, which is now used standardly to analyse decisions, and media professionals and accredited experts devote a good deal of their time to discussing their correctness. On the whole, unless the officials are foreign, in which case chauvinism tends to creep into reportage, their authority is vindicated by the media, and mistakes by officials are, with a few exceptions, treated with sympathetic understanding. Indeed, more and more frequently officials are criticized in media sport for not 'stamping their authority' on the proceedings, or on the conduct of sports generally. The logic dictates that infringements and how they are dealt with – arguments between players and officials, 'incidents' between participants and especially infringements involving violence – are selected and highlighted, not only because they are dramatic, but also as occasions for demonstrating the correct resolution of conflict, that is, it encodes a reassurance that the rule of law and not anarchy and chaos prevails. Stories of confrontations, shots of players, or players and officials eyeball-to-eyeball, fouls, temper tantrums and so on, are all at a premium. At the same time the standard practice is to strongly denounce and disapprove of such behaviour as 'childish', 'unsporting', 'gratuitous violence', etc. The routine practice dictates that justice must also be seen to be done, so punishment rituals are accorded a very special place in this construction – players being shown the card, individuals being publicly warned by officials, dismissals from the scene of action, players emerging from disciplinary hearings etc. Exemplary punishments are singled out for detailed attention and lengthy discussion, and universally now, 'violent' and 'undisciplined play' is condemned as a 'bad example' with calls for severer punishments and firmer handling.

A common device used to bring off the moralizing is the practice of depicting actors in stereotypical terms as heroes and villains. Heroic status accrues to those participants in the drama whose conduct exemplifies the conventions, and these are the figures who are more usually singled out for praise. In fact, where the media give their own annual awards for sportsman and sportswoman of the year, one of the main criteria of selection is the 'example' set by the individual. Rebels and nonconformists on the other hand tend to be cast as the villains. One sees examples of this kind of stereotyping in the media's treatment of individuals like George Best, Ilie Nastase, John McEnroe and others who have been subjected to a stream of adverse publicity and criticism bordering on vilification for being 'undisciplined', 'playboys', 'unsportsmanlike', etc. But in its portrayal of the villain, media sport again achieves a form of accommodation with British working-class culture, which traditionally has shown a certain tolerance of, and even covert support for, the deviant. The subtext of media condemnation is often a sneaking admiration for the villain and rule-breaker, who cocks a snook at authority, but this relatively safe form of accommodation comes down eventually mostly on the side of authority. As it has always done, while supporting the powers that be, the media, especially the popular press, exploits the attractions deviance possesses for the audience. The language of the football reports and stories is just as violent, if not more so, than the very phenomenon it is at such pains to condemn, and in this sense it is all part of the same phenomenon.

Although the problem of 'indiscipline' and bad behaviour applies increasingly across the board, often now in more middle-class sports like tennis as well, it is the working-class game of football that receives by far the majority of the media's attention, and it is with respect to this sport that the media's presentation most directly and explicitly articulates with the political debate concerning the present 'state of society'. Football hooliganism began to be reported regularly in the 1960s and it has been a regular main news item throughout the 1970s and 1980s providing one of the most consistent examples of sport getting mixed up with what are social and, more lately, political issues in the media. Its treatment is completely at one with the way deviance, crime and law and order are constructed in the media from the consensual viewpoint. 'Football hooliganism' is a gift to the media, to the press especially, driven by competition from within its own ranks and particularly from TV, to search out the 'big bang' story; and the way football hooliganism has come to be treated has important consequences for the phenomenon itself and for the treatment of law and order issues. In constructing its account, the press relies typically a great deal on primary definers – football-club managers, the Football Association and the Football League, the police, judges and magistrates, politicians and the transport authorities. Reports of court proceedings and especially the judge's pronouncements and details of the sentences meted out, are dwelt on. What the press adds on its own part, that is apart from its principles of selection, is an account worked up in a stereotyped vocabulary, which stigmatizes young working-class football supporters as animals and lunatics. This exaggerates the problem, over-simplifies the causes, draws attention away from the question of causation and concentrates instead on the 'threat to society' angle and how repressive the solution should be. The 1970s opened with headlines like:[28] 'SAVAGES! ANIMALS!' (*Daily Mirror*); 'SMASH THESE THUGS!', 'MURDER ON SOCCER TRAIN', 'BIRCH 'EM!', and 'FANS GO MAD' (*The Sun*).

The mid-1980s has seen the media giving the maximum possible exposure, in graphic detail, to the lethal results of Liverpool supporters' assault on Juventus supporters at the Heysal Stadium in Brussels, and to the British Prime Minister's vehement (and metaphorically speaking, violent) denuncia-tions of hooligans and to her threats of punitive action against offenders. Press photos and video complete the theme of mindless, frightening violence – police battling with sections of the crowd, the piles of bodies and the wreckage of the stadium and the agony of the bereaved. One type of press photo providing a particularly striking image of mindless violence is the 'dart photo', used repeatedly: a spectator's face is shown in close-up, with a dart (thrown during the match) embedded near the corner of one eye. Another shows a young policeman, in head and shoulders close-up, with a dart, again thrown by a spectator, embedded in the lower cheek. The thrust of this presentation is to suggest that conflict around football is so anti-social, irrational and threatening that the only way it can be dealt with effectively is by tougher disciplinary measures. When causes of the problem enter this discourse they figure merely as fillers between the drama. It is the solution, that becomes the major focus of the media's attention. The absence of an account in terms of power and process and the attribution of cause solely to the irrationality and moral defectiveness of the deviants, is typical of the media's construction of matters with a complex causation involving civil disorders and of social conflict in general.[29]

TV is no exception in this respect, although it employs a less violent vocabulary than the press. In a BBC TV discussion in an edition of the 'Sports-night' programme devoted to 'The State of Football', for example, Graham Taylor, the Manager of Watford United Football Club at the time, somewhat unpredictably departed from the programme's agenda by explaining the problem in terms of the commercialization of the game and how it had alienated the supporter. As soon as Taylor mentioned the viciousness of the game in this context, the presenter interpreted this as a reference to soccer hooliganism, which had not in fact been mentioned at all by Taylor, and immediately cued in the accredited experts, who had been lined up to define the game's problems as being due to hooliganism. Almost the entire focus of the programme thereafter was shifted to discussion of the need to find a solution to this and to calls for punitive sanctions.[30] A similar programme on ITV during the same year (1980) was skewed even more heavily towards attributing the cause of 'football's decline' to hooliganism. Under continual prompting and questioning from the presenter, six of the ten accredited experts/spokesmen/primary definers blamed hooliganism and put forward heavier sentencing as the solution. Attempts to suggest other causes were made by some of the participants, but they were set aside by the presenter, who adhered closely to his agenda. It was concluded that football hooliganism was a reflection of the 'moral decline of the country'.[31] In an ironic sense this was, indeed, the point: in an economically and politically declining Britain, as the social costs become increasingly evident, the football hooligan has been constructed in the media as one of a series of 'folk devils' (others are 'muggers', drug-takers and pushers, strikers, pickets and terrorists) who are somehow responsible for, and symbolic of, the 'decline in moral standards'. By stigmatizing one section of the population as the villains, and by recommending a hard stamping-down by authority as the solution, the media have played a major part in constructing politics in a law and order mood.[32] The violence around football is not a media invention – it is a serious problem with political implications, not least for working-class people. The point is that the media's intervention has ideological effects: it displaces the incipient conflict between dominant and subordinate groups over problems generated by the present crisis, to the level of concern with law abiding and helps to mobilize mass support for authoritarian solutions to the predicament of subordinate groups. One is sometimes tempted to think that if football violence had not existed it would have been necessary to invent it.

Individualism and Civil Privatism

Individualism and civil privatism is constructed through the media-sport professionals' assumption that personalities constitute the core of the audience's interest, that interest is sustained by entertainment and that sport is basically about achievement through struggle. Media sport nowadays is largely built around the individual's attributes, the person's thoughts and feelings. Getting to the top is attributed to their talents, of course, but above all, to their competitiveness and perseverance, the appropriate reward for which is seen as money in large amounts, prestige and glamour. We have seen that even in a game like football where team-work is so important, attention is, nevertheless, focused on the individual, through the routine practice in British TV coverage of making frequent close-ups of players, showing their problems, achievements and failures. The press' treatment is substantially the same, except that personalization and dramatization are carried further in competition with TV and rival newspapers. Paradoxically, the relatively large number of photos in the sports sections almost never depict action, despite the obsession with it in the written text. Instead they disclose personalities, posed for the camera outside the context of action, or taken from actual action shots, usually showing only head and shoulders, or the single figure of the personality.[33] The written text completes the personality angle: it is packed with details of individuals' achievements, successes and failures, their opinions and feelings, details of their private lives and most importantly of their salaries. It was typical, for example, that the coverage of the Wightman Cup focused on the question of whether Virginia Wade's career was over or not. The journalists themselves figure as personalities as well. Many of the columns in the sports sections are headed by photos or graphics of the writer, whose feelings, reactions and assessments are again, conveyed through a highly personalized style.

The entertainment values that underpin media sport articulate with a shift in the historical development of individualism towards promoting the family as the individual's source of well-being, and away from the ideal that individuality is promoted by extending opportunities to participate in public life. The individualism–familism–civil privatism syndrome draws on the working-class ideal of respectability which entails, among other things, the injunction to be independent as an individual, to live up to decent standards, to be as good as others in this respect and to do as much as possible for one's family. But secondly, in working-class culture there is a strong traditional belief also that life is not just a matter of work and ambition, it is also to be enjoyed at the moment; so entertainment and the leisure in which to enjoy it is also valued highly. The message that 'keeping up with the Jones', by maximizing consumption within the family unit is enjoyable, manages the tension between respectability and hedonism. At the same time it subsumes them, together with the competitive, egoistic dimensions of individualism, into a coherent whole, ultimately prescribing civil privatism and fulfillment in leisure as the good way of life. The tendency among media-sport professionals to perceive the audience as strictly limited in its capacity to attend to anything for more than a little while and as therefore requiring constant stimulation with entertainment, is fully consonant with consumerist, civil privatist ideology. Media sports professionals have been at the forefront of reform campaigns to transform sport as a whole into family-oriented entertainment on middle-class lines. One of the routine practices signalling this value loudly is to literally give marks for 'entertainment value' and to continually raise the question: was it entertaining enough? Entertainment is brought off with linguistic practices aimed at creating the impression of action, excitement and suspense – it is brought off with the language of the battlefield: tackles are 'bone-crunching', opponents are 'demolished', 'crushed', and 'humiliated', and terms like 'blitz', 'blast', 'charge' and so on, proliferate. Goals are 'slammed', athletes 'power' their way to the tape, opponents are 'annihilated'. No work has been carried out so far in this country comparing the linguistic structure of media sport with working-class linguistic usage. Some work in Britain analyzing sports writing in the Sunday newspapers and the language used to report on football matches and football hooliganism, points to its lexical and conceptual poverty. With some exceptions the language, even when compared with usage in the rest of the media, is notoriously stereotyped.[34] The vocabulary is limited, reference is overwhelmingly to the concrete as opposed to the abstract and it contains relatively few qualifiers and modifiers. What in aesthetic terms could be categorized as repetitive, cliché-ridden, over-written prose, constitutes in socio-linguistic terms a restricted code.[35] It is doubtful whether the restricted code can be attributed solely to the working-class nature of the audience: there is little reason to think 'sportugese' coincides with working-class usage and the extent to which working-class linguistic codes are 'restricted' is disputable anyway.[36] Rather, what 'sportugese' seems to represent in socio-linguistic terms is an attempt on the part of the media-sports professionals to make sports entertaining for the working-class audience – an attempt which, on the whole, has been quite successful in terms of attracting and keeping that audience.

Sex and Gender

The media constitute one of the prime sites for the reproduction of gender divisions and sexism. Men figure far more than women as participants and even more so as media-sport professionals. Apart from crime reporting, sport is probably the most male-dominated sector of the media and it remains so, despite the rising number of women participants in sport, the greater amount of interest in sport among women in general and, above all, the existence of a significant number of women sports stars. The few women who have gained entry to this male media preserve tend to be restricted to reporting and commenting on 'women's sports'. The fact that it has proved harder for women to break into media sport as professionals than to break into sport itself is a good indication that media sport plays a strong conservative role in the reproduction of inequality between the sexes. Male commentators in male-dominated sports like cricket and football are, no doubt, what the majority of the audience expects, and in fulfilling this expectation the media accommodate to the prevailing pattern of gender division. But men also report and comment more frequently on women's sporting activity than vice versa, and even when sports are very popular with women, say, women's tennis, or gymnastics, as opposed to women's cricket, which is not popular, male commentators are far more prominent. The image of women in media sport is, therefore, predominantly constructed by men. Experience in other sectors of the media suggests that if more women were employed in media sport, sexist stereotyping would not necessarily disappear, but what would be likely to change is the conservative rigidity with which it goes on.

The rigid division between men's and women's sports in the culture, with all the connotations it carries of what constitutes 'manliness' and 'femininity', is replicated in media sport largely without question. Conventionalism and to a lesser extent titillation, does the main ideological work in reinforcing the idea that physical differences are the basis of inequality between the sexes. Whenever sportswomen appear in the media they are judged, not on their proficiency in sport, but also on their ability to conform to conventional definitions of what constitutes a 'real' woman. Performance must be compatible with what is taken to be feminine and deviant cases are treated very critically from a conventionalist standpoint. The first way this is accomplished is in the routine practice of commenting on the attractiveness of sportswomen. Attention is drawn in linguistic and visual presentation to the face and body shape, size, deportment, dress, hair-style and so on. The particular favourites of the media – more likely to be photographed for the press or to appear on TV to be interviewed – tend to be the conventionally pretty, or more sexually attractive sportswomen. The practice is highlighted by the way certain types of East European sportswomen are depicted. Alan Weeks of BBC TV gasps to the audience, as an East German competitor appears on camera: 'Now she's a very big girl indeed!' Martin Amis rails in *The Observer* against 'the breastless, well-hung iron curtain harridans'.[37] In contrast, those that are attractive in more conventional terms, like the Russian gymnasts, are presented positively. Secondly, it is routine practice to represent the sportswoman in relation to the role of wife, mother, girl-friend, that is, in relation to a conventional supporting role to the man. Of special interest here is whether married women athletes have children, which is regarded as a particularly meritorious achievement when pursuing a career in sport, since it confirms their essentially 'womanly', that is familial role. Where a sportswoman does not qualify on grounds of femininity or compatibility with playing a supporting role to the man, then she is in danger of acquiring a deviant, pejorative sexual image. Regularly, stories crop up in this connection concerning women athletes failing 'sex tests'.[38] There is no equivalent in the coverage of men's sport in the media to the allegations of sexual deviance that have been made about sportswomen. The fact that there is no media witch-hunt to discover homosexuals and transexuals, or commentary in terms of male competitors' attractiveness, shows that in a male-dominated sphere achievement confirms male identity, whereas it impugns women's femininity, unless they conform to their ascribed role. On somewhat rare occasions the issue of sexual discrimination does become mixed-up in sport and then it breaks out of the sport section. The case of the girl footballer who was banned from playing for her school team in the local schools league by the FA, took the case to court, won and then lost on appeal, was run as a major story. Another involved a woman judo judge, who brought a case against the British Judo Federation in the courts under the Sex Discrimination Act, because as a woman she had been banned from judging in top competitions. In both cases as they were reported, the conventional justification for discrimination given by the authorities, which were defending, received very prominent exposure in the press, and it is plain that the stories were considered news-worthy, not because they involved sexual discrimination, but precisely because the one instance was considered bizarre, and the other titillating:

RED CARD FOR THE FIRST LADY OF SOCCER

Soccer rebel Theresa Bennett, the tough-tackling schoolgirl who floored the mighty Football Association was beaten in the replay in court yesterday.

this was accompanied by a head and shoulders photo of bespectacled Theresa in football kit.[39] The headline 'BLACK BELTS HOLD THE FLOOR AT JUDO TRIBUNAL' was accompanied by a large photo of an attractive woman with a male demonstrator on either side of her.[40]

Images of gender in media sport reproduce the current pattern of male hegemony by articulating firmly with the discourse and practice of familism--civil privatism, which naturalize the sexual division of labour – that is the tendency of women to be more closely confined to their familial roles and to less rewarding jobs and their consequent unequal position in society. On the other hand, women's stronger anchorage within the family confers on them a major role in the construction of 'normal' family life. In fact it makes them the major relay through which consumer culture penetrates and pervades family life and through which men are induced under high pressure from women to achieve individual success on their behalf.

The sharp gender divisions constructed in the media are likely to resonate more strongly with conceptions of gender subscribed to by the more culturally and politically conservative sections of the population. Among dominant groups these are the forces which resist further advance by women into top business and professional positions, political life, etc. Among the working class, where more widespread assent is given to rigid gender divisions and a subordinate role for women, working-class conservatives are likely to assent more strongly still. Media sport accommodates to this important aspect of working-class culture particularly closely. We will return to the way gender divisions reproduced through sports relate to class in the final chapter.

Constructing the Nation

A sense of unity conferred by the feeling of belonging to the nation, cutting across class, ethnic, gender and other loyalties is, perhaps, the very linchpin of a hegemonic system, and the media are, arguably, the most important institution reproducing national identity today. Since the 1950s especially, with the expansion of TV coverage of international events, media sport has increasingly provided opportunities for people to identify with the nation through sport.

Coverage of the great annual sporting occasions, such as the Cup Final, the Derby, the Oxford and Cambridge Boat Race, etc., tends to convey a sense of a national way of life, but it is in coverage of international events in which 'we' compete against foreigners that 'Britishness' or 'Englishness' constitute conventional reference points signifying membership of a unique community, sharing a common, valued and specific way of life, which supersedes or takes precedence over all other loyalties and identities. The notion of the 'national interest', frequently invoked in media discourse on political topics, is transposed into media-sports discourse when 'our' competitors and representatives are made the focus of the media's attention on international occasions: how are 'we' going to fare? and how have 'we' done? are the issues as, for example, the Olympic medal table is scrutinized to keep track of 'our' achievements, *vis-à-vis* the other elite nations. As we have noted already, when a gold medal or a major competition is won, that is precisely the occasion when the episode breaks out of its separate reality and achieves the status of 'national' news. The ceremonial and ritual surrounding these occasions, prominently displaying the national symbols – the flags, the parades, the uniforms, the patriotic hymns and anthems, the participation of elite figures symbolic of national unity – especially members of the royal family, but also the Prime Minister and others – signal preferred conceptions of national unity which powerfully invoke feeings of identity. A particularly significant aspect of mediasport proceedings is the award ceremony which signifies not only individual or team achievement, but above all national achievement and glory. When media sport concentrates attention on these particular ceremonial and ritual aspects as opposed to other respects – the behaviour of the crowd, the action in progress, etc. – it invokes national unity in a manner more consistent with the dominant class's preferred view. For this aspect, compared with others on which the media focus, is more subject to control and influence by dominant groups. It is predominantly their cultural capital that is being put to work in the elaborately staged ceremonial, for example the Wimbledon Finals ceremony on the Centre Court when, immediately prior to presenting the trophy to the victor, the Duke and Duchess of Kent, having descended from the royal box, enter the court. Silence reigns, and while we all wait, literally in our millions all over the country, they pause casually on their way between the two ranks of ballboys to 'have a word' with one or two of them, as if there were no one else there, before proceeding to confer honour on the victor, on our behalf, to tumultuous applause. Dominant groups' symbolic work is not simply transmitted in pure unmediated form, but is merged in a construction of the nation which also embodies an accommodation to working-class and other groups' feelings of national identity. The latter aspect tends, on the whole, to be reproduced more in the way the action is depicted. More about this in a moment.

The construction of the nation in media sport is not unproblematic. A difficulty is presented, for example, by a degree of ambiguity about being British, which is not present in the conception of being English, and in some ways the consensus on what constitutes the nation is more firmly rooted in the latter than the former conception. In order to resolve the tension between what it means to be English, as opposed to being Welsh, Scottish, or Irish, ideological work is required, for indigenous national identities are strongly represented in some sports. When, for example, Wales and England clash on the rugby field at Cardiff Arms Park, media coverage of royalty's attendance and the accompanying ritual and ceremony, forms an integral part of the symbolic work carried out to ease tensions between these different nationalisms within the United Kingdom, which are expressed on this occasion. But the presence of more than one nation within a single political unit also has its advantages. Where there is no representative of England in major international competitions, the media's problem of finding a conventional reference point with which the audience can identify, is solved by searching out the 'British connection'. For example, in the 1974 and 1978 World Cup competitions, from which the English team had been eliminated early on, the Scottish team was made to stand for Britain.

The simultaneous necessity to construct 'Scottishness' was accomplished through the portrayal of Scots playing-style – 'brilliant individualism', 'fighting spirit', 'tempestuousness' and 'inconsistency'. Consistent with this type of signification in the 1974 World Cup, it was the better-known Scottish players employed by English League clubs who were made the focus of attention for what was, after all, a predominantly English audience.[41] However, when Scotland failed badly after a massive build-up in the media for the 1978 World Cup, this was widely interpreted in the media as a Scottish national disaster, rather than a British one.

Media sport strongly contrasts 'us' with other nations, peoples and races in the way that playing styles of other peoples and nations are depicted. Television coverage of the World Cup, for example, maps the world in a fashion that largely depicts North and Western Europe against Southern and Eastern Europe, and Europe versus Latin America, and unlike the Olympics it does not represent the conflict between the superpowers. Instead, other sorts of divisions are constructed: within Europe between the 'Nordic' and the 'Latin', and within Latin America, between Spanish-speaking and Portuguese-speaking multiracial Brazil.[42] The major motivating signifiers here are hair and skin colour: 'Latin' connotes 'fiery' and also 'bad' (cynical, dishonest, dirty – the England football manager, Alf Ramsey's celebrated castigation of the Argentinians as 'animals' partakes of this kind of discourse). 'Nordic' is 'cool' and 'good' (professional, open, disciplined). This division also corresponds very roughly with the distinction between the richer and poorer countries. The problem with forcing playing styles into such moulds is that in reality the 'Nordic', 'cool' and 'rich' Dutch, for example, have a good deal in common, in terms of playing style with the 'Latin', 'fiery', 'poor' Brazilians, and similarly the 'Latin', Italians have much in common with the 'Nordic' Scots.

The Russians, with the exception of their gymnasts, tend normally to be cast as robots, backed by a ruthless, totalitarian state prepared to spend vast resources on sport for prestige and propaganda. Pitted against them are the plucky individuals from Britain, the underdogs who come through adversity at the end, relying on their own resources and initiative. Normally, a kind of truce operates, restricting the more gross propagandistic expressions of such stereotypes, but the incipient chauvinism which tends to characterize media sport is more likely to be transformed into outright propaganda where the competition features those countries defined as 'our enemies'; and this applies particularly, of course, to the USSR. Media coverage of the Moscow Olympic Games in 1980 became overtly politicized however, when the British Government supported the American's attempt to have the event boycotted.[43] Sport was in this instance subjected to the routine practices of news and current affairs for the treatment of a hostile power. In broadcasting coverage, for example, the 'no politics in sport' rule was revoked and with one accord media sport became strongly partisan. The contrast between the way an event of this magnitude would normally be treated in the run-up stages, with the way it happened on this occasion, could be noted. There was no massive build-up, rather there was a deliberate playing-down of its importance, despite the decision of most of the British sports bodies to participate and the evident interest of the public in these games. The political definition of reality and the evident political pressures on the media, in particular on broadcasting, overrode the routine practices of media sport. Coverage as originally planned by the TV networks was scaled down drastically, and the media as a whole sought news angles consonant with the conventional political definitions and stereotypes. The events and everything connected with them were covered in a consistently hostile and critical manner. Media-sports professionals on this occasion, both in the press and broadcasting, saw their role as counter-propagandists and deliberately set out to mobilize support for an anti-Russian position.[44] Banner headlines taking up half the front page of the *Daily Mirror*, for example, screamed: 'OLYMPIC CHEATS Russia accused of tricks at Games.' This was about a dispute between the Romanians and Soviet organizers over the marking of women's gymnastics.[45] The Games arrangements, and especially the security arrangements, which had become more stringent anyway in the previous Montreal Olympics in 1976, as a result of the killing of Israeli athletes at Munich in 1972, came in for especially sharp criticism and were defined as being typical of Soviet totalitarianism. The life of the country, the nature of the system, the happiness of the people came under close scrutiny. The contrast between this treatment and the coverage of events held under other oppressive regimes not defined as hostile to Britain, such as the Mexico Olympics in 1968 and the World Cup in Argentina in 1978, was very marked.

TV coverage was especially interesting in this respect, since it provided the starkest contrast with the way sport is normally treated. Both BBC and ITV refused to take the complete opening ceremony, which normally would have been given great prominence, on the grounds that they could not be complicit in a propaganda exercise. By all accounts they, in effect, censored the kind of artistic display at which the Russians excel, and which normally serves to wet the audience's appetite for the games. The BBC took the unprecedented step of setting the agenda for the next fortnight in explicitly political terms, by putting on a discussion at the outset between one of their political journalists and an accredited expert on Soviet affairs, who was extremely hostile to the USSR.[46] From the start the interpretive framework was dominated by the issue of the boycott and its possible effects. At both the opening and the closing of the Games BBC commentator David Coleman informed the audience that 'half the world stayed away', an inaccurate assessment of the effectiveness of the boycott. It was stressed that some of the events had been 'degraded' by the boycott, and that medals had been 'devalued' when key competitors were missing. Attention was constantly drawn to the boycott of the opening ceremony by some teams and some individuals. And it was these representatives, rather than the majority who did participate in the opening ceremony, that were interviewed and questioned about the boycott. Attention was drawn frequently to the fact that some teams had decided to use the Olympic flag rather than their own. Both the press and broadcasting's ethnocentrism picked up immediately on the totalitarian connotations that the Soviets' goose-stepping marching style has for a British audience and derided it in the opening and closing ceremonies. The BBC's David Coleman summed up the closing ceremony in a critical editorial:

> The Russians' slogan of peace has nothing to do with reality...the obligatory doves were a mythical message incongruously speeded on their way...there was no sign of them flying south to Afghanistan...the impressive tableau was the work of 4,000 well-rehearsed soldiers...the tear from Misha the bear is a moment to remember the grief elsewhere which has led half the world to stay away...Russia is a country that tries so hard to impress but does so much to depress.[47]

The TV commentary constantly struggled to counteract Russian TV's attempts to put across a favourable impression by frequently contradicting rather than completing the sense of what was on-camera, a practice which is contrary to the normal televisual code. The constant reference to what the Soviet cameras were not showing and to the propaganda effect they were aiming at, to some extent tended to undermine the claim to reality implicit in the pictures, that is the strategy of negating the preferred reading encoded in the visual content was actually successful. There was, however, a contradiction between interpreting the proceedings in terms of a denigratory framework on the one hand, and on the other, the practice of focusing on the nation's fortunes in what was, after all, Britain's most successful Olympic performance to date. The more the occasion was denigrated, the more it detracted from the prestige accruing to the nation's victories and the more difficult it was to trade off the normal interpretive framework of media sport. It also became relatively easy to read the highly politicized commentary as a propaganda exercise. The dilemma remained unresolved, and the customary enthusiasm over possible and actual British winners carried on throughout the fortnight, on many occasions with the British commentary focused single-mindedly on the fortunes of 'our' representative, bearing little relation to what was on camera.

Contrary to working-class people's common perception of ethnic minorities as not forming part of the nation, media sport welcomes the presence of members of ethnic minorities in British teams, treating them equally as 'our' representatives. On the whole, South Africa does not get much sympathy in media sport and the activities of the National Front at football matches are usually deplored. Since sports are one of the few publicly recognized areas of achievement for black people, their depiction as representatives of Britain in international competition signals that progress is being made in achieving racial equality and racial harmony, whereas the facts on the position of black people and the state of race relations in general are quite the opposite.[48] Notably, racism is widespread among the working class. On such a sensitive political issue media sport accommodates more to dominant discourse on race and not so much to its working-class audience. Nevertheless, it does follow the latter course in the sense that by portraying blacks as being successful in sports and failing to portray them as being successful otherwise, it reproduces the myth – widespread in Britain – that blacks, being naturally better at physical pursuits and less so at intellectually demanding ones, are closer to nature and therefore less civilized than whites. The media practice that reinforces the myth is, of course, the absence of black people and, indeed, of ethnic minorities in general from the ranks of media-sports professionals. It is whites almost exclusively who construct images of non-whites in media sport, a reflection of a general tendency in the media to exclude ethnic minorities from the more prestigious influential controlling positions. Their absence suggests that media-sport management fears alienating its predominantly white audience and accommodates to it accordingly. The consequent ethnic stereotyping of black British as well as black non-British nationals that goes on is not very surprising. In cricket reporting, for example, West Indian and black British cricket supporters are typically depicted in terms of their 'exuberance', their 'excitability', and their 'colourfulness'. The connotations of immaturity and indiscipline that such labelling has, is unlikely to be lost on a British audience, which has still not shaken off a good deal of its imperialist cultural heritage, as the camera pans around laughing black spectators, jumping up and down, gesticulating, shouting, playing drums, etc., all of which is accompanied by an attitude of good-natured, amused tolerance on the part of the commentator.

Media sport often gives voice to the view, also widespread in Britain, that sports bring people of different nations and peoples closer together; whereas it is extremely unlikely that media sport counteracts chauvinist, ethnocentric, and occasionally racist-tinged conceptions of national identity and of national differences held by the population at large – and by the working-class in particular. Indeed since such sentiments tend to be encoded in media-sport discourse practice itself, the prevailing exclusionist sense of national identity, uniting indigenous subordinate groups behind dominant groups against 'outsiders' within an over-arching hegemony, is more likely to be reinforced from this direction. The code of media sport is but one aspect of a multi-layered process, whereby an exclusionist sense of national identity is reproduced by the media. In contrast to the public technology of an earlier era (the railways, streetlighting, etc.), the privatizing technology of broadcasting, whereby a centralized transmitter sends messages to scattered household receivers,[49] strongly articulates with that aspect of the political culture which identifies a privatized life-style with being English – an identification succinctly expressed in the old adage 'an Englishman's home is his castle'.

The paucity of firm, well-grounded conclusions in research on the effects of mass communication so far, dictates caution when interepreting the relation between media sport and working-class culture and the likely effects of media sport on the working-class audience. A process of selective accommodation to working-class culture certainly takes place, but it is selective in the sense that the accommodation is to those aspects of working-class culture which are compatible with media-sport professionals' values and which do not jeopardize their relationship with dominant groups. It is these elements that are more likely to be reinforced. Dominant groups are more likely to be accommodated to when sport becomes politicized, as in the case of football violence and the Moscow Olympics, and it is then that media sport is deployed in support of dominant groups' interests, and that it amplifies, rather than simply reinforces social forces. Media sport then, is likely to make an input to the more conservative aspects of working class culture and in particular to exert an overall conservative effect on the relation between sport and working-class culture.

8

Schooling the Body

Progressive Physical Education

The rational recreation ethic and athleticism in a modified form, had been absorbed in the state schools in the inter-war period in the interests of disciplining working-class children. A Swedish-derived form of therapeutic gymnastics was officially favoured and a therapeutic model of 'Physical Education for Organic Solidarity' tended to take over as the paradigm for the developing discipline at the teacher-training college level and the Inspectorate at the Board of Education.[1] The stress in the 1933 Physical Education (PE) syllabus was on discipline, alertness, precision, the soundness of body parts and their harmonious functioning to produce a healthy efficient whole. Against a background of high unemployment and potential political disaffection there was also some concern with recreation and enjoyment. This development in the state schools unified two previously separate disciplinary discourses and technologies – the medical and the educational – for the production of normal individuals, something that had only occurred so far in private schools for bourgeois girls and with a rather different objective.

But also in the 1930s the ground was being laid for a departure from rigid 'scientific' body management. A new discourse and technology was emerging at Dartington Hall in Devon, in the late 1930s around the ideas of Rudolf Laban, a key founding-father figure of what was to become 'movement education'.[2]

Arguably, the promise of greater educational opportunity did more to win the consent of the mass of the population to the post-war settlement between capital and labour and to the accommodation that was achieved between dominant and subordinate groups, than any other single factor.[3] Physical education (PE) developed as part of that achievement. The social context in the aftermath of war provided the essential conditions and ingredients for a new model of PE. Social policy initiatives were being taken to cope with the pent-up expectations of major changes among the

population. Dissatisfaction existed within the profession with the therapeutic
paradigm which felt out of step with contemporary educational trends
– in effect there was a theoretical vacuum in the field of PE and a heightened
search for status among professional practitioners. Support was forthcoming
from key personnel at the Ministry of Education for a dedicated, competent
group of professionals, capable of providing a convincing theoretical
justification and practical demonstrations of a new type of work.[4] Under
the auspices of a liberal–reformist , 'child-centred' educational philosophy,
namely, 'progressivism', the more conventional strand in physical education
(based on therapeutic gymnastics, fitness-and-skills training and team games)
was brought together with the newly developed 'movement education'
(based on Laban's work) and the other initiatives that had been made towards
developing a more problem-solving approach to the subject.[5] PE for
individual responsibility replaced PE for organic solidarity.[6] It was
women professionals, strategically well placed in the Ministry of Education,
the local authority inspectorates and some of the women's specialist colleges
who provided the main driving force in the elaboration and successful
diffusion of movement education throughout the women's teacher-training
and primary teacher-training sectors and thence into girls' secondary
education and the primary schools.

Although progressivist, child-centred ideas and practices hegemonized
men's and boys' PE, and movement education dominated primary-school
PE, movement ideas as such, attracted relatively few men disciples. Given
its institutional base, its arts orientation, its arrival in the wake of the strong
games-playing tradition in Britain and its domination by bourgeois women,
movement education achieved its strongest expression in dance and the
PE lesson in the gym. It is the most militantly progressivist aspect of
the subject, stressing child-centred, unobtrusive teaching, greater freedom
of expression and creativity and the necessity of individual problem-solving.
It is this aspect of physical education which corresponds most closely with
Berstein's characterization of the new progressivist pedagogy as a trend
towards the adoption of an 'integrated code'.[7] The loosening of the subject's boundaries, of the time and space framework in the lesson and the
greater informality therein, is a method for developing in the individual
child the qualities of flexibility and adaptability, the ability to explore and
solve problems independently, and to co-operate with others – qualities
which are seen as being required for competent occupational role performance among the new middle class. This model of physical education
functions so that body management symbolized individual responsibility
as the basis of a harmonious social order.

Movement education in fact coexisted in tension with the therapeutic
fitness-and-skills/games tradition, the latter having become more entrenched
in the men's teacher-training and boys' secondary schools. It is this wing

of the profession which more strongly articulates with and is more attuned to, working-class culture. One way this occurs is through the pattern of male recruitment into the profession, which draws to some extent on young, respectable working-class men with an interest in and competence at organized sport. This side of the profession tends to lean more on the natural sciences (anatomy, physiology, kinaesiology, biomechanics, etc.) and on behavioural psychology and social psychology, for its theoretical base. The absence of a firm agreement on what constitutes the theoretical basis of the subject, in fact, has always made for problems of professional identity and status *vis-à-vis* other subjects, which are possibly felt less acutely by the more solidly middle-class movement-education wing, than by the rest of the profession.[8]

If we are to understand the nature of the input that PE makes to the power network, we must distinguish PE knowledge and discourse into which recruits to the profession are inducted, from the routine practice of PE in the schools, since there is a significant disjunction between them. Although one of the functions of the former is to establish the credentials of practitioners with significant other groups, PE knowledge orders a field and structures a programme of control over subjects coming within the field, according to its own protocols – that is, it is conceived by practitioners as being in the general interest – it is not consciously designed to further the interests of dominant groups. It is in the course of implementing the programme that discrepancies arise between knowledge/discourse and practice, with pertinent effects on power relations. PE teachers are encouraged in their training and by leading elements in the professional community to see society and the school and their own role therein, in specific ways. However, at the level of routine practice in the schools they are influenced also by their experience of the problems of carrying out their role on the ground, notably the problem of controlling and managing pupils, which involves accommodating to pupil culture. Secondly, they are influenced by the problem of fitting into the hierarchy of the school, to which they also must accommodate in order to make a reasonably successful career. These two sets of influences, the 'theoretical' and the practical, together shape the way the role is carried out and consequently shape the effects of PE on the pupils. It is first necessary then, to examine PE discourse, next the nature of body-work carried out in PE ritual and finally the outcome in terms of the effects on subjects.

The Discourse of Physical Education

PE theory, its objectives and recommended practices, constitute a programme of control through sustained work on the body. Apart from religious education, PE is the only subject which, in effect, is statutorily included in the curriculum, and in terms of the attention and resources devoted to it, it is one of the most important elements.[9] A large-scale survey by the Schools Council found that PE ranked third, behind only maths and English, in the proportion of the timetable devoted to it.[10] Again, apart from religious education, it is the only subject on the curriculum which appears to be purposely designed to serve a social integration function: no other aspect of the curriculum is theorized so overwhelmingly in terms of its moral and psycho-social significance. The aims and objectives of physical education, as annunciated in official publications and by leading members of the profession in texts and journals, not only encode, but in many cases are explicitly committed to, views concerning the nature of the social order, which find ready agreement among dominant groups.[11] The multiplicity of value claims made for the subject in the professional literature fall readily into categories concerning fitness and health, skill acquisition and its benefits, the aesthetic qualities in physical activity, and the moral, psychological and social benefits allegedly promoted by physical education. However, even when the discourse is ostensibly otherwise, the sub-text is concerned to a very large extent with the theme of socialization and social control. The subject is conceived overwhelmingly as providing opportunities for monitoring and influencing pupils' social behaviour, for them to experience role-play and for learning to adjust to the 'demands of society'. Such terms and phrases as 'preparation for society', 'knowledge of right and wrong', 'socially acceptable behaviour', 'emotional and social adjustment' and 'integrating the odd man out', pepper the discourse. The cognitive, emotional and moral qualities to be developed are those which are seen as maximizing role performance – 'initiative', 'creativity', 'competence' and 'efficiency', 'adaptability', 'concentration', 'self-management', 'confidence', 'discipline', 'loyalty', 'courage', 'determination', 'cooperation', etc.

Discourse on the function of the subject at the secondary school stage focuses much more on the problem of integrating the less academic pupils. PE's contribution is seen as compensating those who, for want of academic achievement, are destined to spend their lives in unrewarding work, by preparing them to use their leisure. Leisure, from this point of view, provides opportunities for safely chanelling and productively employing emotions, tensions and aggressive feelings created by academic discipline and social disadvantage. In this respect the PE programme thus aims at a formal unity between school and consumer culture.

The predominant value underpinning this discourse is clearly individualism, but it is hardly the competitive, achievement-oriented variety applauded in media sport; rather, it is a more socially responsible variety considered appropriate for 'educational' aims. The reservations concerning competition are because competitive sport interferes with the new programme for producing normal individuals. By definition, competitive sport, because it is achivement-oriented, cannot compensate the majority of pupils who fail academically. Also, it is too specialized and formally structured to allow the integration of knowledge, the training in motivation and attitudes and the opportunity for personal exploration, discovery and expression pre-scribed by progressivist pedagogy. In other words, it does not expose the individual child sufficiently to the teacher's surveillance that is, to the gaze of authority. Competitive sport as such is not rejected (PE theory accepts the elitist distinction between the 'gifted' minority and the rest, in common with modern educational theory as a whole), rather it is played down as being less relevant for educational purposes and is recommended as a separate activity for the 'gifted', or alternatively, as a purely extra-curricular activity.[12] In addition a small, growing minority of social-science-trained PE theorists are especially aware that competitive sport alienates the non-achievers and for this reason they recommend jettisoning teacher-centred competitive sport, even as an extra-curricular activity, in the interests of furthering the integration of the 'school and community'.[13] Progressive as it may seem, all this is a specifically British education tradition. In contrast to the North American system the preferred solution to the problem of inequality of opportunity is to seal off the 'non-academic', that is, the working-class majority, from further exposure to competition and failure, and in Durkheimian fashion to engineer social integration by lowering pupils' expectations, getting them to 'accept their limitations', and by providing a system of surrogate rewards.[14]

The individualistic nature of PE discourse accomplishes the virtual dis-appearance of the social structure, that is, social processes and social phenomena are radically individualized, reducing them to the attributes of persons and of interaction between them. The school as a social organiza-tion, knowledge of the nature of the social context of the education process and of the cultural characteristics of the pupils, forms no part of the discourse.[15] The absence of reference to the existence of social classes and different ethnic groups for example, signals their irrelevance to education; and yet at the same time there are continual elliptical coded references to class inequality and the existence of subordinate groups in the employment of terms and phrases like 'the most advantaged group', 'our average and our less than average pupils', 'those who do not easily achieve expression in words', 'pupils of quite modest talent'. It is precisely the abstraction of the individual child from its socio-cultural context that enables this discourse to construct social integration from a middle-class standpoint: its silences assume that the character of society can be taken for granted, and that a consensus exists on the appropriate pattern of socialization. Where the discourse does touch on social structure it is in terms of a pervasive 'communitarianism', whereby the school and its pupils are depicted as forming part of a vague, undefined entity – 'the community'.

Likewise, PE theory, progressivist or otherwise, almost without exception replicates conventional notions about gender differences, authorizing the actually very active part schools play in encouraging gender divisions through the PE programme. While as much desegregation of the sexes as possible is recommended where it is considered to be appropriate, that is where it is customary, differences are to be maintained: 'where "sensitive" contact between teachers and taught is necessary' and where competition between males and females leads to the latter becoming 'over-pressurized' and leads them to 'overt-exert' themselves.[16] The Department of Education and Science (DES), in stating that eight- to thirteen-year-olds should have separate showers, that separate changing rooms are desirable for ten- to thirteen-year-olds, that there should be facilities for football and cricket and for hockey and netball as well, is signalling that the traditional divisions between the sexes should be adhered to. The separation of boys and girls in the late stages of the middle school is suggested on the grounds of their developing different interests and their physical differences and of course, the problem of taking showers.[17] Segregation of the sexes is sometimes justified, in addition, on aesthetic grounds. The tacit following of established social practices becomes explicit advocacy to do so when making recommendations for the secondary stage, at which coeducational organization is seen as only appropriate where 'adult men and women normally participate together.'[18] Puritan taboos about bodily contact between the sexes are invoked here as well – physical contact between pupil and pupil and between girls and male teachers is considered particularly hazardous.[19] Most of this is, in fact, in marked contrast to the response in education circles to the differences between the sexes, with respect to interest and attainment, in other areas of the curriculum. Differences in attainment between the sexes in maths and science, for example, are considered problematic and in need of remedy.

The Physical Education Ritual

Any mode of investiture of power in the body requires a technology incorporating relevant knowledge and ritual practices. PE deploys quite an elaborate technology, drawn from athleticist, fitness-and-exercise, recreational and movement technology; and it is also one of the most ritualized aspects of the school curriculum. Ritual here functions as a restricted code, that is, although it is not inherently the case, ritual practices sustaining work on the body constitute a particularly effective non-discursive form of communication and therefore are potentially a strong form of control.[20]

Although the movement lesson in the primary school and the PE lesson in the gymnasium tend to be structured more on progressivist lines, contrary to what is often supposed about the de-ritualizing effects of the more informal progressive pedagogy, this aspect is, nevertheless, highly ritualized. Also, substantial parts of the PE programme at the secondary level, particularly games, swimming and athletics, are inherently limited in the extent to which rigid classification and framing of the subject can be eliminated, so traditional forms of pedagogy and organization tend to predominate and here ritual activity is particularly marked. One indication that PE and school sport are bastions of ritualism is provided in an extensive survey of secondary schools of all kinds, which found that the announcement of inter-school and inter-house competition results, award ceremonies, and the prominent display and use of ceremonial regalia and sporting symbols, are an important part of school assemblies each day.[21]

Strictly speaking, communication in PE is not restricted to body language alone – verbal and non-verbal channels of communication are normally open simultaneously, as in any lesson, and as in most ritual activity. The verbal element in physical education, however, tends to be curtailed rather drastically: there is a matter-of-fact curtness exemplified in the use of imperatives at key points in the lesson, like 'Begin', 'Stop', 'Look this way', etc., and the use of non-vocal aids like whistles, starting-guns, etc. The opportunities for verbal interaction between teacher and pupil are relatively restricted in this sense, and also in the sense that the direction of the communication flow is more controlled by the teacher, so that it tends to be more a one-way process from teacher to pupil. Also, distortion or 'noise' enters the communication process, because in this subject rules of conduct and procedures are to a very large extent articulated in technical-functional terms.[22] For example, stipulations about what constitutes appropriate accoutrement and the proper use of equipment are justified often on grounds of safety to oneself and others, or on health and medical grounds. The restricted character of communication is then, not confined to the non-verbal aspects alone, but when the restricted character of the non-verbal aspect is added we have an example of a non-discursive, 'hidden curriculum' *par excellence*, which is more difficult in some ways for the pupil to penetrate critically than classroom teaching. One exploratory study of pupil-teacher interaction during the physical education lesson using videotape, classified observed behaviour roughly into 'teacher talk', 'demonstration', 'class talk', and 'class movement'.[23] It was found that 'teacher talk' accounted for 48 per cent of the lesson and 'class movement' for 41 per cent, leaving a very small amount of time for 'demonstration' and 'class talk'. Significantly, there was no time allowed for the class to initiate ideas verbally: the teacher initiated behaviour and this was nearly always physical, and 26 per cent of this was in direct response to instructions given, with very little choice of interpretation. Only 15 per cent was class-initiated movement and it came from playing a game, in what seems to have been 'free time' at the end of the lesson.

The physical education ritual is highly coded. The units are organized to a great extent to standard types in advance of use, and this is true even of the much-vaunted creative, pupil-initiated movement lesson, since it is rarely taught as officially prescribed due to a lack of properly trained, committed teachers and inadequate facilities. In many respects, the lexical meanings are local and particular, and the syntax is rigid, offering a small range of alternative forms. Organized games are the most obvious example, programmed according to standardized rules and tight classification of space and time; there are relatively set procedures and techniques for teaching and practising skills in general and for assessing standards of technical competence. On the other hand the constituent symbols of body-language in PE are highly condensed, that is, denotation is striking and connotations are multifarious, making for an instant, powerful communication at the cognitive, aesthetic and emotional levels. Colour-coding is especially important. The symbolism of the colour white, for example, is central in the iconography of the culture as a whole, but in PE this general significance can be cashed dramatically. Thus 'whites' (clothing used in cricket, tennis, gym work, etc.) denote 'cleanliness' and simultaneously connote 'discipline', 'health' and 'attractiveness' – the significance given to certain value syndromes can be amplified dramatically in the context of body rituals. The classification of space in PE is rigid, setting body-work off from the rest of the school's activities in clearly marked *loci* – playing-field, swimming-pool, gym and sports hall, running-track, changing-room – each with a distinct working ambience of its own. Specified conditions of access and rules of usage apply to these spaces whereby pupil behaviour can be closely monitored and controlled. The system of rules surrounding changing and the wearing of special types of accoutrement – track suits, shirts, swimming-trunks and suits, gym shorts, plimsolls, football boots, brief garments of various kinds, bare feet, showering and hygiene practices – manages the body through control over its appearance. A high degree of control over what is worn and how the body is adorned is a common feature of institutions in which the level of compulsion and control over individuals is relatively high, such as prison, barracks, asylums, hospitals, old-peoples' homes, convents and monasteries and schools of all kinds.[24] The individual's control over how the body is adorned is a major source of personal identity and therefore is an important defence mechanism against institutional control and dependency.[25] Regulations about mode of dress then, restrict the pupil's opportunity to construct an identity independently of the institution and the capacity to broadcast messages counteracting those transmitted through body-work carried out under institutional control. In PE control over how the self is presented is limited drastically. Loss of control over this aspect of life renders the subject more vulnerable to pressure to conform, more vulnerable in particular to the weapons of shaming and humiliating. The school, via the PE lesson, literally makes more of the pupil visible to the gaze of authority and, therefore, more available for control; and it narrowly circumscribes the scope for self-presentation. It should not come as any surprise to learn that there is a prolonged struggle between teachers and pupils over what is worn, and that this struggle is particularly sharp where PE is concerned, that is, there is conflict over the body, the outcome of which PE teachers tend to regard as a crucial test of their ability to exert control and as a sign in the pupil of conformity or rebellion.

There is little direct empirical evidence available on the signifying process in PE, but we can obtain an indirect impression of what body-language symbolizes in PE with the aid of photographic material contained in official publications, PE texts and professional journals, showing activities in progress in the schools and colleges – materials obviously constructed to present an ideal image.[26]

The photos of young children and adolescents engaged in physical activity show intense involvement in a wide variety of forms of physical activity. Facial expressions are especially important in conveying an impression of concentration and involvement, a feature conveyed also by the fact that children hardly ever stand about – their bodies are shown in constant movement. In repose they are usually observing a demonstration closely or listening to the teacher or coach with rapt attention, signalling the value of willing, enthusiastic effort and achievement. Secondly, the photos are full of happy, smiling, interested children and young people working together; there are no dejected, unhappy-looking, unsure-looking pupils in this world. The message is about the power of 'positive thinking', it advocates co-operation as the source of well-being. The settings are full of space and light, stocked with clean, shiny, new equipment, giving the impression of social advance and opportunities there for the taking. The wearing of special clothing or little clothing at all, tends to mask social differences and buttresses the impression of harmony and lack of social division (PE dress, however, does construct gender differences, which will be examined in a moment). Few fat or thin children are in evidence and dirty children not at all. The only time that malfunctioning or poor performance appears in the photos, is when specialized remedial work with the handicapped, mentally retarded or 'educationally subnormal' pupils is depicted. To all intents and purposes then, this is a middle-class children's world. In these authorized official depictions of the PE ritual the importance of effort, discipline, achievement, compliance, co-operation, harmony and role competence is symbolized. One ritual symbol above all condenses these values – the mesomorphic image of the body – and what is connoted by this image is probably more significant than what is denoted. This image of the ideal body cuts right across the movement education versus conventional PE divide in the profession. The preferred recruit to the profession for example, is a perceived physically adept performer, and notions of physical competence are strongly associated with a preference for the mesomorphic body type, i.e. a muscular torso and limbs, small waist and broad shoulders in the case of males, a less pronounced musculature, yet well-built and well-proportioned frame, with more rounded contoured shape, in the case of females. Photos of PE students and of children in the texts and journals amply confirm this preference. The image functions to devalue two other body images in the culture, those of the ectomorph, the thin or 'skinny' body, and the endomorph, the fat body-type.[27] Body concept is important in the process of identity-formation in the individual and is a significant determinant of social interaction. The high prestige which attaches to mesomorphy is likely to advantage socially those individuals who approximate most closely to the image. They are consequently likely to be more confident socially, have a higher sense of self-esteem and a securer self-identity and to be more sought after as friends. It has been suggested also that mesomorphs are more likely to be unsympathetic to those who are perceived as thin, fat or physically incompetent and are likely to be more conformist and authoritarian.[28] The mesomorphic image resonates strongly with ideologically conservative notions concerning achievement, drive and dynamism, discipline, conformity, cleanliness, efficiency, good adjustment, manliness and femininity. On the other hand, ectomorphic images connote weakness, lack of adjustment and neuroticism, antisocial tendencies, unattractiveness and coldness; and endomorphic images connote laziness, inefficiency, self-indulgence, unhealthiness and unattractiveness. The more individuals deviate from the preferred image, the greater the risk of social exclusion and humiliation. In schools PE teachers and the more physically competent, attractive-looking pupils inadvertently collude through the PE ritual in the construction of individual identities and the pattern of social relationships. The lives of excessively thin or fat children and of the clumsy, can be made almost unbearable in school and great pressure can be brought to bear on the rest to live up to the norm. In schools this pressure is felt at its maximum in PE, but it is also a generalized cultural constraint, very evident for instance, in consumer culture. There are differences between the body as a PE icon and as a consumer-culture icon – for a start, the latter is more eroticized – but their correspondences suggest these fields are now more closely articulated into one more extensive force-field. Witness the widespread preference for a more trained-looking body-shape in consumer culture; and the spread of glamour fashion-wear in the form of leotards and high-tech brand-name equipment with which the body is increasingly adorned, into PE. The ideal body is a social construction, yet it is a construction which naturalizes social relationships and characteristics: it facilitates the process whereby physical educationists exert what is, in fact, a social control, enabling them to construct social competence and social relationships.

The organization of space and time in PE, compared with other subjects in the curriculum also makes more of the pupil available for socialization and control – in extra-curricula activity at the end of the school day, in special clubs, training sessions, weekend matches, expeditions and outdoor pursuits away from the school and home and during holiday time. The great variety of settings in which supervised physical activity takes place, the relative fluidity of spatial relations between pupil and teacher, the play and the fun atmosphere often present, the cameraderie and the intimacy generated in shared physical work involving bodily contact and mutual reliance – all these provide the PE teacher with opportunities for entering the pupil culture and for exerting informal influence and control. PE teachers regard this feature as an integral part of their job, as the equivalent of the time spent by classroom teachers in marking and preparation, and as conferring a certain advantage over the latter, in that it provides an opportunity to make good relationships with pupils. This feature is well recognized by head teachers, who consequently tend to look to the PE department as a major stabilizing influence in the school.

The Efficacy of the PE Programme

It is important to bear in mind that the expansion of power afforded by the development of the modern PE programme constitutes both power *over* pupils and also power *for* them to make advances, beyond what was previously possible. In the latter respect the aims of progressive education were probably taken more seriously and were realized more fully in the primary school PE lesson than in almost any other aspect of schooling. Facilities for participating in physical activity have improved immensely; the subject largely escapes the kind of pressure and strain pupils experience when taking academic subjects and preparing for public examinations. There is a great deal of freedom of choice: many activities are voluntary and there is considerable variety, so that probably more all-round enjoyment and satisfaction is derived from the subject than ever before. The improvements are likely to have benefitted particularly those social categories relatively deprived of opportunities for fulfilling physical activity because of social circumstances – working-class children, those of ethnic minorities and girls.

The efficacy of the PE programme cannot be simply read off the stated objectives in the discourse or the nature of the PE ritual. Physical education constitutes a field through which a number of social forces interact to produce a definite input to the power network: the career strategies and routine practices of PE professionals, the pressure on individuals for achievement, generated within the education system by the examination system and the school culture; the differential response to schooling the body from different social classes and social categories among the pupils – all these elements become linked up in a process whereby relations between subordinate and dominant groups are constructed in physical education.

Notwithstanding the perceived efficacy of PE as a form of control within education circles, the subject has a low status *vis-à-vis* others on the curriculum, and this presents the PE teacher with the problem of demonstrating professional competence to other colleagues in order to gain their acceptance, and to the school hierarchy and education employers in order to advance in career. Attempts to transform PE into an examinable subject hardly solve the problem, indeed, this path is counter-productive, since a proportion of examinees necessarily do not receive good results and what is more important, examinations induce an achievement orientation in the subject, so that the physically able pupil with low academic ability is penalized; and those who are not achievement-oriented because of their cultural backgrounds are alienated. Thus PE loses most of the advantages it has over other subjects.[29] In fact, the established way in which the problem of status is solved in PE is to demonstrate competence and success publicly by getting good team results in inter-school competitions and by organizing prestigious intra-school occasions (sports day, demonstrations of work, swimming galas, inter-house competitions, etc.) at which parents, colleagues, local notables and the school hierarchy are present. Sporting success can bring prestige to the school among the local community and in educational circles and for that reason it tends to be valued by head teachers. Such activity can also encourage certain groups of pupils to identify more with the school. More about this in a moment.

It is the indirect constraint of the public examination system which induces PE teachers to adopt this strategy, since success in examinations is ultimately the font of prestige in which the whole curriculum is bathed; and therefore PE teachers are forced to seek a functional equivalent. The pressure is at its greatest at the secondary level, but at the primary level too teachers can obtain advancement by establishing a reputation for organizing extra-curricular physical activities. Given the limited resources, if prestige is to be gained in this way it can only be achieved by concentrating on those pupils who are identified as possessing the correct motivation and superior potential ability. Sporting activities therefore, whether they are extra-curricular or timetabled, tend to take on a competitive, achievement-oriented, teacher-dominated character and competitive individualism and elitism enter informally as an unintended consequence. It is not simply that PE teachers share elitist values – many, no doubt, do – it is that individualism and elitism are built into the system of constraints and thus they come to pervade the ethos of the PE programme. Classes are far too large for teachers to be able to give all pupils sufficient individual attention to raise their standards of performance significantly and facilities, in any case, do not permit it. It has been estimated for example, that in the typical London comprehensive school, where the only way pupils can be given access to adequate games and playing facilities is to bus them to playing-fields on the outskirts of London, over half the timetable allocation is spent on travelling and changing. In such circumstances elitism is a response to the twin problems of class management and career advancement.

Elitism is built into the programme through the ideological work performed by the dominant body concept of mesomorphism. There is no evidence that mesomorphism correlates with teaching ability or that mesomorphic characteristics are even functionally necessary to teach the subject.[30] There is also reason to think that they can actually be dysfunctional for teaching children with a wide range of abilities: recruits with this body-type are often high-performance oriented, tend to be more interested in those pupils who are taken to be 'physically gifted', and to be relatively unsympathetic to the 'less able' or not naturally-endowed pupils – and there is evidence that pupils perceive this.[31] Also, elitist tendencies in PE have strengthened since the mid-1970s. With the success of the right-wing backlash against progressive education, the utilitarian drive to strengthen the instrumental as opposed to the expressive function of education and the boom in fitness and health concerns, the natural science-based, fitness-and-skills model of the subject is being refurbished and is now being more strongly asserted as the most appropriate paradigm for PE in the 1980s.[32] The top levels of the profession now attach a greater importance to catering for the 'gifted child' and to the pursuit of 'excellence'. Beliefs in a natural hierarchy of ability, legitimized by natural science-based training, remain strong, and there is an increasing commitment to the idea that an unequal structure of provision is necessary to cater for the 'gifted', and that PE in schools should be linked to the programme for building national teams and improving the country's performance at international level.[33]

Class Divisions

Elitism, competitive individualism and an achievement orientation ultimately confer a differentiating function on the PE ritual. A wealth of empirical evidence over the last twenty-five years shows that, contrary to the aim of PE professionals and in spite of the widespread opinion that physical education and sport is of special value to the 'non-academic child', the level of working-class children's involvement in school-organized physical activities of both a voluntary and compulsory nature is far lower than for middle-class and 'able' children.[34] In the early 1960s Newsom discovered that over half the children in non-selective secondary education in England and Wales did not belong to any club or society, school-based or otherwise.[35] In 1970 just under half of the pupils in two large comprehensive schools in the north of England were found not to participate in extra-curricular activities of a physical kind; in 1979 a survey of four comprehensives in Scotland found over half the fourth-year working-class boys took no part, nor did 75 per cent of the girls of this social class.[36] Membership of house and school teams, as well as attendance at extra-curricular clubs and activities is much lower for working-class pupils, working-class girls hardly participating at all. After leaving school, interest in organized physical activity drops away and relatively few continue with it.[37] The differential rate of participation is largely attributable to the clash between certain elements within working-class culture and the school culture. Hargreaves and Lacey in the mid-1960s and Willis and Corrigan in the 1970s have demonstrated that the less academically successful, male working-class pupils prefer unorganized or more commercialized physical activities and pursuits, like street football and watching professional football, snooker, fighting and pop music, in their spare time. These kinds of activities give them the opportunity to play, as they see it, more adult roles, to combat boredom better and to gain control over their own lives. They reject competition, supervision, and organization being imposed upon them and they are hostile to school sport, not because they lack ability, but because it is associated with school values and the school status hierarchy. They well recognize that school sports are not simply an attempt to allow them the chance to enjoy themselves and that they are meant to instil a certain attitude to sports and to life.[38] A lot of these boys are competent per-formers who like sport, but they reject the school style and ethos: for them, for example, organized school football is just not normal, enjoyable football. But crucially, what these studies also reveal is that pupils in the upper streams of schools in predominantly working-class areas, who must therefore come mostly from working-class homes, are not uniformly hostile to school sport and that a proportion do have a relatively higher level of involvement. All the available evidence confirms that although the global rate of partici-pation for working-class pupils is low compared with middle-class pupils, nevertheless a significant proportion of those who are positively involved are working class. Saunders and Witherington found, for example, that the rate of participation in all types of secondary schools was higher for 'academic' boys and that the difference between academic and non-academic boys was greater in comprehensive schools, where working-class involvement was much lower. Nevertheless, in the comprehensives in this study, which were solidly working class, just over half of the boys were successfully involved in extra-curricular physical activities and almost all the working-class boys in the other types of schools were involved. The only reasonable conclusion to be drawn from this is that physical education and school sport is relatively popular with a section of working-class pupils, that is, those who, on the whole, tend to do better academically and who comply with the achievement norms and values of the school. Physical-education teachers' perception of the attractiveness of their subject to fairly large numbers of pupils, who are not necessarily middle class, has a sound basis. Just as different modes of involvement in sport divide the adult working class, so physical education and school sport divides working-class children. Studies of working-class youth's alienation from the school and the development of a counter-culture among them, correct as they are for that section of the working-class youth who reject school, underplay this important difference in the way the upper and lower working class relates to schooling.

If this is correct, far from there being a clash between working-class culture as such and the school, there are in fact, in important respects, linkages between the school culture and the culture of a significant proportion of the working class, which means there is also pressure and demand for competitive sport from the more achievement-oriented pupils and their parents. After all, if the schools were simply transmitters of middle-class culture they would presumably give greater primacy to games other than football as the major game, and they do not.[39] Schools recognize the centrality of football to working-class pupils, for many teachers themselves are of working-class origin; and it is accordingly the established major game in the state schools. One is drawn to the conclusion then, that the values we have identified as those encoded in physical education could not be transmitted and received by a good proportion of working-class pupils unless there was to some considerable extent an anchorage for them already in certain aspects of working-class culture. Voluntary involvement of male working-class pupils in school sport and relative compliance with models of behaviour promoted in the PE programme then, need not imply a one-way imposition of school or middle-class values. What it does mean is that a process of accommodation is going on, which draws the middle class, as represented by the school, and the upper working class, closer together and which produces a quite sharp division among working-class pupils in the school. The antagonism of the lower-working class 'lads' towards working-class boys who conformed with the school's demands, as revealed in Willis' and Corrigan's studies especially, bordered on hatred, and it exemplifies the power of the fragmenting process which the school and PE help to foster.

Gender Divisions

Gender and class are, in fact, inextricably bound together in this process, whereby the working class is fragmented. In PE, gender divisions are still largely understood to be rooted in biological differences – women are commonly held to be naturally weaker and less suited to strenuous exercise. Whatever the outcome of the debate about biological differences – and there obviously are differences – it is equally obvious they are not the basis of gender divisions in PE. We are dealing here with social differentiation. PE follows the dominant perceptions of sexual difference in the culture, and collapses the social into the biological, that is it reduces social relations to relations between things. In fact, there is a good deal of overlap between the sexes in physical capacity and achievement: many women are stronger, faster and more highly skilled than men. It is more likely then, that much of the existing discrepancy in male–female physical performance is socially determined through gender-specific patterns of socialization into physical activity, which narrows girls' achievement. Boys, on the other hand, are positively encouraged throughout school to regard sports as a natural pursuit for a normal boy and are channelled into a male preserve where, in terms of the culture, proficiency at sport equals manliness. The school's role here via the PE programme is crucial.

PE is consistently the most sex-specialized subject on the school curriculum. This is more marked at the secondary stage, although even at the primary stage, it is quite well established. The sexes as a matter of course are differentiated progressively and segregated spatially, both when pursuing the same kind of activity – gym, athletics, swimming, etc. – and also by being channelled progressively into a different pattern of physical activity considered suitable for girls, which in some ways is more conservative than the pattern in society at large. In parallel with recent changes in the sexual division of labour and in sex roles generally, the traditional rigid divisions between the sexes in the subject has, to some extent, been eroded. Girls, for example, now do cross-country running, not long ago thought to be completely unsuitable for females; they play games like basketball and volley-ball; and at sixth-form level they mix in sport more like adults. But the division and inequalities are still very marked and fundamental changes cannot be said to have occurred.

The time spent in physical education by boys and girls is distributed differently among the available activities. Girls spend less of a proportion of their timetable on games and sports and more on gym and dance. Dance in particular is more sex-specific, reflecting the widespread belief in physical education circles that girls are more aesthetically inclined. The girls' programme is narrower, providing less scope for achievement than the boys'. A major survey of secondary schools in the early 1970s showed 9.3 games were available on average for boys and only 6.3 for girls.[40] Some of the games that are available for girls, like rounders and netball – games developed and popularized as female sports – are arguably less skillful, interesting and exciting. In primary schools the male teachers are much more actively involved in extra-curricular physical activities than the women teachers. In one survey 83.4 per cent of the men were involved compared with only 45.8 per cent of the women.[41] Although the men are taking girls during this time as well, it is likely that the difference in teacher involvement already depresses the level of involvement of girls at the primary stage. And the gap in provision gets wider with age.[42]

The incipient battle between the sexes around football illustrates the highly structured and constrained nature of gender divisions in school sport. It was the Schools Football Association which banned competent girl foot-ballers from playing in school league football, a decision obtained from the Appeal court, no less, after it had lost the original action in the High Court.[43] The FA recognized a separate Women's Football Association in 1969, but this did nothing to change football as a focus of male chauvinism. As in other sports, historically, sealing off women in a separate organiza-tion is a device which, while conceding male monopoly over the whole sport, also seals off the established game as a male preserve. It is particu-larly important, from the point of view of maintaining the status quo, to prevent interruption of the established processes of male-identity formation and socialization in the schools; for to be effective, socialization with respect to this process has to take place from a relatively early age. De-differentiation at the school level in physical activity poses a threat to one of the main bases of gender divisions. As in most power relations there is accommoda-tion to and complicity in the relation on the part of the subordinate group. There are some indications, for example, that women physical-education teachers strongly support the established sexual divisions. A study of the members of a women's football club found that when they were in school they experienced considerable hostility and opposition from women physical-education teachers to their interest in playing football and that they were discouraged from doing so.[44] In this sphere physical education may not be functioning simply to maintain the status quo, but intervening more actively to contain change. The potential for change is indicated by a recent survey among comprehensive schoolgirls, which found that over half of them want to play football.[45] There is some additional supporting evidence suggesting the conservative role of women physical-education teachers, from the School Council's survey of physical-education teachers' attitudes and values. Men favoured a more direct teaching style and women a more 'guided discovery approach'. It is, perhaps, not stretching the evidence too far to interpret the difference in terms of men favouring a 'tougher' approach, more appropriate for preparing boys for 'manhood', and women a more 'lady-like' approach more suited to fulfilling the established female role.[46] Also, intuitively, one suspects that boys, particularly working-class boys, are pressurized by girls into demonstrating their manliness and that competence at sport serves this purpose. More needs to be known about this aspect.

That gender divisions inhibit girls from participating, can be seen in the difference in girls involvement in organized physical activity between single-sex and mixed schools. In the former, class differences in levels of participation show up very clearly: middle-class boys and girls are much more involved, as are all 'academically able' pupils, a category which includes a proportion of working-class children. It seems that in the single-sex school, sport serves, in Bernstein's terms, the expressive order of the school, that is, in girls' schools involvement demonstrates achievement and compliance with the school's norms and values and girls are showing how good they are in comparison, not with boys, but with other girls. Similarly in boys' schools, such as the ones Hargreaves, Lacey, Willis and Corrigan studied, school sport is important in differentiating boys in achievement terms, and in their compliance with the school culture and in the process of male-identity-formation. In mixed schools, overall, boys are more involved than girls and here the gender divisions overlay class divisions in participation. In the mixed setting sport seems to become more important in establishing male-female identity and differentiation: greater discrepancies show up in the pattern of involvement between the sexes, in particular girls are not as involved as they are in single-sex schools. It is as if the interaction of the sexes in mixed schools creates greater pressure on both boys and girls to conform to the dominant stereotype and it is in this sense that girls are more disadvantaged in terms of opportunities for achievement in sport in this type of school. The same argument has been made with respect to the lower achievement of girls in maths and science.[47]

It is plain that sport and PE play a much more central part in boys' education than in girls'. Willis ingeniously argues, with respect to working-class boys' schooling and its function in the reproduction of unskilled labour, that the strongly sexist element in working-class culture has a large part to play in their school and work fates. In their case sexism is the active element in the way they are able to counter the school's attempt to incorporate them: they make the equation academic work/mental labour equals women's work/not 'real men's' work. But when we examine more closely the relation between gender divisions, sexism and PE, we can see that it plays a bigger role than Willis attributes to it. It can be seen as having just as important an influence, if not a more important influence, in a different direction altogether – it functions as well to integrate the 'more able' working-class boys, the comformists, into the school culture. There is no reason to suppose that sexism, as such, is less of a potent force among the respectable working class – across the class spectrum, competence in physical activity is equated with the manly virtues – but note that the appeal of school sport is skewed in the direction of those who are relatively successful in academic terms among working-class pupils, because school sport is also achievement oriented. It is precisely the latter aspect that kills school sport as far as the 'lads' are concerned. So, in the case of the achieving working-class boy, PE is able to harness sexism to the school culture. Whereas in the case of 'the lads', the centripetal force of sexism in PE is cancelled out for them by the achievement orientation of the subject, and consequently their particular version of sexism leads in the opposite direction, to a break with the school culture. Sexism plays a different role in each case and in doing so it divides working-class male pupils.

Ethnic Divisions

Contrary to the photos in PE texts which show relatively few members of ethnic minorities,[48] and where the impression conveyed is of harmonious relationships, racial inequality and conflict in Britain enters school sport as well. There is little recognition of the problematic relationship between race and PE in the PE world. Indeed, the different and specific needs of ethnic minorities in physical activity are on the whole misrecognized systematically. The lack of provision for ethnic dance in schools illustrates this well. In one investigation covering fifty schools, over half the dance teachers reported difficulties in teaching dance to immigrant children, and one of the greatest difficulties, apparently, was with the Indian girls' parents' social and moral objections. There was also great difficulty in getting Indian girls to stay for extra-curricular activities. Ethnic dance is actually very important to both Asian and West Indian girls, and dance was on the timetable in 62 per cent of the schools surveyed, but it was almost exclusively modern educational dance. Ethnic dance appeared very rarely – in only four schools and only for one period a week. In the words of this study: 'Very little effort was made to make use of the vast dance culture these children have to offer.'[49] Typically, the 'problem of race' is conceived in integrationist terms: the children of immigrant groups are identified as a behaviour problem and ways are sought of involving them in the school via the PE programme and school sport. There is some awareness of how PE in schools responds differentially to the needs of ethnic minority groups, but the predominant understanding of ethnic differences, as far as PE is concerned, is in terms of ethnic groups' physical differences: blacks are said to be less buoyant in the water than whites; Asian girls are said to be less able to adopt certain postures than other groups; West Indian pupils' natural movement tendency is said to be located in the lower half of the body; Asians' 'effort attitudes' are said to tend towards 'indulging attitudes'; and West Indian 'effort attitudes' are said to be towards 'fighting attitudes'.[50] The absence of a critical–analytical perspective on race in physical education is crippling here.

The differential involvement of ethnic groups in PE and school sport is due to social and cultural differences and not physical differences. Attitudes and ideas concerning physical activity and the care of the body vary widely from one ethnic group to another. What is considered appropriate physical activity for children in general, for boys as opposed to girls, towards revelation of the body, towards body contact and to personal hygiene, are all matters over which there is tension and conflict between some ethnic groups and the school.[51] A growing amount of sociologically informed research on PE and race shows this, and in particular, the role that school sport plays in helping to perpetuate the subordinate position of blacks and in reproducing racism in schools.[52] The level of achievement in school sport is closely related to ethnic-group membership. Among pupils of West Indian origin it is markedly higher than their level of academic attainment, and compared with white pupils their sporting achievement is higher and the level of academic attainment lower. The reasons for the relatively poor academic performance are complex: in general terms it is determined by job discrimination against adult black people, the nature of relations between black children and their parents – that is, the character of black families – and the clash between black culture and that of the school.[53] The relatively better performance in sports seems to be a function of a number of factors. The perceived restricted opportunities for success in other fields after leaving school encourages black children to see sport as an alternative way of achieving. In the case of the boys, sporting prowess is strongly identified with manliness. PE teachers widely assume that blacks are naturally better at sports, and promote black participation as an alternative success system for these pupils, as a way of integrating them into the school culture and of gaining prestige for themselves and the school. However, when head teachers and PE teachers implement this policy they inadvertently depress the level of academic achievement among black pupils, that is, they sponsor the child of West Indian origin as 'non-academic' and in this way help to reproduce the very set of problems resulting from black people's subordinate position in the society, that schools are ostensibly trying to alleviate. The response of black youth itself to school sport closes the vicious circle of racial inequality, indeed gives the process an additional impetus, an extra twist in the spiral of discrimination and conflict. Black pupils come to define school sport as their territory within the school and seek to exclude whites from it. This does not seem to affect so much the attitude of achievement-oriented, able working-class white pupils, but it does have repercussions as far as the other working-class pupils are concerned, whose alienation from school sport and incipient racism is reinforced by the perception that black pupils dominate in, and attempt to exclude them from this sector.[54] School sport therefore, is inadvertently divisive, rather than integrative of pupils from different cultures as it is intended to be: it integrates black sport-oriented pupils at the expense of further vitiating the chances of integrating lower-working-class whites by this method. PE teachers are not exceptional in their attitudes to ethnic minorities such as blacks: what are, in effect, racist practices are not caused simply by prejudiced teachers. They are sustained through structural and cultural processes which lock both PE teachers and their black pupils within a self-reinforcing set of constraints in which they are both complicit: it is in the interaction between them that the 'superiority' of black people at sport is constructed, lower-working-class white and black pupils are divided and their subordinate position reproduced. This 'solution' is never simply imposed, nor is it necessarily smooth-running: a mutual process of accommodation goes on between the school and black pupils. The pupils and their parents to some extent, are aware that school sport as an alternative success system reinforces the tendency to low academic attainment, and accordingly they resent and resist it.[55] Institutionalized low academic attainment among blacks is responsible for a further link in the chain of subordination, namely, the remarkable contrast between the prominence in school sport of black pupils and the virtual absence of blacks among the ranks of PE teachers – an absence, that is, of entrants to the profession who would be likely to be more attuned to the needs of black pupils.

9

State Intervention

The Structure and Rationale of Intervention

Apart from PE and sport in schools, the state intervenes on an increasing scale in sport and physical recreation through the local government and central government apparatus and through a variety of quasi-governmental and non-governmental organizations. The Home Office funds youth and community programmes involving sporting activity, it deploys physical training as a disciplinary instrument in youth custody centres and prisons, and is responsible for the Gaming Board and the Horse-race Betting Levy Board. The Ministry of Defence manages extensive sporting facilities and, like the Ministry of Agriculture, controls access to large outdoor recreation areas. The DHSS (Department of Health and Social Security) is concerned with health and fitness aspects of sport. Other government bodies impinging on sport and recreation include the Countryside Commission, the Nature Conservancy, the Water Authorities, the Tourist Boards, the British Inland Waterways Board, the National Parks Commission, and the Regional Planning Authorities. Increased intervention is due to the interplay of a number of social forces. First, profound social change was manifesting itself fully by the mid-1950s, in particular in a more egalitarian, independent, materialist spirit among subordinate groups, a fact demonstrated, above all, in the behaviour of organized labour, which was felt by dominant groups to constitute a potential threat to social order. The way this kind of perception came to be articulated, which has a direct bearing on state intervention in the field of sport and physical recreation, is in terms of the so-called 'problem of leisure'. It was recognized that the increasing demand from the population as a whole for greater opportunities to enjoy leisure – opportunities which working-class people had been relatively denied – had to be met concretely if their consent was to be won and the structure of hegemony was to be maintained intact. More specifically, the uses that some categories among subordinate groups made of their free time – notably working-class youth – were seen either as in some instances, positively 'antisocial' (then, as now, the rising incidence of juvenile crime was taken as definite confirmation of this), or as potentially undermining social order in the long run, because it failed to involve individuals to a sufficient degree in 'constructive' forms of leisure activity.

A number of official inquiries voicing these concerns were launched in the later 1950s, to the extent that their remit included the question of how subordinate groups spent their leisure, and their recommendations influenced the direction that policy on sport and physical recreation was to take subsequently.[1] The Wolfenden and Albermarle Reports for example, both focused on a dangerous gap in the apparatus of control between school and work: [We]...are not suggesting it [criminal behaviour]...would disappear if there were more tennis-courts and running-tracks...and at the same time it is a reasonable assumption that if more young people had opportunities for playing games fewer of them would develop criminal habits.'[2] Quite remarkable weight is given to sport and physical recreation as socializing agencies, Wolfenden's commitment to athleticist ideology being virtually total:

Certainly it can be said that in Britain there is an ingrained respect for certain attitudes which have their roots in sport...it is easy to ridicule the 'That's not cricket old boy' attitude. But in its deeper (and usually inarticulate) significance it still provides something like the foundations of an ethical standard which may not be highly intellectual but which does have a considerable influence on the day-to-day behaviour of millions of people.[3]

All the familiar claims are made concerning the valuable qualities to the individual and society that participation in sport is alleged to encourage – endurance, self-discipline, determination, self-reliance, loyalty etc.[4] Both reports, in singling out physical recreation as the key element in leisure, attribute to it a cathartic, compensatory function. As in PE theory, the claim is made that it offers the 'non-academic' and the less-skilled some significant element of compensation for their lack of achievement in school and work, in that it constitutes an alternative sphere in which commitments can be made and achievement gained. Crucially, sport and physical education are seen as activities affording valuable opportunities for social mixing across class lines and this is to be encouraged as a means of creating social harmony.[5]

A further motive for state intervention was the realization in ruling circles that in a more competitive sporting world, unless sport was state-aided to some extent, British prestige abroad would be likely to suffer – indeed that success in sport might go some way toward offsetting Britain's relatively declining influence in the economic, political and military spheres.[6]

The definition of the problem as one of social control in such inquiries, the instrumental and utilitarian view of sport that this entailed, the focus on the danger of some social categories escaping supervision during their free time and the stress on the need for leadership and guidance from authority, resonated with the structure of feeling among dominant groups. Such concerns underpinned policy formation and programming of sport and recreation thereafter. The proposals that emerged from Wolfenden were, in fact, very much in tune with what the two major political parties were beginning to advocate with respect to this realm – an advisory Sports Council, the rejection of a continental-style Minister of Sport, and some modest expansion of state aid.[7]

Thirdly, pressure to intervene in the everyday life of the citizen through the Welfare State apparatus was also building up, within the state apparatus itself, in the interests of administrative efficiency and of safeguarding legitimacy. The era, in fact, witnessed a major restructuring of the state apparatus along corporatist lines, as a strategy for defusing and depoliticizing growing class conflict. That is, Parliament was increasingly bypassed as a relatively inefficient instrument for coping with this problem and instead, the representation of conflicting interests was secured on the basis of their function in the division of labour, within state apparatuses specifically designed to facilitate the process of accommodation between them. The National Economic Development Council and later the Prices and Incomes Board, both of which brought capital and labour together, are examples of the strategy.[8]

Lastly, the sports lobby itself, i.e., those interests organized around sport and physical recreation, themselves subjected to strong economic pressure as a result of rising costs, falling incomes, and changing patterns of leisure and confronted by increasingly stiff international competition, skillfully applied pressure on government to obtain aid.

A relatively minor change at the centre in quantitative terms facilitated a qualitatively new departure in state intervention from 1965 onwards. A continental-style Ministry of Sport was abjured as alien to British democratic tradition and instead, a new state apparatus, a quasi-governmental organiza-tion, the Sports Council, was progressively installed at the centre. Leading figures from the existing quasi-non-governmental organization in the field, the Central Council of Physical Recreation (CCPR) and from other sport and recreation interests were appointed to it on a voluntary, unpaid basis. The CCPR's technical and administrative staff were mostly transferred to the Sports Council and a Junior Minister at the Department of the Environ-ment (DOE) was made politically responsible.[9] The Council's powers are limited by its small budget. However, the significance of the innovation lies not in the magnitude of its operations but in its strategic function: it formulates policy, co-ordinates the private and public sectors of provision, is responsible for long-term planning, research and development and target-setting; and it stimulates and advises providers. Direct management and control from the centre, is still largely absent: this is still either in the hands of voluntary organizations or local government (in fact, the major proportion of state expenditure in this sphere is still under the control of local government).

The restructuring was not simply a matter of the state unilaterally taking over the function of an independent body. The CCPR successfully stipulated conditions, which allowed the sport and recreation lobby to continue to play a key part in the new structure. Like its predecessor, the CCPR, the Sports Council's membership is informally representative of dominant groups and the special interests around sport and physical recreation. But the fact that the Council's members (about thirty, including the chairman and vice-chairman) are state appointees and that even in the early stages the CCPR and governing bodies of sport were reliant on state aid funelled through the Sports Council, means that sport now articulates with the power network in a way that accords the state a greater role. The membership has strong links with the establishment, with the business world, including commercial interests in sport itself, and with the two main political parties, but the sports and recreation lobby, in the shape of the CCPR and governing bodies of sport, secures the largest representation.[10] The latter nominates a third of the membership, provides the longest-serving and some of the most active and influential members and the top officials have a CCPR background. The PE profession and the sports elite are also well represented, but very few non-PE academics are included, apart from a geographer/planner. Representation of subordinate groups on the other hand, is negligible: women are a tiny minority with two or three members, ethnic minorities are hardly represented at all, and no working-class organizations, such as trade unions and working men's clubs are represented, unless the Labour Party members are counted. Clearly, the membership is related to the middle and upper strata of society, but the basis of representation, and therefore of intervention, cannot be characterized purely in class terms; rather, it is mostly based on function in the field of intervention. Strictly speaking then, although this is not a corporatist institution, whichever government was in power, from the mid-1960s a corporatist style of intervention developed in this field, going progressively beyond what was originally envisaged. It formed part of a social democratic programme until the late 1970s and became subject to the New Right's direction in the 1980s. The main lines of development were set when social democracy hegemonized the political scene – fostering equality of opportunity, achieving a degree of cultural democratization and creating a sense of community through welfare programming.[11] The strategy rested on the ability of government to synchronize state intervention and the private sector of the economy, so that sufficient resources were generated to enable appropriate levels of investment in the Welfare State to be made.[12] The strategic objectives with regard to sport and physical recreation are, first, to maximize participation, and to even-up somewhat the grosser inequalities in participation through a limited expansion of collective consumption in this sphere. The 'Sport for All' campaign, which exemplifies this strategy, also illustrates the method of achieving the second objective, namely the co-ordination of the public and private sectors of provision. On the production side, state intervention is designed to fill the gaps left by the private and voluntary sectors, not to replace them; and state intervention tends to assimilate collective and private consumption by promoting sport and physical recreation as a family-centred form of entertainment.[13] Thirdly, programmes designed to foster community identity are targetted specifically on sections of the population categorized as the 'unattached'. These put more stress on participatory democracy, and they view sport overwhelmingly in instrumental terms, that is, as an antidote to a variety of social problems, such as alienation, loneliness, juvenile crime, vandalism and hooliganism. Fourthly, the programmed provision of national facilities – the Sports Council's own National Centres, Sports Council subsidies to other major facilities in private as well as public hands, the promoting of 'centres of excellence', aid to governing bodies of sport for the development of national squads and the encouragement of business sponsorship of elite sport – all have as their main objective the development of a national sports elite capable of projecting a favourable image of Britain abroad, of serving as a model of positive achievement which the nation's youth can emulate and of serving as a focus of national unity.

The state sport and recreation sector has expanded significantly under this initiative in terms of the provision of public facilities, growth in the number of personnel, global opportunities for participation and the development of a national sports elite. Capital expenditure rose in absolute terms and as a proportion of total capital expenditure in the early 1970s, with new investment in sports facilities, particularly in indoor centres. From 1973–7 the number of sports centres in England trebled and the number of swimming-pools increased by 70 per cent.[14] After the economic crisis of 1975–6, capital expenditure started to fall and in an era of growing economic restraint and political uncertainty the atmosphere of confidence evaporated. Although the momentum of expansion could not be halted immediately, vigorous attempts were made to put the brake on expansion. This change of direction in policy was marked by the Labour Government's White Paper on Sport and Physical Recreation.[15] Much more emphasis was placed on cost-effectiveness, in view of the perceived limited capacity of the state to intervene positively with financial support; equality of opportunity was, in effect, abandoned and resources were henceforth concentrated more on the problems of 'deprived areas', that is, on preventing vandalism and delinquency, dealing with the consequences of unemployment and doing something about the plight of ethnic minorities. Secondly, they were concentrated on promoting the development of a sports elite and on the chances of success in international competition.[16]

Since 1979 when the New Right Conservative Government replaced Labour, and authoritarian populism has hegemonized the political scene in contrast to social democracy, the objective has been to 'roll back the Welfare State' and confront the political opposition as opposed to achieving a consensus, and to subordinate collective to private consumption. Cultural democracy and equality of opportunity are rejected in favour of cutting expenditure absolutely, recommodifying sport and recreation services, and making them, like health care, more of an individual and family responsibility. Rather than dismantling the Sports Council to meet these objectives, the terrain on which it operates has been shifted and in the course of adjusting to its rougher contours the Sports Council's priorities have shifted further away from their social democratic origins. Commodification is given priority in the way policy and programming are framed by an ethic of cost-cutting, capitalistic efficiency: small-scale, cheap schemes are preferred; provision must be more economically priced; business sponsorship must be relied on even more, voluntary schemes and private-sector initiatives are more favoured. The problem of social order is given special priority by injecting Urban Programme aid into schemes designed to pre-empt and defuse urban unrest, schemes of the kind to be observed in the 'brushfire' measures, taken in the aftermath of the Brixton and Toxteth riots of 1981. Equal priority is accorded to maintaining and developing the elite sector, in concert with the government's extreme concern with national pride and with setting an example of disciplined effort to the nation's youth. But despite the rhetoric of public-spending cuts, from 1979/80 capital expenditure in this field has risen, due to the large proportion of Urban Programme money spent on sport and recreation projects, together with money from other sources, like the Manpower Services Commission's (MSC) projects, which use sport to cater for the unemployed. Also, the net expenditure of local authorities on sport and recreation, as a proportion of their net revenue, has continued to rise throughout the 1970s and early 1980s, due to the previous higher level of capital investment in new facilities and the fact that charges to users only cover a small proportion of running costs.[17]

Rescuing the Community

State intervention in sport and physical recreation aims at normalizing individuals in specific ways. The discourse of successive Sports Council Annual Reports, of officially directed and inspired research, of the relevant government reports and of the White Paper, defines a low rate of participation among certain sections of the population as *ipso facto* evidence of mal-integration, and the benefits of sport are singled out as making a fundamental contribution to individual and social welfare.[18] Since intervention is premised on the assumption that every individual and grouping – decision-makers and executors, public and private sectors, users and providers, capital and labour, sponsors and sports bodies – all belong to a single entity, the 'community', programming aims at integrating those individuals and groups who are perceived as 'unattached'.[19]

The notion of individual choice at work here entails a model of the user of public facilities as a consumer, and state intervention aims at articulating perceived consumers' needs with public and private providers' plans. Hence, problems of marketing sport and recreation in terms of providers' definitions of needs tend to dominate the discourse. The Sports Council continually stresses the need for a good marketing job and counsels regularly on the problems of selling sport with the help and advice of recreation entrepreneurs and leisure consultants.[20] The 'Sport for All' campaign uses all available modern marketing and publicity techniques, and under its tutelage local authority leisure and recreation departments now offer 'packages' of activities to target groups in places like unemployment-stricken Corby in Northamptonshire. Individual Sports Council-aided projects like the London Docklands Sports Bus project and the London Interaction Sports Space Programme, function as 'delivery systems', either taking their wares to the consumer or dispensing them at conveniently placed outlets within a given area. Market research and programmed provision are thus supplemented by a dirigist strategy, which recognizes that consumers' needs are aroused and formulated through interaction between provider and user. Experimental provision is favoured, backed by continuous monitoring of use, so that adjustments and modifications can be made and the provision developed according to user response. Flexibility and sensitivity on the part of management is combined with an attempt to involve consumers to some degree in management decisions. This model of participation and control redraws the boundaries of the private realm so that the public realm includes more of the individual, but in a manner that, nevertheless, allows an affirmation of the primacy of the individual consumer and his/her needs.

Consumer culture indeed, permeates the pattern of state intervention whether it is social democratic or New Right-directed. In the former case, state intervention and social consumption, and private provision and individual consumption, complement each other; in the latter, privatization is given priority. Since leisure centres now find it increasingly difficult to cover the cost of sporting activities, they are beginning to give priority to developing non-sporting sources of revenue, in the form of sports-goods sales, providing bars and restaurants, vending-machine sales, solariums and saunas, dance studios, cinema, etc.[21] There is thus a convergence with the private-sector health club and the entertainment industry. Just as the normal individual within consumer culture is, above all, the family-oriented person, state programming aims at maintaining the family as a unit by involving it, as such, in sporting activity. The consumer-culture icon of the fit, healthy, young, well-adjusted, happy, attractive-looking, 'normal family', is now common to both private and social consumption.

Groups among whom significant numbers of individuals are perceived as deviating from the norm are targetted with specific types of programmes. The socially and the economically deprived are variously categorized: the 'unemployed', 'young people', 'those living in densely populated areas', 'the handicapped', 'the retired', 'ethnic minorities', 'those on low incomes', 'housewives', 'women', 'the over-fifties' and so on; but it is clear that the main concern is with the potentially troublesome – the unemployed, young white working-class males, and young working-class blacks. The concentration on aid to 'areas of special need', or 'recreation priority areas' dates from the Cobham era and it took a sharper turn in that direction after the idea was taken up and supported strongly in the White Paper of 1975.[22] The promotion of sport in such areas was specifically recommended by the Sport Council's Advisory Group as a solution to urban deprivation and alienation.[23] In 1976–7 against the background of a worsening economic crisis, local authorities were encouraged to consider small, low-cost schemes, and to appoint: 'leaders to encourage specific groups, e.g. the disaffected and alienated youth, to join socially acceptable activities such as sport.'[24] The formula was low-cost facilities backed up by inspiring leadership. The Department of the Environment (DoE) recast its Urban Programme, in particular, its Partnership Scheme with six metropolitan authorities, to revitalize the inner cities. The kinds of projects that were promoted were outdoor activities, boxing, five-a-side football, weight-lifting, table tennis, etc., that is, the kinds of activities that are not too expensive to put on.[25]

By 1979–80 social problem-solving achieved equal status with fostering national prestige as a Sports Council objective.[26] In its forward planning the Sports Council now virtually commits itself to giving the problems of social unrest and unemployment top priority and plans to shift expenditure over the ten years from 1982 'in favour of the community'.[27] As a start, over a three-year period, its Action Sports Scheme covering over 400 projects so far, aims to 'put leaders on the streets' in London and the West Midlands at a cost of £3 m.: '[Leadership]...is one of the most important factors in solving some of our social problems.'[28] In the wake of the Toxteth riots the DoE made its 'Merseyside initiative': £1 m., to be matched by the same amount from private and voluntary sources, was put in the hands of the Sports Council to provide sports facilities in the area.[29] This scheme has been extended to Bristol and Tyneside as a result of its perceived success on Merseyside.

The development of a cadre of young sports leaders or 'motivators' as agents of social integration, who are co-cultural with the target population, now has top priority, and the CCPR's award scheme is being developed to provide the requisite training.[30] Those who have either experience of unemployment, or belong to an ethnic minority group, or are women, are preferred. Also, a special scheme designed to ascertain how the unemployed can be attracted to sport has been started in three areas. These two schemes are monitored carefully in order to provide lessons for future patterns of intervention.[31] The longest-standing monitored scheme, 'Football in the Community', reveals the character of state intervention policy. In June 1978 following warnings on the explosive state of the inner cities, the Labour Government suddenly made available, at short notice, a special subvention of £2 m., over and above the Sports Council's budget, to encourage Football League clubs to develop their facilities for 'community use', in socially deprived areas.[32] The target was identified as unemployed youth, and a number of League clubs were selected for grant-aid. At Aston Villa Football Club the largest sports hall in the West Midlands has been constructed under the scheme, which was worked out between the club, Associated Dairies of Leeds, the local authority and the Sports Council. In return for giving £½ m. towards the cost of the new sports hall and to resurfacing the club car-park, Associated Dairies was allowed to lease the car-park and build a supermarket in one corner. The club was allowed exclusive use of the car-park on match days and 15 per cent of the use of the sports hall, which for the rest of the time was available for public use. The Sports Council's contribution was £250,000 and the local authority, Birmingham City Council, gave £400,000, which it obtained from central government's Inner City Partnership Fund.[33] In the same vein, a private body, the Football Trust, has given over £½ m. to the Sports Council, and another £¼ m. to be matched with the same amount by the Sports Council, for development of community facilities closely associated with Football League clubs.[34] It is, of course, not accidental that intervention focuses on football, the game with which the working class has traditionally identified, and which exerts such a strong pull on working-class youth today; for of all local institutions the clubs' prestige and their symbolic power would seem to afford good opportunities for bringing off social integration. State intervention aims at rejuvenating these local institutions, which have traditionally solidified the local community, by giving some financial assistance, but more importantly by restoring the link between the clubs and local people, from whom they have become remote. Other ways in which the Sports Council attempts to alleviate social and recreational deprivation are by giving grants to local voluntary organizations. The Sports Council is not the only source of state aid in this respect. MSC schemes often involve sports also, and both the Sports Council and the MSC collaborate on such schemes. The Home Office's Family Advisory Centres work in deprived areas building up contacts and relationships with local people and stimulating social activity. Sport and physical recreation activities again figure prominently: one account reveals that out of sixteen community and youth-work projects in one locality, roughly 40 per cent were of this type.[35] Another Home Office project, targetted at teenagers in the inner city, has the object of understanding their leisure patterns in order to attract them away from delinquency and to find equally attractive alternative activities. Working on the principle that the peer group is a fundamental influence in the lives of teenagers, the motivating idea of the scheme is to introduce sport to a group whose members know each other and to work through the peer group with a sympathetic adult, with the object of organizing alternative activities.[36] Such methods of penetrating and quietly missionizing within working-class communities by accommodating to their culture, with the object of reconstituting the community, have a long history indeed. They afford dominant groups entrée to communities normally closed to bureaucratized forms of intervention, and opportunities for exercising influence and leadership that are not seen as being imposed from above.

In the National Interest

'The nation lifts its head up high when our national teams succeed. It also takes to the court, pitch and swimming pool.'[37] From its inception the Sports Council has been concerned with promoting the 'national interest' through sport. It was in 1975, however, that the Labour Government, returned to power in an acute economic and political crisis, decided to give priority to the development of the elite sector, and thereafter it was accorded *de jure* equal first priority with solving social problems.

> Success in international competition has an important part to play in national morale. . . in the sporting world the pinnacle of achievement is to represent one's country. . . The government feel it right to give special encouragement to sportsmen and sportswomen capable of performing at international level and expect clubs and other bodies to give priority to international calls over local interests.[38]

Expenditure on the elite sector absorbs a major part of the Sports Council's annual budget. We have it on no less authority than that of the former Director of the Sports Council, Emlyn Jones, that: 'Governing bodies are about elitism at whatever level.'[39] The amount spent on the National Sports

Centres, run in the main for elite-level activity, together with grant-aid to the governing bodies of sport for 'sports development' – that is for developing the top levels – amounts to roughly half the Sports Council's grant from the government. Whereas its expenditure on regional and local facilities actually fell between 1982/3 and 1983/4.[40] In addition, very large grants are regularly given for the development of other national facilities considered necessary for staging international-level events. For example, £450,000 was earmarked for the development of Wembley Stadium as a national indoor centre, £1m. for the Lea Valley Ice Centre and £655,000 for an indoor tennis centre.[41] It is noticeable that financial stringency does not affect this category of expenditure as much as the non-elite sector.

The White Paper inaugurated the Centres of Excellence policy, a decision directly linked in the minds of its makers with national morale and prestige. The idea was to cater specifically for the 'gifted' by giving them special opportunities for high-level training, coaching and competition. In 1976 the then Minister for Sport, Denis Howell, approached all institutions of higher education to seek support in making provision for the 'gifted' and sought to encourage local authorities to give grants to such students to attend them. In 1978/9 the Sports Council received a special supplement of £1 m. to its grant to spend on schemes for the 'gifted'. There are currently over eighty Centres of Excellence specializing in about thirty sports and the Sports Council justifies such expenditure in terms of the boost they give to success in international competition.[42]

The development of young talent to serve the national interest has been a constant Sports Council theme: 'It is essential to provide a structure that allows talent to be identified, harnessed and developed from the lowest to the highest level.'[43] School teams were grant-aided for international competition almost from the start. In 1976–7 the Sports Council's overview of governing bodies' national squad plans was extended to take in their plans for youth squads. The Council has concerned itself with identifying and encouraging talent through the PE programme, in pursuance of which it argues that just as academically 'gifted' children are specially looked after, so the physically 'gifted' child should be.[44] The recent creation of a National Coaching Foundation is an important step further in programming the development of young talent. There are also plans to take the next step, namely research into stress on young sports performers at top levels.[45]

Sponsorship of top-level sport by business has become much more important as a result of government cut-backs. At almost exactly the time the elite turn was taken, sponsorship was more firmly integrated into the elite development programme, when in 1976–7 the establishment of the Sports Aid Foundation (SAF) was announced jointly by the Minister for Sport, the Chairman of the Sports Council, the CCPR and the British

Olympic Association (BOA). Its purpose is to raise funds from industry, commerce, voluntary organizations and the general public, to enable top competitors to attend university, to travel, and/or generally support themselves in the short term while they are competing as 'amateurs'. The Sports Council passed over £425,000 to the SAF in 1977/8 and thereafter has subsidized it on a smaller scale (about £30,000 annually). Since the Montreal Olympics, when seventy athletes were aided in this way, the number has at least doubled.[46] All concerned attach enormous importance to this scheme and to sponsorship, as such, for national success. In addition, the Sports Council and the government use sport to enhance Britain's influence abroad, through participation in international sports bodies such as the Council of Europe Committeee for the Development of Sport, through co-operation with the British Council in arranging study visits and courses in sports administration and management for foreign visitors, by sending delegations to international conferences, by organizing international seminars, through meetings of European Sports Ministers, and by assisting developing countries such as those in the Middle East, with their sports development programmes.[47]

The Effectivity of Intervention

Tempting as it is to do so, the effectivity of programmed intervention cannot simply be read off the programming. There are several dimensions of the practice of intervention to consider: the relationship between the Sports Council and (i) the central state apparatus (ii) the local state (iii) the sports lobby and (iv) the target population. Secondly there is the relation between central and local state. It must also be borne in mind that programmed intervention is not the only form intervention takes: politics can be overtly brought into sport, as in the case of the Moscow boycott and the boycott of South Africa; and the sporting event may function as a species of political ritual, as in the case of the Cup Final.

The Sports Council has a similar status to the BBC and the Arts Council, that is, it possesses a significant degree of independence, which enables it to act as a buffer between government and its clientele, in that the members of the governing body are voluntary, unpaid, prestigious part-time figures, whose co-operation is required if it is to function properly. It formulates policy to a large extent and is left to allocate its budget accordingly. On the other hand, the members are government appointees, government controls the finances and the staff have Civil Servant status. Governments come and go, but their powers to appoint and to finance are crucial controls. Under a social democratic strategy appointments were on a consensual basis, that is they were 'politically safe' rather than party-political. With the exception of some friction when the Labour Minister, Denis Howell, vetoed the Council's appointment of Nicolas Stacey as Director and insisted on Emlyn Jones instead, the working relationship between Council and government was relatively smooth. Under the New Right Conservative Government a chairman has been sacked – the first to go in this way – and the incumbent director and another top official, not necessarily sympathetic to the Conservatives, were removed; and in 1985 a more right-wing Minister for Sport replaced Neil McFarlane. With the appointment of the chairman of Liverpool Football Club as the new chairman, and of the former managing director of Wembley Stadium and of the sports agency West Nally as vice-chairman, the head of a football-pools firm as a new member, and the appointment of a more business-efficiency oriented new director, the Council's policy increasingly reflects the New Right's economic philosophy. The Council's grant from the government has also been kept within strict bounds.

A degree of autonomy has been exhibited by the Council, notably in its refusal to countenance the Conservative Government's attempt to enforce a boycott of the Moscow Olympics, and also by its out-of-step attempts to end the isolation of South Africa. But the chairman in question has been removed. Clearly the Sports Council has less autonomy and has become more integrated into the apparatus of the state.

Secondly, via the Sports Council, the state exerts a greater degree of control over the voluntary sports bodies than ever before. Again, he who pays the piper calls the tune. The CCPR, a formally independent body representing the sport and recreation interests, receives half its annual income from the Sports Council in the form of grant-aid. The main individual governing bodies are heavily dependent upon Sports Council grants: it pays 75 per cent of the salaries of 400 full-time officials;[48] provides many of the governing bodies with their headquarters accommodation; pays for travel, training and preparation for international events and for the development of national squads; it makes large capital grants for facilities; it runs the National Centres that these bodies mostly use. As the scale and significance of aid has increased, the more the Sports Council has scrutinized the recipient's development plans as a condition for giving aid, until now, it insists that they formulate objectives for years ahead and match financial aid to them.[49] Clearly, the potential withdrawal of financial support is a powerful inducement to comply and in the normal course of events sanctions have not even been threatened, let alone applied. The failure to take sanctions against the Rugby Football Union for contravening the Gleneagles Agreement when it sent teams to South Africa, may appear to contradict this, but it must be remembered that neither the government nor the Sports Council give the agreement other than nominal support, so contraventions hardly constitute a serious case of non-compliance with official policy. On the other hand, both government and the Sports Council strongly oppose drug use in sport and governing bodies who refuse to submit to monitoring for drug use have been publicly threatened with withdrawal of their grant.[50]

The CCPR and governing bodies are by no means supine and totally dependent on the state, for the restructuring of the state apparatus threw them back on other sources of support especially on sponsors. A running battle over finance and over the perceived growing weight of the Sports Council has developed. The CCPR went over the head of the Sports Council to complain to the Minister about the way the Council allocates its expenditure – and it has influential allies. The Duke of Edinburgh, its President, has called for a Royal Commission on the administration of sport; and the CCPR in 1980 and the former Labour Minister for Sport in 1985, have both called for a merger of the Sports Council and the CCPR and for a greater say for the latter in the new organization.[51] The CCPR and other sport and recreation interests are powerfully represented on the Sports Council itself and publicly orchestrated opposition can embarrass the Council and the government. Also, the co-operation and expertise of these interests is required if policy is to be implemented successfully. Having said this, it is noticeable that these interests have been conspicuously unsuccessful in raising the general level of state aid to sport from the centre.

Bearing in mind the relatively low level of expenditure, there can be no doubt of the Sports Council's effectivity in one respect, namely, it has presided over the development of a national sports elite which has transformed Britain into a major sporting power. More about this in a moment.

The Sports Council's influence on local authorities is small in quantitative terms since its grant-giving capacity is limited compared to what many local authorities, particularly the metropolitan authorities, spend. The influence it exerts is mainly through the growing centralization of technical services which it now has at its command, and consequently through the advice and information it is able to provide on all aspects, from facilities and coaching, to administration and marketing. It exerts influence also to a large extent, through the 'demonstration effect' of the projects it sets up, supports and monitors, at the local level.

Central government obviously exerts an enormous effect in general terms on local government operations through its control of the rate-support grant and it has done so with sport and recreation. More about this in a moment concerning the effects on the target population. Nevertheless, local authority provision varies enormously, for example London has the highest expenditure on leisure facilities (over twice that of the average non-metropolitan authority). Some authorities have used their relative autonomy, in effect, to continue to pursue a social democratic policy in opposition to the Conservative Government. The Greater London Council (GLC) is a notable example. However, precisely because of this opposition, central government has accumulated more power to bring expenditure under control by abolishing the metropolitan authorities and rate-capping authorities which have, in its opinion, over-spent. This means that although a rising proportion of net revenue has been spent on sport and recreation at the local level, total revenue out of which this is found is being constantly restricted by central government. Also, under the Urban Programme and through other agencies like the MSC, it is the centre which is able to decide which localities are to receive injections of special aid for sport. Thus Merseyside, Manchester and Salford and Hackney have benefitted disproportionately from the Urban Programme, compared with other needy areas.[52]

The effects of intervention on the target population are extremely complex and far more information is needed in order to assess them. First though, it is worth remembering that the state's capacity to intervene and control social consumption effectively in this field is limited by the structure of the British state. The price it pays for a relatively light-weight flexible apparatus is a relative lack of co-ordination at the centre, the different major ministries with some role in the field still acting independently of each other in many cases, so that, for example, the Sports Council finds difficulty to integrate its policy with the Department of Education and Science's (DES) policy on physical education.

The fundamental limitation on the capacity of programming to achieve its goals, in terms of normalizing the target population, is however, financial. Paradoxically, although the limited nature of public expenditure results in a failure to achieve the ostensible aims, it nevertheless makes an input to the power network possible, because it appears to be doing otherwise. And the one respect in which programming is successful, the production of a sports elite, makes a positive input to the power network by providing a focus for national unity.

From the mid-1960s there was no boom period in public expenditure on leisure and recreation; there was no major shift of resources in favour of subordinate groups; and therefore there was no significant equalization of opportunity.[53] Sport and recreation was, indeed, one of the first victims of the Labour Government's expenditure cuts in response to the economic crisis of the mid-1970s. As a result, Sports Council targets for provision failed to be met, and the gap between estimated need and current provision is now unbridgeable at current levels of input.[54] As in the case of educational expansion, what was achieved was a by no means insignificant absolute rise in the scale of provision, from a relatively low original level. The benefits of this expansion however, are distributed unequally. The main beneficiaries are, in fact, firstly, the middle-class and upper-working-class white men whose social advantages enable them to make fuller use of state provision, and secondly, a number of specific interests: the elite sector, which takes the lion's share of Sports Council expenditure, certain commercial interests which obtain subsidies for maintaining otherwise uneconomic facilities, and in general the business community, which has gained better opportunities to advertise. Vast inequalities remain in the pattern of involvement.

All the evidence on user patterns in the public sector points to a division between semi- and unskilled workers – that is, roughly speaking, the lower working class, who are under-represented as users and the rest of the population.[55] The lower rate of participation among the lower working class, among women and ethnic minorities remains true even when special programmes to involve them are mounted. Schemes for the unemployed, the 'Merseyside Initiative', and the Action Sport scheme, may attract attention and interest among the target population initially, but there is no evidence as yet that they attach them in any real sense.[56] The state lacks the organic connection with these groups to be effective: they are not even represented on the Sports Council for example, so it is forced into trying either to rejuvenate the existing organizations, such as they are, at the local level, or it creates organizations of its own, such as the various leadership schemes discussed above. Neither means of entrée to these groups' cultures has been conspicuously successful so far.

The communitarian ethic in this kind of official discourse and practice, if anything, articulates with, and operates 'localism', that is, it plays on whatever sense of corporate identity remains – and at the risk of quite serious unintended consequences. For example, in labelling the black minority as a problem requiring special programmed intervention and in promoting sport as of special utility in this regard in places like Merseyside, the West Midlands and London, Sports Council discourse and programming unwittingly reinforces feeling among white working-class people that blacks are a problem. It also complements the role of the schools in sponsoring blacks as 'non-academic', further sidetracking blacks into avenues leading to poorer educational and employment prospects. At the same time there is some awareness within the Sports Council of how ethnic minorities' interest and ability in sports can be exploited in the national interest. In the words of a one-time Director of the Council: 'In terms of excellence we cannot afford to ignore the ethnic minorities...we can get quite a component of our excellence, our prestige factor, from this source.'[57] The discourse and programming therefore perform ideological work at reproducing blacks' subordinate position.

Programming of 'Sport For All' has probably evened up equality of opportunity between the sexes in this sphere, but like the schools, it reproduces gender divisions by tacitly accepting the sporting conventions regarding the differences and encouraging development along conventional lines. At the elite level programming does challenge sexism in so far as better results demonstrate that women are capable of very high levels of performance, often commensurate with, or surpassing, those of men. Whether this counteracts gender divisions to any significant extent is doubtful. One indication that it may not, is the acceptance at the elite level of sexist practices like sex-testing women athletes – a practice the Sports Council, for example, has not opposed. Another is the generally low rate of participation among working-class women in particular.[58]

These programmes signal to subordinate groups that significant changes in opportunity can be brought about without the need for structural change. The causes of deprivation, disadvantage, community disintegration, dislocation and alienation, and of inequality of opportunity in sport and physical recreation, are absent from this discourse. Instead, problems are defined and prescribed for in a way which suggests they arise more or less fortuitously, and that they possess little or no systemic relationship to the character of the society. Social class and references to the structural position of other subordinate categories, which are inserted into the discourse in the coded form of 'deprivation' and 'disadvantage', play down their causal significance. The relevant problem is then taken to be how to cater for, and integrate, the recreationally deprived non-participators. And so attention is shifted from causes to treating perceived effects – notably delinquency, vandalism, football violence and urban rioting and disturbance – and with *ad hoc* solutions commensurate with the preferences of dominant groups. Thus, more sports centres, and cheaper facilities, and changing the attitudes of non-participants, are preferred to raising the incomes of target groups or the lowering prices of key resources which they lack, such as land prices in the inner city. The social structure is conjured away and what is left are individuals with their problems.

In prescribing family-centred sport and recreation as a solution to social problems, programming articulates firmly with consumer culture. 'Sport for All', after all, implicitly entails the opportunity to be unequal, that is, together with 'excellence' these are slogans which bring into play within this cultural field the ideology and the practices of competitive individualism in an extremely powerful form. 'Helping the deprived' is simply a corollary slogan. These notions legitimize, not only the social order, but also the state's structured selectivity in response to pressure-group activity around this particular sphere, whereby a relatively high proportion of the public funds available is channelled to the sports lobby and invested in a privileged few, who have succeeded in the competition.

Furthermore, and most importantly, 'excellence' discourse and programming, in so far as it successfully produces a national sports elite, provides a focus for the reproduction of national unity and for promoting Britain's prestige and cultural influence abroad. Intervention reproduces that aspect of the political culture in which sporting activity is symbolic of the national virtues and the superiority of the political system. To see how this works we must consider now the two other forms of intervention referred to previously, namely the political ritual that surrounds sporting activity and also the overt politicization of sport, both of which articulate on programmed intervention.

The modern version of the 'theatre of the great' whereby sport continues to be appropriated by dominant groups as a standard component of the political cultural repertoire, is, of course, neither programmed through the state sports apparatus nor appears as 'political': the achievement of such ritual practices is precisely to appear to be 'above politics'. The opportunities for extending the scope of sport as a species of political ritual have been enhanced by the state-programmed development of sports, so that ritual activity encompasses not only the great sporting occasions, but also occasions such as the opening of the local sports centre, the Olympic gold-medal winner receiving honours at Buckingham Palace, and the Minister for the Environment's visit to Merseyside to inspect the new sports facilities and so on. However, sporting events as such, do still constitute the hub of this form of ritual and they articulate on the structure of hegemony in particular, when they are staged around the great national festive sporting occasions and/or occasions when the prestige of the nation is symbolically at stake – the Derby, the FA Cup Final, the Wimbledon Championships, the Olympic Games, the World Cup, etc. On such occasions the national symbols and the pageantry are vividly brought into play by weaving them into the sportive occasion. The monarchy, members of the political elite and other national leading figures are usually in prominent attendance and/or participate in the ceremonial. Emblems such as flags, colours, uniforms, opening and closing ceremonies, parades, national anthems, hymns, martial music, victory accolades and presentation ceremonies, all form a constituent part of a political ritual whose ideological work celebrates, above all, national unity and the legitimacy of the existing social order. The subtle interpenetration of political culture and sports culture can be seen in the way sports discourse forms an integral part of political discourse in Britain. The metaphor of the nation or the local community as a team enterprise in which everyone 'pulls together' subordinating individual and group interests for the common good (the 'national interest') occurs with great frequency in government leaders' appeals for unity at times of conflict and crisis. The English language is replete with sporting expressions commonly employed in prescriptive discourse on social and political issues: 'playing fair', 'being a good sport', 'keeping to the mark', being 'on the ball', 'playing on a sticky wicket', hitting 'below the belt', 'pulling one's weight', 'pulling one's punches', 'getting carpeted' and so on. Social conflict, as well as social harmony, can be projected and reproduced in sports, and this means that they can also be drawn on by dominant groups to construct images of what constitutes a threat to the social order. More about this in a moment.

This brings us to 'political' intervention in sports and its relation to the power network. With the exception of the anti-apartheid campaign's effect on sports, sports in Britain were hardly politicized at all until recently. With recent events that era seems to have gone for good.

The Conservative Government's attempt to enforce a boycott of the Moscow Olympics illustrates how a sports event may be used to unify the nation, and how it may be made to function as an instrument of foreign policy by mobilizing chauvinist sentiments against a perceived foreign enemy. In this instance government pressure was brought to bear on sports bodies and individuals to make them comply, in a way that called into question the supposedly non-directive role of the state with regard to this sphere. The Foreign Office and the DoE at first even contemplated the idea of organizing an alternative Olympics, and the British Olympic Association (BOA), the voluntary body in charge of Britain's entry, was persuaded to defer its decision on whether to participate, while the government built up further pressure by getting a motion through the House of Commons calling for the boycott. Funds to the BOA were cut off by the British Olympic Appeal Committee (Chairman, Sir Anthony Tuke, Chairman of Barclays Bank) on the grounds that it was obliged to follow government policy.[59] The BOA's decision to go nevertheless, was publicly condemned by the DoE, the Prime Minister wrote personally to its chairman in the same vein, and when this failed, government sanctions were operated: diplomatic aid for the British contingent was withdrawn; the Defence and Civil Service departments, which normally allow special leave for competitors in their employ, refused it, and even prevented competitors using their holiday entitlement to go; funds collected voluntarily by servicemen and their families were blocked; and servicemen competitors were warned not to speak to the media. The chairman of the BOA was vilified in the House of Commons with the Prime Minister's support, and she appealed over his head directly to the athletes: 'Medals won at Moscow will be of inferior worth and the ceremonies a charade.' As the departure date neared the chairman of the BOA was called to the Foreign Office, and the Minister for Sport joined calls for the BOA to withdraw. A group of prominent businessmen wrote to athletes individually asking them to consider 'loyalty to their country'.[60]

In terms of its immediate objectives the campaign backfired almost completely: it incurred the implacable opposition of the main sports body concerned, the BOA, and it failed to stop the British contingent going; it alienated the majority of the competitors and it was opposed by the Sports Council. One of the most important counter-productive effects was that it made it impossible for the latter to operate on the basis that sport and politics are separate, in fact, it made it virtually impossible to claim any longer that sport is 'non-political'. Instead, it brought political conflict right to the heart of the state sports apparatus, since it inevitably involved the Sports Council. The latter, in fact, had become involved as early as October 1978 when a Conservative MP and member of the Council put before it a resolution urging the government to organize an international boycott.[61] The Labour Government at the time opposed the move, the Sports Council followed this lead and the motion was withdrawn. By adopting a neutral, detached position, the government and the Sports Council at this point thus preserved the traditional insulation between sport and politics. However, the Conservative Government's policy and actions revealed the somewhat anomalous position of the Sports Council: *de jure* it is an independent adviser to government; *de facto* its function had been increasingly to actively intervene in carrying out government policy on sport. If it were now to reverse its previous decision it would incur the opposition of the sports lobby, which would make it difficult, it not impossible, to carry out its function in the future. If it did not, it would incur the displeasure of the government which controls its purse-strings. In the circumstances it came down against the government and thereby, albeit unwittingly undermined the policy (as well, no doubt, as storing up a fund of ill-will against itself in that quarter).[62] The fact that the government did not achieve its immediate goal does not mean it necessarily lost popular support over the issue. Indeed, it may very well have strengthened anti-Soviet sentiment in the country, nevertheless, across party lines. The media's treatment, as we have seen, was uniformly hostile when compared with, say, the celebration that marked its presentation of the Los Angeles Olympics in 1984. And the campaign had the support of influential figures outside the Tory ranks, such as the then Labour Shadow Foreign Secretary, David Owen.

In contrast to this episode, the Sports Council itself took on a supporting role to government in a drama of national unity concerning Northern Ireland. In 1981, when the Republican hunger-strikes seemed to be effectively mobilizing world sympathy for the Republican cause, there was anxiety that government policy on Northern Ireland was losing its legitimacy. In the tension following the death of the hunger-striking MP, Bobby Sands, the English and Welsh football teams due to play there in the British Championships withdrew, and the Championships collapsed.[63] The cancellation of a major sports event in this context signalled to the world that Northern Ireland was not only an abnormal political entity, but that the IRA was winning. The government, recognizing the ideological importance of sporting events in this context, put political pressure on the Amateur Athletic Association (AAA) not to cancel its championships, which were due to take place in the province the following month. It was decided to launch a counter-propaganda campaign around them to convey the message that Northern Ireland was stabilized. The Minister for Sport attended the meeting personally, together with the Chairman of the Northern Ireland Sports Council and the province's best known athlete, Mary Peters, who also happened to be a member of the Sports Council. The view expressed by these spokesmen, that these championships had brought the community together and that sport was a peace-maker, was given great prominence in the media coverage of the event.[64] Steve Ovett, the Olympic gold medallist at the time, was held up as an example for all boys to follow, on the grounds that, as the chairman of the Northern Ireland Sports Council asserted: 'If schoolboys were attached to sport they would not go in for throwing stones at the army and the police.'[65]

In so far as this exercise in persuasion demonstrated the authorities' capacity to ensure the staging of major public events without disruption by the IRA, it signalled 'normality' to the world; and if Britain's international prestige did not exactly receive a boost, it is likely to have prevented further slippage, at least for the time being. The media certainly presented it as such: 'a little triumph for those trying to tell the world that life in Northern Ireland is mostly normal and that protest and violence are contained in certain areas'.[66] The reality, of course, is quite different. Sport, like almost every other aspect of life there, contributes to sectarianism and to the fragmentation of the province's extremely militant working class along sectarian lines, setting Catholic/Republican against Protestant/Loyalist. Sectarianism pervades sport there. For example, Craigavon Borough Council refused a grant of £300 to Lurgan Road Cycling Club on the grounds that it had previously organized a tour of Armagh which ended on a Sunday, and that its application was for an all-Ireland event.[67] The conflict spills over into British mainland football in cities like Glasgow, Edinburgh and Liverpool, where support for some League teams divides on Catholic/Irish v. Protestant/English lines.

The contrast between the Sports Council's and the government's role in relation to football violence shows how conflict around sport may be used by an authoritarian populist government to draw attention away from consideration of the causes of conflict by promising salvation through repression and retribution.[68]

State intervention over the problem of football violence, under the auspices of the new conservatism, has acquired a new dimension, in which the Sports Council, as such, plays little part. The issue is defined primarily as a law and order problem and outbreaks of violence in sport are used to popularize an authoritarian approach to social and political issues. Football hooliganism is regularly denounced by government spokes people, notably by the Prime Minister herself, in virtually the same vocabulary as that reserved for terrorists, strikers, 'muggers' and other folk devils. These moralistic tirades (themselves not without a menacing undertone of violence) exploit fears of football violence and of undisciplined, disorderly behaviour on the part of working-class youth. Their function is to mobilize support among the more respectable, conservative and vulnerable working class for a policy of confronting 'trouble-makers' in general, using the repressive apparatus of the state. Thus we have pre-emptive policing posing a serious threat to civil liberties: more arrests, the use of specialist units and of modern technology (video surveillance of crowds, computer link-ups, the 'hoolivan', etc.), heavier punishments and statutorily fortified football grounds. In contrast, the Sports Council's mode of intervention in the problem via the 'Football in the Community Scheme' operates at the 'non-political' level.

British sport has been at the centre of anti-apartheid struggles through which South Africa has been successfully isolated internationally in the sporting realm since the early 1970s, and with little positive assistance from government or state agencies.[69] The Labour Government's response to the 'Stop the Seventies Tour' demonstrations was to call on sports bodies to withdraw invitations to visiting South African teams because of the threat they posed to law and order. Official policy from then on has been to dis-approve of sporting contacts with South Africa and to support the Gleneagles and Lusaka Agreements between Commonwealth countries, opposing apartheid in sport while leaving individual sportsmen and teams free to visit that country and maintain links. The South African Government, with the complicity of some British sports bodies and individuals, has made strenuous efforts to re-establish sporting links with Britain. The hoped-for reversal of South Africa's isolation was boosted by the return of a Conservative Government, in that it refused to bow to pressure from the Anti-Apartheid Movement and it accepted confrontation with demonstrators in accordance with its tough stance on law and order.

The Sports Council has mostly kept out of the controversy, preferring to tacitly follow official policy. However, in 1979 it moved onto the centre of the stage by deciding to send a 'fact-finding' mission to South Africa for 'the purpose of examining and establishing independently progress made at all levels with the multi-racial integration of sport'.[70] At the same time a motion by the only black member of the Council, to withdraw the Rugby Union's £200,000 grant for organizing a British tour for the South African Barbarians' team was thrown out. Whether it intended to or not, the Sports Council aided the strategy of the South African Government and its supporters in this country, by giving an official blessing to the reopening of the issue, and indeed, a year later the Council was advocating the readmission of South Africa to the international sporting arena. Thus it entered the political arena, by opposing the multiracial sports organiza-tions in South Africa which wanted a stronger boycott, the non-white Commonwealth nations and the Anti-Apartheid Movement; and it accepted the South African Government's propaganda that progress was being made in multiracial sport.

The intervention, curiously enough, is consistent with the ideology that sport and politics are separate (a view strongly endorsed by South Africa) and also with the position it took on the Moscow affair. Boycotts of influential sporting nations are opposed because they threaten the international structure of sport, upon which elite development depends. Since it is also in Britain's interest not to alienate nations which support the boycott of South Africa – for unilateral breaches by Britain could also threaten the structure of international sport and Britain's substantial investment in it – the policy is to adhere formally to the Gleneagles and Lusake Agreements while working to persuade the international bodies to end the boycott.

10

Sport and Hegemony

Main Trends in the Relationship between Sport and Power

During the transition to, and the early phase of, industrial capitalism, sporting and recreational activity was characterized by class conflict. The movement launched among the dominant class to reconstruct popular sports and pastimes along 'rational recreation lines' met strong resistance among the emergent working class, and this, coupled with a degree of disunity among dominant groups, reduced its impact. However, divisions within the working class placed limits on the extent of that resistance and on the capacity of working-class people to innovate in this area, and so significant changes in the way subordinate groups related to sport and recreation were induced along rational recreation lines. The working class was integrated into the new social order more by repressive means then, and the reform of popular sports and pastimes was accorded quite limited legitimacy within the class as a whole. Integration was aided, in addition, by an accommodation at this level between the religiously inclined and the radically inclined working class, with that section of the dominant class which supported 'reform' and which was behind the rational recreation programme. In response, a bond was simultaneously created between the 'disorderly', 'disreputable' working class and that element among dominant groups which was prepared to defend popular culture as part of a rearguard action to maintain the traditional way of life. During this period, as far as this particular cultural sphere is concerned, the rationalizing elements neither established a hegemony over the dominant classes as a whole or over the subordinate class.

The successful achievement of bourgeois hegemony within the power bloc, as such, in the mid-Victorian period was signalled, notably, by the ascendency of the ideology of gentlemanly amateurism. Popular sports were reconstructed in the public schools and the older universities; a network of clubs and organizations catering for reconstructed sports, and for other new, more rationalized sports was created and organizations co-ordinating individual sports at the national level were founded. This institutional network catered overwhelmingly for dominant-class men: through it, the cult of athleticism became one of the most important sources of ruling-class male unity. With the exception of skilled artisans, who showed some signs of being attracted to, and accepted within, reconstructed sports, sporting activity therefore served to radically differentiate dominant from subordinate groups. The repression of 'disorderly', 'disreputable' forms of popular sport continued in the mid-Victorian era, but gradually became less important in the reconstruction process. A considerable degree of continuity with traditionally popular sporting forms was, in fact, maintained; indeed popular sports developed further, especially in parts of the country where the grip of the factory culture had yet to take a firm hold. Where the latter form of compulsion was experienced, sporting activity, while still differentiating the classes, provided at the same time a means whereby they accommodated in a manner which preserved the dominance of elites at the local level. But the unity produced among dominant groups as such, with the help of athleticism had yet to be translated into bourgeois hegemony over the working class.

Mass involvement in, and strong allegiance to, certain forms of modern organized sport, both as participants and as spectators, only crystallized in the 1880s and it coincided with the arrival of a more organized, independent working class on the national political scene. Skilled male manual workers and workers with a more respectable life-style, together with lower-middle-class male employees, were far more strongly attracted, and it was these groups therefore, that tended to constitute the mass following. Among them attachment to organized sports became a major source of male identity and a major basis for gender division. Although sports reproduced gender divisions between bourgeois men and women, they did not do so to the same extent, since the latter made significant advances in this field in this period. The demand for sports as entertainment was now backed by greater disposable income and by more free time, factors which spurred the commercialization of sports and which, together with the increasing presence of working-class people in this sphere and the development of professionalism, threatened to undermine amateur–gentleman hegemony in some major sports. The more thrusting capitalistic elements, which favoured a more business-oriented form of organization, moved into the domain of amateur sports to gain prestige and exert social influence at the local level, or simply as a business venture; and these elements acquired greater financial control, exerting more general influence over this sphere thereafter. Gentlemanly amateurism saved itself by conceding some ground to the new forces, and so the effects of commercialization were restricted and the hegemonic structure remained intact, since control over the voluntary sports apparatus remained mostly in the hands of gentlemen amateurs. Support for this pattern of conservation came also from the rational recreation lobby, which was deeply suspicious of what was seen as the deleterious influence of commercialism on the working class. Athleticism thus reached its zenith in the late-Victorian and Edwardian eras, when the British amateur-gentleman model exerted its greatest ideological and cultural influence, both at home and abroad. Moreover, it is precisely at this time that bourgeois hegemony over the working class is successfully achieved.

Missionary activity to the working class in various forms, using the appeal of sports, registered a significant degree of success in organizing the free time of young, respectable working-class men and skilled workers, in a manner which reinforced existing divisions between these groups and the rest of the class and further extended such divisions into the use of free time. Popular sports culture was appropriated too by the Liberal and Conservative Parties in their election campaigns and put to use in the political clubs they created to mobilize support from the newly enfranchised working class. Increasingly, notable sports events attracting large crowds were the scene of a form of appropriation by the political elite, around whose appearances on these occasions a species of political ritual was constructed, adding these popular settings to the already rich resources of the political culture. Working-class demands for more opportunities to enjoy sport were exploited by commercial interests and the business model of organization was adopted increasingly. Like the patronage model, the business model not only excluded working-class people from direct participation in decision-making, more importantly, in the spectator-sports sector it exerted a more impersonal form of control, encouraging the atomization of working-class clientele into separate consumption units. Concurrently with this pattern of expansion sports became identified more widely with a sense of a national way of life.

Such tendencies continued on an expanding scale in the inter-war period and organized sports at both participant and spectator level spread more evenly among the working class, as well as attracting greater numbers of women. Concomitantly, sports emerged as a central component of the national popular culture, which now functioned less equivocally to include the class within the nation. These developments were facilitated especially by the accelerating commercialization of sports, a process in which press and radio played key parts. The state also contributed to some extent to this dissemination of organized sports by promoting them in the schools and through local state provision. Although sports still functioned to differentiate social classes and in doing so encouraged a certain solidarity among the working class, on the whole differentiation functioned in a way that encouraged accommodation rather than conflict between classes, and the pattern of hegemony at this level thus remained essentially the same.

The 1950s marked a major turning-point. Since then, the more business-

oriented, commercially conscious tendency within the power bloc has
become hegemonic and sports have become much more firmly integrated
into consumer culture. The role of the state is now qualitatively different,
in that it is now consistently interventionist. The expansion of the sports
sphere, national and international, which affects all classes and groups,
places it in an even more central position in the national popular culture
and this, together with state intervention, has in some respects led to a
greater politicization of sports. Inter-class and intra-class differentiation
remains the hallmark of this domain: notably, sporting activity continues
to divide and fragment the working class rather sharply. The role of sports
as a source of divisive non-class identities has become relatively more
important, especially in relation to gender, age and race.

Division, Fragmentation and the Achievement of Hegemony

We have been at considerable pains to point out that this pattern of
development and of the contemporary relationship between sports and power
cannot be attributed validly in a determinist manner to any single factor
or process, or agent's action. It cannot be explained in terms of the dominant
class's capacity to bourgeoisify the working class. Nor is there evidence
of a conspiring, unified dominant group successfully putting its master plan
into operation step by step. No predetermined inevitable unfolding of
historical destiny (the dialectic, modernization, etc.) or 'hidden hand' was
at work. On the contrary, we have tried to show how this relation has a
contingent character: that is, it is the outcome of continual interaction
between opposed interests (of which class interests are the most important,
but by no means the only ones) adopting strategies in pursuit of their
objectives; that strategies are discursively arrived at in given conditions
of struggle and that the outcome is determined also by the autonomous
character of sport as a specific kind of cultural formation. Just as bourgeois
hegemony over the social formation, as such, is never guaranteed, so it
is not guaranteed over any specific realm, like sport, either. Rather, it is
a matter of continuous achievement, of work and practice at the structural,
institutional and discursive/ideological levels.

The turning-points in the relationship between sports and the power
network have occurred when a threat to the established social order has
manifested itself, and when the consequent interaction between dominant
and subordinate groups has implicated sports. At each of the turning-points
we have identified the sports apparatus was strategically redeployed: new
programmes were drafted and set in motion and new discourses circulated.
As the targets of the programmes resisted, even becoming recalcitrant and
attempting to bring their own alternative programmes into play, the elements

comprising the power network were strategically elaborated. The successful achievement of hegemony is contingent in the sense that the process has a 'value-added' character: the efficacy of single inputs or components depends on the prior installation of other components. Thus without the cult of athleticism, organized sports could not have developed. Without the rational recreation movement and athleticist missionizing, organized sports could not have penetrated and become part of working-class culture. Without a penchant for a popular version of organized sports among subordinate groups, and their move into some of the amateur–gentleman-controlled sports, the commercial development of 'mass sport' could not have taken place. And without 'mass sport' the political elite would have been deprived of the use of a rich cultural resource and the state of opportunities for intervening in elite sport in the 'national interest'. This is a contingent rather than necessary process, in that each link in the network depended on the creativity of different agents, on their ability to recognize and to seize opportunities open to them and to deploy their resources to maximum effect. Sports are not a central determining factor in the achievement of hegemony – they are more determined, if you like, than determining, but the relationship between them over the long term has become closer, as sports have become a weightier component in the national popular culture.

Sports have contributed to bourgeois hegemony in two different but nevertheless related ways: on the one hand by helping to fragment the working class in particular, as well as subordinate groups in general; and on the other hand, by reconstituting them within a unified social formation under bourgeois hegemony. On the whole, sports unify dominant groups and supporting classes, while disorganizing and fragmenting subordinate ones. In this sense, the divisions in the social formation – in particular, those among subordinate groups – and the dispersal of power throughout the social formation, are just as important as consensus among groups, and the concentration of power in the hands of any one group in the achievement of hegemony.[1]

Historically, different modes of participation in sports and the differing class identities and loyalties they have helped to generate, have divided the upper from the lower strata of the class: the respectable from the rough; skilled wage-labour from semi- and unskilled; working-class women from working-class men; and it has divided the class along local and regional lines as well. In addition today, it divides the traditional from the new, privatized working class, and in particular skilled workers and the non-manual working class from the rest. In all these ways it reproduces in broad outline the division of labour. This is not a question of a process reducing the class to passivity. Rather it is the specific nature of working-class responses to subordination (which have often been combative) that have enabled sports to be deployed strategically by dominant groups to control working-class people's free time.

It must be said that the conditions of struggle in Britain were not as propitious for contesting the cultural level as they were elsewhere. The political and cultural systems were relatively well developed and powerfully entrenched prior to the emergence of a working-class movement and the transition to industrial capitalism; so it was easier for dominant groups to channel the main thrust of the working-class challenge into a relatively narrow economic and political front as the nineteenth century progressed, culminating in the remaking of the working class at its end.[2] In contrast, on the Continent the emergence of the working class, the transformation of the economy and political and cultural change, were compressed in a conjuncture that reduced the capacity of dominant groups to channel conflict; and this situation provided a better opening for the working-class challenge to be made on all fronts – economic, political and cultural. The British working class contested strongly at the economic level; although the political challenge was weaker, it was by no means insignificant; but at the cultural level the challenge was weakest of all. Dominant groups made concessions on wages and conditions and on political representation, which in turn opened up potentially greater opportunities for advance on the cultural front. However, in these conditions of struggle, and given the strategies adopted by working-class people and by the leadership of the working-class movement, it was possible for dominant groups to retain a relatively strong control at the cultural level, which made an important input to their capacity to controll overall. The decisive turning-point in the relationship between working-class involvement in sports and bourgeois hegemony came in the late-Victorian and Edwardian eras, in the sense that the outcome at this point set the mould for the subsequent development of the relationship between the apparatus of sports and the power network. The political and economic resources at the disposal of the working-class movement were not negligible, but the ineffectiveness of its strategy at the cultural level and with respect to the significance of sport in particular, stemmed from and was an integral part of, the corporatist, economistic and labourist character of the class and of the movement.

Sporadic, often violent protest, more characteristic of working-class people's early involvement in sports and not unknown today, as well as other forms of illegality (attachment to 'cruel sports', disorderly conduct of various kinds around sport, illegal gambling) have at times induced dominant groups to make concessions ('collective bargaining by riot', as Hobsbawm terms it). But such forms of resistance have a limited efficacy: they lack direction and organization, are difficult to sustain, ultimately dissipate energies, and can be brought under control relatively easily through the developing technology of power. More importantly, they can be exploited by dominant groups, in that they alienate the more law-abiding, disciplined elements among the working class. Alternatively, the strategy represented by instrumental behaviour – exemplified in the colonization of bourgeois-controlled institutions dispensing sports, and which can be observed especially with regard to football – although it won concessions, was at the same time eminently exploitable by dominant groups. We will return to this very important point in a moment. The gains won through independent working-class initiatives in this sphere, which in the main took the form of locally controlled sporting activities based on the working-class community, were relatively small. Much of this type of activity was 'improving' and respectable in a way that made it virtually indistinguishable in terms of its efficacy as a form of resistance, from the rational recreation recommended and enforced by dominant groups and their allies. Again, energies were absorbed in unrealistic efforts at local control, it was difficult to co-ordinate and sustain all the separate efforts, and they were overtaken and subverted by commercialization relatively easily. This brings us to the significant absence of any alternative strategy and tactics at the leadership level, the lack of an alternative form of discourse to that of rational recreation and commerce, which proved to be a crucial negative constraint. From the emergence of the working-class movement in the early nineteenth century to the foundation of socialist parties – the Independent Labour Party (ILP), the Social Democratic Federation (SDF), the Socialist League and finally the Labour Party – there was little, if any interest in the way the working classes were involved in sports: socialist culture either could not accommodate sports and the body because of a rationalist, intellectualist bias (organized sport was either dismissed as a business swindle or a Tory plot); or it was viewed through virtually the same spectacles as the rational recreationists. The earnest, middle-class, Fabian, reforming elements that increasingly aligned themselves with labour towards the end of the century, and which exerted such an inordinate influence on the latter, simply grafted onto the pragmatic, reformist, often Methodist-inspired labourism of working-class leaders, a concern with extending to the masses the kinds of opportunities that they had enjoyed. The gains made on this basis were decidedly meagre, but above all, social democracy here could not mobilize popular support over this issue because it was not organically linked to working-class culture and to working-class people's experience of leisure. The few qualitatively different independent, radical initiatives that were launched failed to attract working-class support because of their apparently 'cranky' orientation and their overwhelmingly middle-class ethos.

Up to the First World War, as far as one can see, the organized working-class movement had virtually no effect on working-class people's involvement in sports, and consequently this cultural terrain was to remain uncontested. This was in marked contrast to other relevantly similar countries, like Germany and France, where specifically socialist sports organizations had been formed before the war, which were to be influential afterwards. In France large numbers of working-class people were mobilized for the defence of the Third Republic against right-wing and clerical reaction, through state subsidies to sports organizations sympathetic to the Third Republic, to which they were attached.[3] Also, compared with continental countries the working-class movement in Britain was virtually uninvolved in the sports organizations and activities of the Second International.[4] That this pattern was not inevitable and that there are unique features in the British case, is indicated by the qualitative difference between the struggles around sports in Britain at the end of the nineteenth century and subsequently in the inter-war period, and those that took place on the Continent. In Britain between the wars there was nothing like the opposition to dominant groups that was organized around sporting activities on the Continent, where an independent working-class sports movement emerged. Strong autonomous socialist and communist sports bodies were formed to combat right-wing and fascist attempts to gain the allegiance of workers through sports. By 1920 revolutionary communist sports groups had been formed in Germany, France, Czechoslovakia, Sweden, Finland, Italy and Hungary. In Germany in the late 1920s the membership of the *Social Democrat-Arbeiter Turner und Sports Bund* alone stood at 800,000. The workers' sports bodies in the different countries were linked through their own Sports Internationals, which even organized their own Olympic Games. In contrast, neither the British Labour Party nor the Communist Party exerted any effective influence over a domain which was assuming at that very time a rapidly growing importance in the way workers used their free time. The contrast is, perhaps, highlighted best by the role sport played during the most serious class confrontation in Britain in the twentieth century, the General Strike of 1926. Rather than sports providing a rallying point for working-class resistance to employers and the government, it was thought desirable on both sides to organize football matches between police and strikers.[6]

Meanwhile a socialist transformation of sport was attempted in pre-Stalinist revolutionary Russia where, freed from commercial constraints, under the influence of the Proletkultists and Hygienists, competition was minimized, practices dangerous to physical health were curbed and the health and fitness of the population were promoted through sports.[7] A British team, in fact, visited the 1928 Workers' Spartakiad where twenty-one different competition sports were played. Pageants and displays, carnivals and mass games were organized, all forming an integral part of the proceedings. There were motor-cycle and motor rallies, demonstrations of folk games, music and dancing, poetry readings and mock battles between the 'world proletariat' and the 'world bourgeoisie', in which all participated.[8] In the 1920s the Social Democratic Lucerne Sports International aimed at creating a sports movement equal in importance to political and economic organization, as part of a proletarian subculture. It envisaged and, in fact, organized, workers' Olympiads, with parades, red flags, mass exercises, performances of plays and mass choirs singing socialist songs. It is not our task here to go into the question of the viability of such emancipatory projects. We simply note that the Workers' Sports Movement in Germany was suppressed by the Nazis and the experiments in the USSR terminated by Stalin. The relevant counter-factual evidence on sports as a potential arena of resistance to control by dominant groups is to be observed in France. Under the Popular Front in the later 1930s socialist workers' sports clubs embraced 103,000 members, and Lagrange's massive programme of sport for all, aimed at improving sport and physical recreation facilities and stimulating active participation, was launched against the threat from the Right, with great elan and success.[10] With the exception of the Communist Party-inspired British Workers' Sports Federation, (which, in fact, had little influence on sports overall) no such developments occurred in Britain, let alone were initiatied from within the working-class movement. Here, although dominant groups did not overtly politicize sports as on the Continent, informally they had exerted a conservative influence through sporting activity for a long time, and in contrast, the attempts to counteract influence at this level by progressive forces were minuscule.

Social democratic and reformist as it undoubtedly was, the Popular Front's sports policy had a qualitatively different function at this conjuncture, because it presented a real alternative rallying point for working-class resistance to the threat of fascism and thus it was able to contest this terrain effectively. The policy caught the imagination and did much to sustain the allegiance of French workers in that struggle, and it left a legacy of goodwill among the French working class towards the Left, as well as a widespread awareness among the population of its cultural importance. One of the results is a higher level of public spending on sport than in Britain. Another is the fact that some of the most critically penetrating analyses of sports as cultural forms have tended to emanate from France.

It was not until the 1960s that an attempt was made to extend sport to all in Britain and it was under a Labour Government. Unlike the Popular Front's sports programme it signally failed to catch the imagination and hold the allegiance of the working class. No qualitatively different alternative was posed to what was by now a more developed, dense imbrication of sports in civil society. Limited in scale, lacking in vision, it failed to make a political impact: having no alternative set of priorities to those articulated in rational recreation and commercial discourse, it merely represented a pallid synthesis of the two. Unlike the 1930s, the contrast with the Continent is not so startling today, which of course raises the question of whether the workers' sports movement was specific to the conditions of the 1930s. Today as we have pointed out, there is still a difference between the two countries – the greater level of public spending in France and the more sophisticated understanding on the Left of the social and political significance of sport. And the latter point is true of Italy as well.

Undoubtedly, working-class people have made gains in this domain: opportunities for enjoyment have been enhanced and extended and sporting careers have been opened up to more working-class people. But these gains were made in an expansive process of accommodation, through which bourgeois hegemony was achieved. The new techniques of control, in successive strategic elaborations, defused conflict by increasing the capillarity of the power network. The fragmentation of the working class reproduced in sporting activity through differences in the mode of involvement within the class, help to disorganize the class at this level and help to reassemble it within the hegemonic structure.

Among the non-class, autonomous factors contributing to the process of fragmentation, gender has been crucial. Sporting activity played relatively little direct part in the disciplining of women and girls in the nineteenth century, a task which was carried out mainly by the family. However, the burgeoning of organized sports as a male preserve, first in the production of 'gentlemen' in the public schools, and then in the last quarter of the century among the working class, increased their importance in reproducing gender divisions and chauvinist versions of masculinity. Working-class women in particular, were excluded from equal participation in this growing popular sphere of free-time activity. Middle- and upper-class 'ladies' managed to resist and overcome exclusion to a significant extent and by the First World War had achieved a limited entry, on terms which still largely accommodated to the prevailing division between 'ladies' and 'gentlemen'. Further gains between the wars and since, have narrowed the differential more.

It is particularly among working-class people that sporting activity sharply differentiates the sexes in a manner which subordinates women. Class identity for working-class men is strongly tied up with sexual identity (a common critical perception of the dominant class among working-class men is that they are effeminate) and it profoundly affects the manner in which the two halves of the class relate. In response to their subordination working-class women have tended to adopt the strategy of constructing a version of respectable family life, a strategy which dovetails with that which has received wide support among dominant groups for disciplining the working-class man, notably through state regulation of the family. Class and gender relations are thus constructed together and a double conservatizing influence is exerted over the class as a whole. For working-class women's subordination is mediated by their subordination to working-class men, and an important dimension of this division is the unequal access to free-time activities such as sports. The subordination of the class as a whole is thus reproduced, for women's subordination evidently inhibits the extent to which they can be fully participant class actors. In an era when traditional male identity is increasingly threatened by occupational change and by feminism, sporting activity is one of the main ways in which a male chauvinist identity is constituted. Functioning in a corporatist manner, as a haven into which working-class men can retreat and gain relief from social pressure and thereby acquire some sense of dignity and achievement, sports compensate working-class men for their subordination at the expense of working-class women. Starting early in childhood the process is strongly reinforced during adolescence and is one of the major ways young men are inducted into male roles. The resulting sexual divisions are particularly marked in working-class youth culture: working-class girls are the least involved sector of the population in sports (with the exception of Asian girls). These divisions are powerfully reproduced in school sports, the PE programme being one of the few remaining areas of the school curriculum to formally segregate the sexes and restrict opportunities to participate equally with boys.

Media sport reproduces conventional images of masculinity and femininity and it assimilates its depiction of sports to the depiction of male–female roles circulating in consumer culture. Although state intervention has extended opportunities to women and girls in the sports sphere, the extension takes place within a framework which does little, if anything, to challenge the global structure of gender inequality in sports. On the whole then, the gender factor in sports adds yet another force to those which fragment and disorganize the working class.

In the nineteenth century the problem of what to do with working-class youth increasingly occupied the attention of dominant groups and their allies. A battery of voluntary youth organizations drew on the burgeoning sports culture as one of the main instruments of control, a tradition which lives on in the state schools, the youth service, and the Sports Council in the present century. The main result of the interaction of working-class culture with voluntary organizations, missionary work, commercial ventures in the field and the various forms of state intervention, is to reproduce the intra-class divisions already outlined. Since the 1950s the interplay between these forces also produces a distinct working-class youth culture, in which football functions as a major reference point, which in some ways is quite opposed to adult working-class culture. Once a game which unified younger and older working-class men, football now expresses, to some extent, lower-working-class youth's frustration with, and rebellion against, its condition and its extreme subordination. It is also a source of conflict and of sharp antagonistic intra-class divisions between older and younger generations.

Sporting pastimes have traditionally promoted a sense of corporate identity at the local community level among working-class people, which tends to isolate one local community from another and, indeed, to promote rivalries between them. In this way sports have traditionally encouraged a stronger sense of class solidarity at local and regional levels than they have nationally.

Since non-white ethnic groups tend to be widely regarded within working-class communities as outsiders, to some extent participation in sports divides along ethnic lines. The division is strongly reproduced in school sport, where black pupils in particular are side-tracked into sports as an alternative to academic achievement, which for them is generally lower than that of whites. The statistical over-representation of blacks in school sports alienates lower-working-class non-achievers even further from organized sport. The division is compounded by media sport, which tends to restrict the transmission of positive images of blacks to their success in sport and entertainment. This, together with the fact that media sport tends to project ethnic stereotypes with racist overtones in its coverage of international sport, reproduces the widespread racism within working-class communities. In identifying young blacks in urban areas as a major social problem, state programming of local community sport implies it is their presence and character, as such, rather than structural and cultural features of the society, that is the cause of racial conflict. In these ways sport tends to reproduce racial divisions and to play some part in distancing working-class whites and blacks.

Integrating Forces and the Achievement of Hegemony

The process whereby the working class, and subordinate groups as a whole, are unified within the social formation under the hegemony of the dominant class, is the other side of the coin of the fragmentation process. Two processes are of particular relevance here with regard to the role of sport: the consolidation of consumer culture and the construction of national identity. In response to potential instability in the social formation in the second half of this century, a further strategic elaboration of power has taken place, which has renewed and refurbished bourgeois hegemony. Since the 1950s the struggle for control over production and for political control has been more firmly displaced to the sphere of distribution and consumption and the latter has become a far more central element in the apparatus of power and control. Consumer culture incorporates key features of popular and of working-class culture, and it therefore cannot be adequately conceptualized simply as capitalist-determined 'mass culture'. It is precisely the autonomy of consumer culture and of sports as a cultural formation, which facilitates the displacement of economic and political struggle to this region, and enables consumer culture to stimulate production and confer legitimacy on the system. Although commercialism and professionalism then, hegemonize organized sports, and all major groups in the social formation are involved in sports as a commodity form, the sports apparatus is not uni-directionally determined by these forces.

Sports as an aspect of consumption are increasingly made to bear the brunt of frustrated desires. The established groups, institutions, individuals, discourses, knowledges and movements that comprise the sports apparatus have been extended and elaborated, new elements added, and the whole ensemble reassembled to form a more dense, complex, subtle and flexible apparatus with a variety of elements. We now have the new breed of leisure and sports entrepreneur, the sports celebrity, administrators and coaches, advertising industry and other sponsors, media-sport professionals, PE professionals, Civil Servants, government ministries, government commissions, local state leisure and recreation professionals, the Sports Council, the modern hygiene and fitness movement, social democracy, and the attendant discourses, knowledges and ideologies. Concomitantly, the sports apparatus has become articulated on a new regime of discipline and surveillance, a shift in the balance of forms of control has taken place – from control by prohibitive, denying techniques associated, broadly speaking, with the cult of the Protestant ethic, to control by stimulation, that is, the power network is a more productive, expansive and positive entity.[11] Consumer culture's strength derives from its ability to harness and channel body needs and desires – for youth and longevity, beauty and sexual fulfillment, health, and the eternal quest for freedom, enjoyment, excitement, achievement and self-expression.[12] Sport, which has become in this age perhaps, the means of body expression *par excellence*, feeds such needs with rewarding experiences of its own – of fitness, movement, energy, force, speed, play, competition and dramatic, ritualized activity. Sports, together with other cultural forms centring on body needs and desires – fashion, cosmetics, dieting, cooking, etc. – are now firmly articulated on consumer culture, in a two-way determined/determining relation. However, jettisoning the Protestant ethic does not entail any fundamental change in the relations of production, or of the political order. Rather, it is that consumer culture makes hedonism respectable, indeed, it makes it virtually mandatory.

It is not accidental that one of the key prescriptive tenets in this culture, the promotion of family-centred life, now makes it appearance increasingly in the theatre of sport. Sport is increasingly sold as a family-oriented activity – media sport is for the family, and participating together as a family is encouraged at the local sports centre or club, or holiday centre. In this manner one of the main thrusts of sporting activity coincides with that of

consumer culture, namely the recomposition of the working class and
subordinate groups as an aggregate of privatized family consumption units,
a network of discreet gender- and age-structured units for the production
of normalized individuals. The family is to be the site where normal male
and female bodies are constructed, where body needs and desires are
channelled and normally fulfilled. Gender relations within the family are
absolutely crucial to this process of class composition through the stimulation
of commodity consumption.

Age relations are significant in this process as well. If working-class youth's
mode of attachment to football divides generations, what unites them about
consumer culture is the cult of eternal youth, which is one of its major
hallmarks; and one of the main ways in which the promise of youth is held
out to the older generation by consumer culture is through the promotion
of sporting activity. Again, it is a process in which the media play a key
part in bringing off this aspect of accommodation. The linkage between
consumer culture and sport then, does not represent an emancipation from
control: it is about the joy of subjecting the body to continual sensation,
of one's own will.[13] The uncompromising quality of the jogging cult, for
example, and the imperative encoded in the way that highly erotic advertising
depicts the body ('Get undressed – but be good-looking slim and tanned')
attest to the formidable regimen of discipline and surveillance that this
culture can entail.[14] The drive within this culture to transform the body
into a receptacle of continuing sensations is a powerful drive to give meaning
to one's life in certain terms: to do something about one's body in this
context is to do something about one's life.[15] Originally aimed at the
middle classes in the 1920s, it must not be supposed that the bounties of
this culture are equally enjoyed by the entire working class, a considerable
proportion of which are still excluded, or only partially included. However,
the majority of the class has been sufficiently implicated since the 1950s
for this experience to be a significant factor over the whole period in the
achievement of hegemony.

The state makes a major contribution to the commodification of sports,
first by providing a network of facilities complementing rather than
competing with the private-sector enterprises. Secondly, it does so through
its policy of promoting sponsorship schemes – and sponsorship, it should
be remembered, is the most important factor in the contemporary commercialization of sport. It does so also by subsidizing financially ailing sports
so that they can survive in the market. Sponsorship is attracted to sport
overwhelmingly at the elite level: it is this level which attracts the attention
of the media, and media sport is the epitome of consumer culture. The
BBC, a state corporation, may have done more to transform sport into
an aspect of consumer culture than any other single institution. Thus, the
state promotes sport as a commodity and it is precisely this aspect of sport

which successfully involves the working class as a whole. The state, by promoting sport as consumer culture, thus makes a major contribution to the process of working-class accommodation to the social order that takes place in general around consumer culture. The recent movement in the state schools to make PE optional, to broaden the programme and to make it more recreational, seems to be both an assimilation to, as well as an attempt to exploit, consumer culture, in order to further the school's own objectives.

From the mid-Victorian period to the First World War the cult of athleticism reproduced a sense of national identity among dominant groups. As jingoistic sentiments reached a crescendo in these circles at the latter end of the period, sports were increasingly looked to among dominant groups as a useful means of uniting an increasingly divided nation. Although it is doubtful whether the attempt to unite the lower and the higher orders by these means was successful in generating an identical sense of nation among both, the immense popular support for the First World War at its outset is one indication, not only of the ease with which dominant groups were able to strike a chauvinist chord among working-class people, but of the latter's very firm sense of inclusion within the nation, to which attachment to sports is likely to have contributed. The sight of British troops advancing over no man's land to attack the enemy trenches, kicking a football ahead of them as they went to their deaths in the First World War, is one of the more macabre indications. In the inter-war period the expansion of international sporting competition strengthened the association between elite-level sport and nationalist sentiment. The effects on the British working class are difficult to estimate. It seems likely that popular sports, like football and cricket, were increasingly coming to express a sense of national unity that was not confined to dominant groups. One indication that this was so is the way those working-class heroes of the 1930s and 1940s – the professional footballers like Stanley Matthews who were household names, were exempted from military duties during World War Two and were deployed, basically, as entertainers to keep up the troops' morale.

The post-war expansion of sporting activity has made high-performance sport almost synonymous with the nation, and the chief mechanism in this process has been the media. The modern propensity of dominant groups to incorporate the great sporting occasions into the panoply of political ritual, makes sports simultaneously a discourse on the state of the nation, its virtues and its interests. One of the prime objectives of the Sports Council's programme to develop sport is to promote national unity and the prestige of the nation abroad. We must distinguish between the reproduction of an integrative national sentiment in sports, and the nationalism of the periphery, expressed in certain sports like Welsh rugby and Scottish football, which comes close to synthesizing a sense of suppressed nationhood with a sense of class oppression in these regions. The 'Britishness' and 'Englishness' expressed in sports has been, until relatively recently, muted in comparison with this, and with the more strident doctrinaire brand of nationalism that surrounds sports in many other countries.

There is little doubt that sports have become more important in constructing the nation and that this tends to cut across class. Today, probably more than any other component of the national popular culture, sports have come to symbolize a national way of life, over which bourgeois hegemony has been achieved. Although this sense is likely to differ between dominant and subordinate classes and groups, the key point is that the working class sense of national unity reproduced around sports is a conservative force, even when, as in the case of football hooliganism, it takes the form of disruption strongly disapproved of by authority. Working-class jingoism and racism thus expressed is the uglier face of national identity. One of the most important contributory factors to the association between sport and national identity is the progressive incorporation of sports into consumer culture which is broadly speaking, coextensive with the nation as a whole, and which encompasses the majority of the working class. Among its multitudinous components, sport is the one which can be made most readily to symbolize the nation.

Emancipatory Potentialities?

Hegemony is never guaranteed: it must be worked for continually and renewed by the hegemonic class or class fraction. So the analysis of its achievement entails the critical question as to what extent an emancipatory politics of sport and the body is possible. The issue, as Hall has cogently pointed out, is the extent to which the politics of the popular provides a point of resistance and challenge to bourgeois hegemony.[16] Clearly, this is dependent upon the extent to which struggles between dominant and subordinate groups in this field link up with struggles in other fields. Hall points to the contradictory character of popular culture: it possesses a critical, dissatisfied, discontented and disruptive side, as well as more conservative, compliant, conformist aspects, which provide positive support for the social order. It is precisely this ambivalent quality that constitutes its strength from the point of view of its integrative function, but it also constitutes a potential weakness, making it susceptible to contestation. As a matter of fact, conflict is rarely absent from some sphere of sport, whether it be over blood sports, or football violence, or South Africa. But there are several ways in which sport as a cultural form is being more systematically transformed into a contested terrain, and which render it problematic as a theatre of accommodation between dominant and subordinate groups. Sport is being moved closer to the centre of the political stage as fissures appear in the apparently apolitical face of sport, through which subordinate groups are able to challenge bourgeois hegemony to a greater extent than previously.

The first fissure is created by the way government handles the problem of the alienated population of the inner cities. There is now what amounts to a surplus population in these areas, in the sense that it cannot be absorbed by the mode of production. Among the unemployed and their families, lower-working-class youth and black youth, in particular, is an extremely volatile element, as has been demonstrated in the series of explosions from Toxteth in 1981 to Tottenham in 1985. An increasing proportion of the population has never experienced the rigours and the integrative force of labour discipline; and low incomes among this group drastically restrict access to consumption. Leisure therefore, instead of providing a means of accommodating them to the social order, is experienced as one more dimension of deprivation and alienation. Bauman has speculated that this surplus population now presents a problem equal, in principle, to that which necessitated the redeployment of power in the seventeenth and eighteenth centuries.[17] There is no doubt that some kind of redeployment is now taking place, with the shift from social democratic, corporatist strategy for dealing with the problem of crisis management and 'legitimacy deficits' (to use Habermas' terminology) towards a more authoritarian mode of intervention under the new conservatism.[18] What is becoming increasingly clear is that the latter form of intervention, which restricts provision for sport and leisure and attempts to reverse the (admittedly half-hearted) previous policy of 'Sport for All' is generating a struggle over provision in this area, just as it has in others. State intervention in sport, rather than accommodating dominant and subordinate groups, tends to polarize them in such circumstances. For example, for blacks, the demand for more opportunities for sport and recreation is not only a demand for a better environment, but organized sport is now also a source of black pride and dignity, a way of asserting a separate identity, and of resisting subordination.

The conflict between central and local government over the provision of social services is a good illustration of the principle that state intervention, rather than solving problems, shifts the conflict to the level of the state apparatus. The more the state intervenes in aspects of the social formation which have traditionally reproduced social relations 'spontaneously', as it were, without state intervention, the more they become polititicized and their legitimizing function threatens to be undermined. The issue of how free time is spent and how the material resources necessary to structure it appropriately are allocated, is now an urgent political issue which can hardly be kept to the margins of the political agenda any longer.

Sport has also become more politicized and has suffered a decline in its legitimacy-conferring function for other reasons of course, as in the case of the Conservative Government's clumsy attempt to secure a boycott of the Moscow Olympics and its negative attitude to the campaign to bring pressure to bear on South Africa through sporting sanctions. The latter conflict has implications for ethnic divisions in this country, in the sense that the Conservative Government can be perceived as being unsympathetic to the plight of both the black British and the black South African populations.

The second set of forces tending to make sport a problematic contested terrain stems from the fact that the attempt to subject sports to a capitalistic pattern of rationalization and to programme sport in the 'national interest' exists in tension with the nature of sport as an autonomous means of expression. The autonomy of sport places limits on its use value, beyond which any legitimizing, accommodating function it may possess tends to be jeopardized and conflict generated instead. The tendency inherent in the commercialization of sport, to transform it into an entertaining spectacle, runs the continual risk of raising the following's expectations of excitement, etc. faster than sport organized along such lines can satisfy them, and therefore of ultimately alienating the audience. Secondly, ruthless sporting competition, whether commercially or politically structured and motivated, can have unforeseen, counter-productive effects. The pursuit of success at all costs against the opponent does not necessarily produce the most exciting spectacle, especially when the strategy adopted is the negative one of avoiding defeat. It may also result in systematic rule-breaking on the part of contestants and the organizations behind them, outbreaks of violence in and around sports, scandals and the growth of insensitive bureaucratic organization which damages participants and alienates supporters. Such consequences make the task of selling sport as an uplifting form of family entertainment and as an exemplification of the national virtues, difficult to sustain. In particular, the ludic element is inherently irreducible to programming for profit and control: the more the desire to play is frustrated and reduced, the less it works as entertainment, and the less efficacious sport is for control purposes. The more the ludic element is present the less efficacious it is as an instrument of control. The ritualistic and dramatic character of sport is delicately constructed and does not automatically reproduce social relations. In certain circumstances the sporting occasion that normally solemnizes and celebrates the social order can be transformed, so that the signs are reversed to signal irreverence and disorder. The contest element always makes, not only the outcome of the sporting event itself unpredictable, but also the efficacy of the whole occasion as political ritual, unpredictable as well.

The third major source of contestation is the growing pressure to transform sport from a male-dominated domain, which constitutes one of the major bases of male hegemony, into one in which women have an equal opportunity to express themselves and satisfy their needs. The project has hardly begun, but it is on the agenda. Given the centrality of sports to male-identity formation, it will be resisted, and over this issue, if the pressure continues, sports are likely to be transformed into a fiercely contested terrain. The outcome of such a struggle will have almost incalculable consequences, in particular, for the character of the recomposition of the working class.

The failure of progressive forces in Britain, theoretically and practically, to accommodate sport and the body as a means of expression, and the associated tendency to reduce questions concerning sport to the issue of class alone, is one of the most important lessons to be learned from analysis. On the basis of analysis alone we would not presume to make policy prescriptions, but we would hope to have made some contribution to rectifying the highly significant absence of critical reflection.

Having perhaps learnt this lesson, one of the most mistaken deductions that could be drawn is to see sports simply as a more efficacious political instrument with which subordinate groups can be mobilized in support of this or that cause, whether it be the short-term consideration of vote-winning, or for more radical purposes. This would be to devalue sport as an autonomous means of expression and once again to profoundly misunderstand its place in the lives of those who are involved. Such a policy ultimately alienates the subordinate groups which are its targets, in that it is simply concerned with dispensing more of what is, in effect, qualitatively no different a commodity. There is no ready-made model available today, now that the amateur tradition, commercialized sport, social democratic 'Sport for All' and communist-bloc sport, have all to a significant extent been discredited in terms of their emancipatory pretensions.

Those who are trying to formulate and implement a relatively progressive sports policy and who take sport seriously as an aspect of culture, are groping their way towards, and badly need an answer. What is certainly needed at the moment is critical reflection and creative thought. Logically, analysis is only the first step in what is, after all, a discursive process – that of policy formation. Policy cannot automatically be deduced from analysis: its formation is a creative process requiring imaginative leaps, and above all, a genuine interaction between policy-makers and subjects.

Notes

Chapter 1

1 Some representative examples of the view that sports aid social integration and/or system integration are to be found in J. W. Loy and G. S. Kenyon, *Sport, Culture and Society* (Macmillan, London, 1969); E. Dunning, (ed.), *The Sociology of Sport* (Cass, London, 1971); J. A. Mangan, (ed.), *Physical Education and Sport: Sociological and Cultural Perspectives* (Basil Blackwell, Oxford, 1973). See also J. Dumazadier, 'The Point of View of the Social Scientist', in E. Jokl and E. Simon, (eds), *International Research in Sport and Physical Recreation* (Thomas, Springfield, Mass., 1964); H. Edwards, *The Sociology of Sport* (Dorsey Press, Illinois, 1973); A. Guttmann, *From Ritual to Record* (Columbia Press, New York, 1978). For the view that sports aid the formation of personal identity and/or group identity in an otherwise alienating world see: G. Stone, 'American Sports, Play and Display', in Dunning (ed.), *The Sociology of Sport*; E. Goffman, 'Where the Action Is', in *Interaction Ritual* (Doubleday, New York, 1972); M. B. Scott, *The Racing Game* (Aldine, Chicago, 1968); P. Marsh, et al., *The Rules of Disorder* (Routledge and Kegan Paul, London, 1978).

2 J. Huizinga, *Homo Ludens* (Paladin, London, 1970): C. Lasch, *The Culture of Narcissism* (Norton, New York, 1980). For a review of some sources of such a critique see J. Hoberman, *Sport and Political Ideology* (Heinemann, London, 1984), ch. 5.

3 P. Hoch, *Rip Off The Big Game* (Doubleday, New York, 1972): J. Brohm, *Sport, A Prisoner of Measured Time* (Ink Links, London, 1978); B. Rigauer, *Sport and Work* (Columbia University Press, New York, 1981).

4 For a critical assessment of the various approaches see my 'Sport, Culture, and Ideology', in J. A. Hargreaves (ed.), *Sport, Culture and Ideology* (Routledge and Kegan Paul, London, 1982).

5 B. Hindess, 'Power, Interests, and the Outcomes of Struggles', *Sociology*, 16 (4), (1982).

6 M. Foucault, *Discipline and Punish* (Allen Lane, London, 1976); see especially, his essays in C. Gordon (ed.), *Power/Knowledge* (Harvester, Brighton, 1980) and his *History of Sexuality* (Penguin, London, 1981), vol. 1.

7 S. Lukes, 'Power and Structure', in his *Essays in Social Theory* (Macmillan,

London, 1977). See also D. Wrong, *Power* (Basil Blackwell, Oxford, 1979).

8 E. P. Thompson in his *The Making of the English Working Class* (Penguin, Harmondsworth, 1968), makes the point magnificently.

9 Gramsci is the major theorist of hegemony. See A. Gramsci, in Q. Hoare and P. Nowell Smith (eds), *The Prison Notebooks* (Lawrence and Wishart, London, 1971). For an incisive appraisal of Gramsci's concept see P. Anderson, 'The Antinomies of Antonio Gramsci', *New Left Review*, 100 (1976). See also E. Laclau and C. Mouffe, *Hegemony and Socialist Strategy* (Verso, London, 1985).

10 The concept is taken from H. Cunningham, *Leisure in The Industrial Revolution* (Croom Helm, London, 1980).

11 R. Williams, *The Sociology of Culture* (Schoken Books, New York, 1982). R. Johnson 'Three Problematics: Elements of a Theory of Working-Class Culture', in *J. Clarke et al. Working Class Culture* (Hutchinson, London, 1979) insightfully raises the issue of the relation between the economic, the political and the cultural.

12 J. Larrain, *The Concept of Ideology* (Hutchinson, London, 1979).

13 P. Burke, *Popular Culture in Early Modern Europe* (Temple Smith, London, 1978): S. Hall, 'Notes on Deconstructing "The Popular"', in R. Samuel (ed.), *People's History and Socialist Theory* (Routledge and Kegan Paul, London, 1981).

14 M. Featherstone, 'The Concept of Consumer Culture', *Theory and Society*, 1 (2), 1983.

15 Huizinga, *Homo Ludens*. See also R. Caillois, *Man, Play and Games* (Free Press, New York, 1961); R. Sennett, *The Fall of Public Man* (Cambridge University Press, Cambridge, 1977).

16 C. Hill, *The World Turned Upside Down* (Penguin, London, 1975); Burke, *Popular Culture in Early Modern Europe*.

17 Stone, 'American Sports, Play, and Display'.

18 V. W. Turner, 'Symbols in Ndembu Ritual', in D. Emmett and A. McIntyre, (eds), *Sociological Theory and Philosophical Analysis* (Macmillan, London, 1970).

19 S. Lukes, 'Political Ritual and Social Integration', *Sociology*, 9 (2), (1975).

20 Foucault is the outstanding exception. See also B. Turner, *The Body and Society* (Basil Blackwell, Oxford, 1984).

21 N. Elias, *The Civilization Process* (Basil Blackwell, Oxford, 1982), vol. 1.

22 J. Benthall and T. Polhemus (eds), *The Body as a Means of Expression* (Allen Lane, London, 1975).

23 M. Douglas, *Natural Symbols* (Penguin, Harmondsworth, 1973).

24 P. Bourdieu, 'Sport and Social Class', *Social Science Information* (17 June 1978) notes this, but does not give it the analytical importance that Foucault does.

25 Z. Bauman, 'Industrialization, Consumerism, and Power', *Theory, Culture, and Society*, 1 (2), (1983). Bauman does not refer to sport, as such, in this connection.

26 See R. Gruneau, *Class, Sport and Social Development* (University of Massachusetts Press, Amherst, 1983) for an insightful analysis of Canadian sport in this respect.

Chapter 2

1 P. Burke, *Popular Culture in Early Modern Europe* (Temple Smith, London, 1978); C. Hill, *Reformation to Industrial Revolution* (Pelican, London, 1969); D. Brailsford, *Sports and Society: Elizabeth to Anne* (Routledge and Kegan Paul, London, 1969), ch. 4.

2 E. P. Thompson, 'Patrician Society Plebian Culture', *Journal of Social History*, 7 (4), (1974).

3 K. Thomas, *The Decline of Magic and Religion* (Peregrine, London, 1978).

4 Thompson, 'Patrician Society Plebian Culture'; Hill, *Reformation to Industrial Revolution*.

5 E. P. Thompson, 'Time, Work Discipline and Industrial Capitalism', *Past and Present*, 38 (1967): K. Thomas, 'Work and Leisure in Pre-Industrial Society', *Past and Present*, 29 (1964).

6 Thompson, 'Patrician Society Plebian Culture'.

7 R. Malcolmson, *Popular Recreations in English Society 1700–1850* (Cambridge University Press, Cambridge, 1973).

8 J. H. Plumb, 'Sports of Fortune', *The Listener* (19 October 1978).

9 H. S. Altham, *A History of Cricket* (Allen and Unwin, London, 1962).

10 W. Vamplew, *The Turf* (Allen Lane, London, 1976).

11 J. Ford, *Prize-fighting* (Newton Abbot, 1971).

12 Thompson, 'Patrician Society Plebian Culture'.

13 E. P. Thompson, 'The Moral Economy of the English Crowd', *Past and Present*, 50 (1971); E. Hobsbawm and G. Rude, *The Crowd in History 1730–1848* (J. Wiley, London, 1964).

14 Thompson, 'Patrician Society Plebian Culture'.

15 Vamplew, *The Turf*.

16 E. P. Thompson, *Whigs and Hunters* (Allen Lane, London, 1976).

17 H. Perkin, *The Origins of Modern English Society* (Routledge and Kegan Paul, London, 1969); E. P. Thompson, *The Making of the English Working Class* (Penguin, London, 1968).

18 Thompson, *The Making of the English Working Class*.

19 Malcolmson, *Popular Recreations in English Society*.

20 Thompson, 'Time and Work Discipline in Industrial Capitalism'; See also the 'Report on Work and Leisure in Industrial Society', *Past and Present*, 30 (1965).

21 P. Bailey, *Leisure and Class in Victorian England* (Hutchinson, London, 1978), p. 12.

22 S. Pollard, 'Factory Discipline in the 'Early Industrial Revolution', *Economic History Review*, second series, 16 (1963–4), p. 268.

23 Malcolmson, *Popular Recreations in English Society*; Bailey, *Leisure and Class in Victorian England*, ch. 1–3.

24 T. W. Lacquer, *Religion and Respectability: Sunday Schools and Working Class Culture 1780–1850* (Yale University Press, 1976), pp. 277–8.

25 Malcolmson, *Popular Recreations in English Society*.

26 D. Reid, 'The Decline of St Monday', *Past and Present*, 71 (1976).

27 Malcolmson, *Popular Recreations in English Society*, pp. 127–34.
28 Ibid., p. 138.
29 R. D. Storch, 'The Policeman as Domestic Missionary: Urban Discipline and Popular Culture in Northern England 1850–1880', *Journal of Social History*, 9 (1976) pp. 491–2.
30 See Malcolmson for further details.
31 H. Cunningham, 'The Metropolitan Fairs, in A. P. Donajgrodski (ed.), *Social Control in Nineteenth Century Britain* (Croom Helm, London, 1978).
32 Malcolmson, *Popular Recreations in English Society*.
33 R. D. Storch, 'The Plague of Blue Locusts 1840–57', *International Review of Social History*, 20 (1975), p. 84.
34 Storch, 'The Policeman as Domestic Missionary', pp. 482–3.
35 Ibid.
36 Storch, 'The Plague of Blue Locusts', p. 77.
37 Storch, 'The Policeman as Domestic Missionary', p. 484.
38 Bailey, *Leisure and Class in Victorian England*, pp. 44–6.
39 P. Joyce, *Work, Society and Politics* (Harvester, London, 1980). On the social origins of factory employers see also J. Foster, *Class Struggles in the Industrial Revolution* (Weidenfeld and Nicolson, London, 1974).
40 For some striking statistical indications see Lacquer, *Religion and Respectability*, pp. 234–40; Foster, *Class Struggles*, p. 214; Joyce, *Work, Society and Politics*, p. 246.
41 Lacquer, *Religion and Respectability*.
42 B. Harrison, 'Religion and Recreation in Nineteenth Century England', *Past and Present*, 38 (1967).
43 Bailey, *Leisure and Class*, p. 36–9.
44 Harrison, 'Religion and Recreation in Nineteenth Century England'.
45 R. Johnson, 'Educational Policy and Social Control in Early Victorian England', *Past and Present*, 49 (1970).
46 Bailey, *Leisure and Class*, pp. 36–9.
47 Ibid.
48 F. Hearn, *Domination, Legitimation and Resistance* (Greenwood Press, London, 1978).
49 Joyce, *Work, Society and Politics*.
50 Ibid.
51 Thompson, *The Making of the English Working Class*, p. 437.
52 Lacquer, *Religion and Respectability*.
53 Thompson, *The Making of The English Working Class*.
54 K. Inglis, *The Churches and the Working Class in Victorian England* (Routledge and Kegan Paul, London, 1963); Foster, *Class Struggles in the Industrial Revolution*.
55 E. Hobsbawm and G. Rude, *Captain Swing* (Allen Lane, London, 1969), pp. 250–1.
56 Joyce, *Work, Society and Politics*, p. 248.
57 Harrison, 'Religion and Recreation in Nineteenth Century England'.
58 Reid, 'The Decline of St Monday'.
59 Bailey, *Leisure and Class*; H. Cunningham, *Leisure in the Industrial Revolution* (Croom Helm, London, 1980).

60 N. Abercrombie, S. Hill, B. Turner, *The Dominant Ideology Thesis* (Allen and Unwin, London, 1980).
61 Bailey, *Leisure and Class*, pp. 49–50.
62 Joyce, *Work, Society and Politics*, pp. 276–8.
63 Bailey, *Leisure and Class*; Cunningham, *Leisure in the Industrial Revolution*; Storch, 'The Policeman as Domestic Missionary'.
64 Vamplew, *The Turf*.
65 Cunningham, *Leisure in the Industrial Revolution*, pp. 25–7; Bailey, *Leisure and Class*.
66 C. C. P. Brookes, 'Cricket as a Vocation', (PhD Thesis, University of Leicester, 1974).
67 Cunningham, *Leisure in the Industrial Revolution*.
68 Ibid.
69 R. Johnson, 'Barrington Moore, Perry Anderson and English Social Development', *Cultural Studies*, 9 (1976).
70 Vamplew, *The Turf*.
71 Bailey, *Leisure and Class*, p. 90.

Chapter 3

1 E. Hobsbawm, *The Age of Capital* (Weidenfeld and Nicolson, London, 1975); see also his *Industry and Empire* (Weidenfeld and Nicolson, London, 1967); W. L. Burn, *The Age of Equipoise* (Allen and Unwin, London, 1964).
2 R. Harrison, *Before the Socialists* (Routledge and Kegan Paul, London, 1965).
3 R. Gray, 'Bourgeois Hegemony in Victorian Britain', in J. Bloomfield (ed.), *Class, Hegemony, and Party* (Lawrence and Wishart, London, 1977).
4 E. C. Mack, *The Public Schools and British Opinion 1760–1860* (Greenwood Press, Westport, 1973); T. W. Bamford, *The Rise of the Public Schools* (Nelson, London, 1967); D. Newsome, *Godliness and Good Learning* (J. Murray, London, 1961); B. Simon and L. Bradley, *The Victorian Public School* (Gill and Macmillan, Dublin, 1975); R. Wilkinson, *The Prefects* (Oxford University Press, Oxford, 1964); A. Briggs, 'Thomas Hughes and the Public Schools', in his *Victorian People* (Pelican, Harmondsworth, 1971); J. Gathorne-Hardy, *The Public School Phenomenon* (Hodder and Stoughton, London, 1977).
5 C. L. R. James, *Beyond a Boundary* (Hutchinson, London, 1976).
6 E. Dunning and K. Sheard, Barbarians, Gentlemen and Players (Martin Robertson, Oxford, 1979).
7 Ibid. For the use of this concept see N. Elias, *The Civilization Process* (Basil Blackwell, Oxford, 1978), vol. 1.
8 James, *Beyond a Boundary*, p. 163.
9 T. Hughes, *Tom Brown's Schooldays* (Puffin, London, 1977), p. 65.
10 Ibid., p. 88.
11 B. Haley, 'Sports and the Victorian World', *Western Humanities Review*, 22 (1968), p. 116.
12 Ibid. See also, P. Bailey, *Leisure and Class in Victorian England*, (Hutchinson, London, 1978), p. 72.

13 M. Vance, 'The Ideal of Manliness', Simon and Bradley, *The Victorian Public School*.

14 W. F. Mandle, 'Games People Played: Cricket and Football in England and Victoria in the Late 19th Century', *Historical Studies*, 15 (1973), pp. 511–35.

15 Wilkinson, *The Prefects*, p. 81.

16 Ibid., p. 84.

17 J. Arlott (ed.), *The Oxford Companion to Sports and Games* (Oxford University Press, Oxford, 1975).

18 C. C. P. Brookes, 'Cricket as a Vocation', (PhD Thesis, University of Leicester, 1974).

19 Ibid., p. 318.

20 R. Q. Gray, *The Labour Aristocracy in 19th Century Edinburgh* (Oxford University Press, Oxford, 1976).

21 Gray, 'Bourgeois Hegemony in Victorian Britain'.

22 Bailey, *Leisure and Class*.

23 Ibid. See also R. Price, *An Imperial War and the British Working Class* (Routledge and Kegan Paul, London, 1972); J. Taylor, 'From Self-Help to Glamour', *History Workshop Pamphlets* 6.

24 Bailey, *Leisure and Class*, p. 100.

25 Ibid.

26 Ibid.

27 J. Walvin, *The People's Game* (Allen Lane, London, 1975), pp. 56–8.

28 G. Best, *Mid-Victorian Britain* (Weidenfeld and Nicolson, London, 1972), pp. 209–11.

29 H. Cunningham, *The Volunteers* (Archon Books, Hamden, 1975).

30 Ibid., p. 28.

31 Bailey, *Leisure and Class*.

32 K. Inglis, *The Churches and the Working Class in Victorian England* (Routledge and Kegan Paul, London, 1963).

33 R. Storch, 'The Policeman as Domestic Missionary: Urban Discipline and Popular Culture in Northern England 1850–80', *Journal of Social History* 9 (1976), pp. 491–2.

34 Bailey, *Leisure and Class*.

35 Storch, 'The Policeman as Domestic Missionary'.

36 H. Cunningham, 'The Metropolitan Fairs', in A. P. Donajgrodski (ed.), *Social Control in 19th Century Britain* (Croom Helm, London, 1978).

37 J. Hutchinson, 'Respectability in Sport', *New Edinburgh Review*, (1974); Bailey, *Leisure and Class*, p. 90; H. Mayhew, *London Labour and the London Poor* (Dover Publications, New York, 1968), vol. 13, pp. 5–10.

38 Best, *Mid-Victorian Britain*, p. 209.

39 J. Ford, *Prizefighting* (Newton Abbott, 1971).

40 W. Vamplew, *The Turf* (Allen Lane, London, 1976).

41 Best, *Mid-Victorian Britain*; Hobsbawm, *The Age of Capital*.

42 Bailey, *Leisure and Class*, pp. 132–3.

43 B. Chambers, 'Hadaway, Harry Lad Hadaway', *The Guardian* (12 Mar. 1979).

44 A. Metcalfe, 'Organized Physical Recreation in the Mining Communities of South Northumberland, 1800–1889', (unpublished paper, University of Windsor, Canada, 1979).

45 Ibid.
46 Ibid.
47 P. Joyce, *Work, Society and Politics* (Harvester, Brighton, 1980).
48 Ibid. p. 273.
49 P. Horn, *Labouring Life in the Victorian Countryside* (Gill and Macmillan, Dublin, 1976), p. 146.

Chapter 4

1 E. Hobsbawm, *Industry and Empire* (Weidenfeld and Nicolson, London, 1967); and 'Trends in the Labour Movement' in his *Labouring Men* (Weidenfeld and Nicolson, London, 1971). See also: W. Kendall, *The Revolutionary Movement in Britain 1900–1921* (Weidenfeld and Nicolson, London, 1969) part 1; J. Hinton, *The First Shop Stewards' Movement* (Allen and Unwin, London, 1973); H. Pelling, *The Origins of the Labour Party* (Macmillan, London, 1954).
2 M. A. Bienefeld, *Working Hours in British Industry* (Weidenfeld and Nicolson, London, 1972); C. Booth, *Life and Labour of the People of London*, selected and edited by A. Fried and R. Elman (Hutchinson, London, 1969); G. Stedman Jones, *Outcast London* (Oxford University Press, Oxford, 1971).
3 G. Dangerfield, *The Strange Death of Liberal England* (Paladin, London, 1972); S. Meacham, 'The Sense of an Impending Clash', *American Historical Review*, 77 (V), pp. 1343–64.
4 J. Walvin, *The People's Game* (Allen Lane, London, 1975); T. Mason, *Association Football and English Society, 1863–1915* (Harvester, Brighton, 1980). Mason estimates that church, chapel and Sunday-school clubs formed a quarter of all organized, regularly playing clubs.
5 K. Inglis, *The Churches and the Working Class in Victorian England* (Routledge and Kegan Paul, London, 1963).
6 F. Dawes, *A Cry from the Streets* (Wayland, Hove, 1975), p. 49–50.
7 H. Meller, *Leisure and the Changing City* (Routledge and Kegan Paul, London, 1976), ch. 6.
8 Daws, *A Cry from the Streets*.
9 Ibid., p. 105.
10 Ibid., p. 90.
11 L. L. Shiman, 'The Band of Hope Movement', *Victorian Studies*, 18 (1975).
12 J. Springhall, *Youth, Empire and Society* (Croom Helm, London, 1977).
13 Meller, *Leisure and the Changing City*, p. 177.
14 Springhall, *Youth, Empire and Society*, pp. 125–6.
15 W. D. Smith, *Stretching Their Bodies* (David and Charles, London, 1974); P. McIntosh, *Physical Education in England since 1800* (Bell and Son, London, 1968), ch. 7.
16 J. R. Gillis, 'The Evolution of Juvenile Delinquency, 1890–1914', *Past and Present*, 67 (1975).
17 R. Roberts, *The Classic Slum* (Manchester University Press, Manchester, 1971), p. 48.
18 Gillis, 'The Evolution of Juvenile Delinquency'.

19 P. Joyce, *Work, Society and Politics* (Harvester, London, 1980). M. Anderson, *Family Structure in 19th Century Lancashire* (Cambridge University Press, Cambridge, 1971).

20 J. Donzelot, *The Policing of Families* (Hutchinson, London, 1981).

21 D. Armstrong, *The Political Anatomy of the Body* (Cambridge University Press, Cambridge, 1983).

22 Mason, *Association Football and English Society*. See also D. C. Coleman, 'Gentlemen and Players', *American Historical Review*, 26 (1973).

23 P. Wilkinson, 'English Youth Movements, 1908–30', *Journal of Contemporary History*, 4 (2), (1969).

24 J. Springhall, 'Lord Meath, Youth and Empire', *Journal of Contemporary History*, 5 (4), (1970).

25 Amateur Athletic Association (1880), Amateur Boxing Assoc. (1880), Amateur Gymnastic Assoc. (1890), Amateur Rowing Assoc. (1882), Badminton Assoc. of England (1893), Hockey Assoc. (1886), National Skating Assoc. (1879), Wimbledon All-England Lawn Tennis and Croquet Club (1882), Lawn Tennis Assoc. (1888), British Lacrosse Union (1892), Yachting Assoc. (1875), Sports Council, *A Guide to Governing Bodies*, 1977; *The Oxford Companion to Sports and Games*, ed. J. Arlott, 1975. A medium-sized town like Reading provides some idea of the proliferation of sporting organizations at the local level: Reading Football Club (1871), Reading Amateur Football Club (1895), Reading Cycling Club (1899), Reading Wheelers Cycling Club, Reading Rovers Cycling Club, Reading United Quoits Club (1892), Reading Amateur Regatta, Reading Working Men's Regatta (1877), Reading Rowing Club (1867), Reading Rifle Club (1901), Reading Swimming Club, Reading Cricket Club, Reading Biscuit Factory Recreation Club, Reading Athletic Club (1882), and Reading Angling Association (1877). S. Yeo, *Religion and Voluntary Organisations in Crisis* (Croom Helm, London, 1976), p. 185.

26 Blackpool (1887), Everton (1878), Fulham (1880), Southampton (1885), Swindon (1881), Burnley (1882), Wolverhampton Wanderers (1877), Leicester City (1884), Queen's Park Rangers (1885), Sunderland (1879), Northampton (1897), West Ham (1895), Preston North End (1881), Crewe Alexandra (1877), Manchester United (1880), Coventry City (1883), Millwall (1885), Arsenal (1886), Sheffield United (1889), Tottenham Hotspur (1882), and many more less famous or since gone.

27 J. Wolvin, *The People's Game*.

28 W. F. Mandle, 'Games People Played: Cricket and Football in England and Victoria in the Late 19th Century' *Historical Studies*, 15 (1973), pp. 511–35.

29 D. Scott with C. Bent, *Borrowed Time, A Social History of Running, Salford Harriers 1884–1984* (Salford Harriers, Moston, 1984).

30 W. Vamplew, *The Turf* (Allen Lane, London, 1976).

31 E. Weber, 'Pierre Coubertin and the Introduction of Organised Sport in France', *Journal of Contemporary History*, 5 (2) (1970).

32 W. Vamplew, *The Turf*.

33 R. Williams, 'The Growth of the Popular Press', in his *The Long Revolution* (Penguin, Harmondsworth, 1961).

34 R. Price, *An Imperial War and the British Working Class* (Routledge and Kegan

Paul, London, 1972); J. Taylor, 'From Self-Help to Glamour', *History Workshop Pamphlets*, 6 (1972).

35 Joyce, *Work, Society and Politics*.

36 Wolvin, *The People's Game*; Mason, *Association Football*.

37 E. Hobsbawm and T. Ranger, *The Invention of Tradition* (Cambridge University Press, Cambridge, 1983) Introduction.

38 P. Bailey, *Leisure and Class in Victorian England* (Hutchinson, London, 1978).

39 Scott, *Borrowed Time*.

40 Wolvin, *The People's Game*; Mason, *Association Football*.

41 B. Dabschek, 'Defensive Manchester: A History of the Professional Footballer's Association' (unpublished paper, Dept of Industrial Relations, London School of Economics, 1978).

42 C. Korr, 'West Ham United and the Beginnings of Professional Football in East London, 1895–1914', *Journal of Contemporary History*, 15 (1978).

43 T. Delaney *The Roots of Rugby League* (T. Delaney, Keighley, 1984); E. Dunning and K. Sheard, *Barbarians, Gentlemen and Players* (Martin Robertson, Oxford, 1979).

44 C. C. P. Brookes, 'Cricket as a Vocation', (PhD Thesis, University of Leicester, 1974).

45 W. F. Mandle, 'The Professional Cricketer in England in the 19th Century', *Labour History*, 27 (1972).

46 P. Atkinson, 'Fitness, Feminism and Schooling', S. Delamont and C. Duffin, *The Nineteenth Century Woman in the Cultural and Physical World* (Croom Helm, London, 1978).

47 Ibid., p. 110.

48 Ibid., p. 118.

49 Dangerfield, *The Strange Death of Liberal England*, part 2, ch. 4.

50 W. Whittam, *Modern Cricket and Other Sports, 1884*, cited in Mandle, 'The Professional Cricketer'. On the lengths to which the games cult was taken in the public schools see J. Gathorn Hardy, *The Public Schools Phenomenon* (Hodder and Stoughton, London, 1977). On the hysteria and the connection with imperialism see, J. Mangan, *Athleticism in the Victorian and the Edwardian Public School* (Cambridge University Press, Cambridge, 1981), (ch. 6 and 8).

51 Hobsbawm, *Industry and Empire*; Joyce, *Work Society and Politics*; G. Stedman Jones, 'Working Class Culture and Working Class Politics in London, 1870–1900', *Journal of Social History*, 7 (4) (1973).

52 R. Q. Gray, *The Labour Aristocracy in 19th Century Edinburgh* (Oxford University Press, Oxford, 1976). See also his *The Aristocracy of Labour in 19th Century Britain* (Macmillan, London, 1981).

53 G. Best, *Mid-Victorian Britain* (Weidenfeld and Nicolson, London, 1972), pp. 209–11.

54 H. F. Moorhouse, 'The Marxist Theory of the Labour Aristocracy', *Social History*, 31 (1978), and 'On the Political Incorporation of the British Working Class: Reply to Gray', *Sociology*, 9 (1), 1975. See also E. Hobsbawm, 'The Labour Aristocracy in 19th Century Britain', *Labouring Men*; J. Foster, *Class Struggles in the Industrial Revolution* (Weidenfeld and Nicolson, London, 1974); G. Crossick, 'The Labour Aristocracy and its Values: A Study of Mid-

Victorian Kentish London, *Victorian Studies*, 19 (1976); H. Pelling, 'The Concept of the Labour Aristocracy', in his *Popular Politics and Society in Victorian Britain* (Macmillan, London, 1968).

55 H. Newby, 'The Deferential Dialectic', *Comparative Studies in History and Society*, 17 (1976); P. Bailey, *Leisure and Class in Victorian England.*

56 Wilkinson, 'English Youth Movements'.

57 Mason, *Association Football.*

58 J. Hutchinson, 'Respectability in Sport' *New Edinburgh Review* (1974). See also Hutchinson's 'Some Aspects of Football Crowds Before 1914' (Paper given to Society for the Study of Labour History, Sussex University, 1975).

59 Gray, *The Labour Aristocracy.*

60 Bailey, *Leisure and Class*, p. 176. See also Price, *An Imperial War*; Taylor, 'From Self-Help to Glamour'; Joyce, in *Work, Society and Politics*, points out the same tendency in the working men's clubs run by the Conservative and Liberal Parties.

61 Crossick, 'The Labour Aristocracy and Its Values', notes the strong constitutionalism of the skilled workers.

62 Bailey, *Leisure and Class in Victorian England*, p. 122.

63 R. Roberts, *The Classic Slum*, describes the feelings graphically.

64 Joyce, *Work, Society and Politics.*

65 Yeo, *Religion and Voluntary Organizations in Crisis*, p. 195.

66 Ibid.

67 Meller, *Leisure and the Changing City*, ch. 11.

68 Mason, *Association Football*, pp. 235–37.

69 D. Prynn, 'The Clarion Clubs, Rambling and the Holiday Associations in Britain Since the 1890s', *Journal of Contemporary History*, 11 (2), (1976).

70 Mason, *Association Football.*

71 D. A. Steinberg, 'The Workers' Sports Internationals', *Journal of Contemporary History*, 13 (1978).

72 Mason, *Association Football.*

73 Yeo, *Religion and Voluntary Organisations*, p. 323.

74 M. Mann, *Consciousness and Action Among the Working Class* (Macmillan, London, 1973); R. Miliband, *Parliamentary Socialism* (Merlin, London, 1964).

75 R. Williams, *Culture and Society* (Penguin, Harmondsworth, 1957); A. Briggs, *Mass Entertainment: The Origins of an Industry* (Adelaide, 1960).

76 Stedman Jones notes the change in the London working class.

77 Price, *An Imperial War*; Stedman Jones, 'Working Class Culture and Working Class Politics': Taylor, 'From Self-Help to Glamour'. William Morris noted it also, see E. P. Thompson, *William Morris* (Merlin Press, London, 1977).

78 A. Gibson and W. Pickford, *Association Football and the Men Who Made It* (1905), vol. 1, p. 79, cited in Hutchinson, 'Respectability in Sport'.

79 Anon., 'Fashions in Pastimes', *Spectator* (1898), cited in Hutchinson, 'Respectability in Sport'.

80 Bailey, *Leisure and Class*, p. 128.

81 Anon., 'A Counterblast to Exercise', *Spectator* (1882), p. 493, cited in Hutchinson, 'Respectability in Sport'.

82 G. Green, *The Official History of the FA Cup* (Naldred Press, London, 1949), p. 69.

83 Hobsbawm and Ranger, *The Invention of Tradition*, p. 300.

84 Wolvin, *The People's Game*, p. 85.

85 T. Barker (ed.), *The Long March of Everyman* (Penguin, Harmondsworth, 1978): E. Hobsbawm, *Industry and Empire* (Weidenfeld and Nicolson, London, 1968). On leisure patterns see: A. Hawkins and J. Lowerson, *Trends in Leisure, 1919–1939* (Sports Council, London, 1979).

86 Walvin, *The People's Game*; C. C. Brookes, *English Cricket – The Game and Its Players Throughout the Ages*, (Weidenfeld and Nicolson, London, 1978); J. Arlott (ed.), *The Oxford Companion to Sports and Games*; J. Lovesey, *The Official History of the AAA* (Guinness Superlatives, London, 1984).

87 Howkins and Lowerson, *Trends in Leisure*.

88 Vamplew, *The Turf*.

89 Walvin, *The People's Game*.

90 B. Watson and M. Gray, *The Penguin Book of the Bicycle* (Penguin, Harmondsworth, 1980).

91 H. Justin Evans, *Service to Sport: The Story of the CCPR 1935–1972* (Sports Council, London, 1974).

92 Evans, *Service to Sport*.

93 Report of the Consultative Council on Medical and Allied Services, para. 141, cited in Armstrong, *The Political Anatomy of the Body*, p. 33.

94 Evans, *Service to Sport*, p. 22.

95 McIntosh, *PE in England Since 1800* (Bell and Son, London, 1968).

96 J. Lowerson, 'Battles for the Countryside', in F. Gloversmith, *Class, Culture and Social Change* (Harvester, Brighton, 1980); D. Rubinstein, 'The Struggle for Ramblers' Rights', *New Society* (15 April 1982).

97 J. Lowerson and A. Howkins 'Leisure in the 30s', in A. Tomlinson (ed.) *Leisure and Social Control*, (Brighton Polytechnic, 1981).

98 J. Hoberman, *Sport and Political Ideology* (Heinemann, London, 1984); R. Holt, Sport and Society in Modern France, 1920–1938 (Macmillan, London, 1981).

Chapter 5

1 OPCS, *General Household Survey, 1977* (HMSO, London, 1979). For an analysis of the data on sport in this survey see A. J. Veal, *Sport and Recreation in England and Wales* (Centre for Urban Studies, University of Birmingham, 1979). A preliminary analysis of the GHS for 1980 is outlined in *Sport and the Community in the Next Ten Years* (Sports Council, London, 1982).

2 Football Association, 'Evidence submitted to the House of Lords Select Committee on Sport and Leisure', November 1976; Sports Council, 'Playing Fields: A New Approach to Assessing Requirements', (Unpublished, 1976), cited in A. Tomlinson, *Leisure and the Role of Clubs and Voluntary Groups* (Sports Council, London, 1979).

3 Central Statistical Office, *Social Trends* (HMSO, London, 1979).

4 S. Wagg, *The Football World* (Harvester, London, 1984).

5 *General Household Survey 1980*, tables 2–3, 7 analysed by T. Veal for the Sports Council.

6 S. Parker, *The Sociology of Leisure*, (Allen and Unwin, London, 1976) p. 137, *Social Trends* 9, (1979), table 12.19; *Royal Commission on Gambling, Final Report*, (HMSO, London, 1978), Cmnd 7200.

7 GHS 1980, cited in Sports Council, *Sport and the Community*, table 20, p. 27.

8 J. Roberts, *A Review of Studies of Sport and Recreation in the Inner City*, (Sports Council Study 17, London, 1978) p. 40.

9 A. Dale, et al., 'Integrating Women into Class Theory', *Sociology*, 19 (3), (1985).

10 T. Nichols, 'Social Class: Official, Sociological and Marxist', in J. Irvine, I. Miles and J. Evans, *Demystifying Social Statistics* (Pluto Press, London, 1979).

11 Veal, *Sport and Recreation in England and Wales*; B. Rees, *Activists and Non-Activists: Variations in Sports Participation in the UK* (Sports Council, London, 1974); M. Young and P. Willmott, *The Symmetrical Family*, (Penguin, Harmondsworth, 1973) p. 215.

12 Veal, *Sport and Recreation in England and Wales*, p. 47.

13 Built Environment Research Group (BERG), *Sport For All In The Inner City* (London, 1978) Sports Council Study 15; *Sport in a Jointly Provided Centre* (London, 1978), Sports Council Study 14; *The Changing Indoor Sports Centre* (London, 1977), Sports Council Study 13; G. Arrowsmith, *Sports Usage and Membership at a Large Urban Leisure Complex: Billingham Forum* (London, 1979), Sports Council Research Working Papers, 17.

14 J. H. Goldthorpe et al., *The Affluent Worker and the Class Structure* (Cambridge University Press, Cambridge, 1969). On the 'Deskilling' thesis see H. Braverman, *Labour and Monopoly Capital* (Monthly Review Press, London, 1974).

15 D. Downes et al., *Gambling, Work, and Leisure* (Routledge and Kegan Paul, London, 1976): *Social Trends*, 9 (1979), table 12.18.

16 Cited in J. Curran and J. Tunstall, 'Mass Media and Leisure', in M. A. Smith et al. (eds), *Leisure and Society in Britain*, (Allen Lane, London, 1973).

17 S. Hutson, *A Review of the Role of Clubs and Voluntary Associations Based on a Study of Two Areas in Swansea* (Sports Council, London, 1980).

18 Goldthorpe, *The Affluent Worker in the Class Structure*.

19 M. Stacey, 'The Myth of Community Studies', *British Journal of Sociology*, 20 (2), (1969); A. N. Birch, *Small Town Politics* (Oxford University Press, London, 1959): R. Frankenberg, *Village on the Border* (Penguin, Harmondsworth, 1957) and his Communities in Britain (Penguin, Harmondworth, 1966); W. Williams, *The Sociology of an English Village: Gosforth* (Routledge and Kegan Paul, London, 1964); R. E. Pahl, *Whose City?* (Longman, London, 1970) p. 39–42.

20 M. Stacey, *Tradition and Change – A Study of Banbury* (Oxford University Press, London, 1960). See also, M. Stacey et al., *Power, Persistence, and Change – A Second Study of Banbury* (Routledge and Kegan Paul, London, 1975).

21 P. Willmott and M. Young, *Family and Class in a London Suburb*, (Routledge and Kegan Paul, London, 1960) p. 97.

22 B. Jackson, *Working Class Community*, (Penguin, Harmondsworth 1968) ch. 6;
    N. Dennis, et al., *Coal is Our Life* (Eyre and Spottiswoode, London, 1956).

23 For a discussion of the transformation of the working class in contemporary
    capitalist societies see A. Gorz, *Farewell To The Working Class* (Pluto Press,
    London, 1980).

24 Goldthorpe, *The Affluent Worker in the Class Structure*.

25 J. Ford, *The Comprehensive School* (Routledge and Kegan Paul, London,
    1969).

26 North West Regional Council for Sport and Recreation, *Moss Side Leisure
    Centre* (NW Regional Sports Council, Manchester, 1978).

27 P. Cohen and D. Robbins, *Knuckle Sandwich* (Penguin, London, 1979).

28 BERG, *Sport For All in The Inner City*, exemplifies the failure.

29 P. Willis and C. Critcher, 'Women in Sport', *Cultural Studies*, 5 (1974) is
    one of the few exceptions.

30 Veal, *Sport and Recreation in England and Wales*. See also A. J. Veal, *Using
    Sports Centres* (Sports Council, London, 1982).

31 For attempts to solve this problem see M. Barrett, *Women's Oppression Today*
    (Verso, London, 1980); J. Lewis, 'The Debate on Sex and Class', *New Left
    Review*, 149 (Jan/Feb 1985).

32 C. Griffin et al., 'Women and Leisure', in J. A. Hargreaves (ed.), *Sport, Culture
    and Ideology* (Routledge and Kegan Paul, London, 1982).

33 On the economic and biological determinants of the sexual division of labour
    see J. Brenner and M. Ramas, 'Rethinking Women's Oppression', *New Left
    Review*, 144 (1984).

34 T. Bottomore, 'Social Stratification in Voluntary Organisations', in D. V. Glass
    (ed.), *Social Mobility in Britain* (Routledge and Kegan Paul, London, 1954);
    Stacey et al., *Power, Persistence and Change*; Hutson, *A Review of Clubs and
    Voluntary Associations*.

35 J. Littlejohn, *Westrigg: The Sociology of A Cheviot Parish* (Routledge and
    Kegan Paul, London, 1963).

36 Equal Rights in Clubs Campaign for Action (ERICCA).

37 J. Platt and M. Slater, 'Football Hooliganism', *Leisure Studies*, 3 (1984).

38 I. Taylor, 'Class, Violence and Sport: The Case of Soccer Hooliganism in
    Britain', in H. Cantelon and R. Gruneau (eds), *Sport, Culture, and the Modern
    State* (University of Toronto Press, London, 1982).

39 Platt and Slater, 'Football Hooliganism'.

40 S. Kew, *Ethnic Groups and Leisure* (Sports Council, London, 1979).

41 See E. Cashmore, *Black Sportsmen* (Routledge and Kegan Paul, London, 1982).

42 'Rollerball Gladiators', *City Limits* (12/18 July 1985).

43 I. Althusser, 'Ideology and Ideological State Apparatuses', *Lenin and
    Philosophy* (New Left Books, London, 1971).

44 K. Roberts, et al., *The Fragmentary Class Structure* (Heinemann, London,
    1977). Goldthorpe, et al., *The Affluent Worker in the Class Structure*.

45 J. Lowerson and A. Howkins, 'Leisure in the 30s' in A. Tomlinson (ed.),
    Leisure and Social Control (Brighton Polytechnic, Brighton, 1980).

Chapter 6

1 Department of Education and Science, 'Report of the Committee on Football' (The Chester Report), (HMSO, London, 1968); Royal Commission on Industrial Relations, 'Professional Football', (HMSO, London, 1974), Report No. 87; R. Sloane, *Sport in the Market?* (Institute of Economic Affairs, London, 1980) Hobart Paper 85; Football League, 'Report of the Committee Into Structure and Finance' (Football League, Lytham St Annes, 1983).

2 J. Rhodda, *The Guardian*, (June 1979).

3 See the Central Council for Physical Recreation, 'Report of the Committee of Enquiry Into Sports Sponsorship' (The Howell Report), (Sports Council, London, 1983), ch. 10, pp. 68–70.

4 J. Arlott, 'The Money Changers in the Temple of Sport', *The Guardian*, (22 September 1979); C. C. P. Brookes, 'Cricket as a Vocation', (PhD Thesis, University of Leicester, 1974), p. 521; D. White, 'Is Cricket Dying?', *New Society*, (22 June 1978); H. Blofeld, *The Packer Affair* (Collins, London, 1978); Sloane, *Sport in the Market?; Wisden's Cricket Almanack*.

5 W. Vamplew, *The Turf* (Allen Lane, London, 1976).

6 J. Arlott, *The Oxford Companion to Sports and Games* (Oxford University Press, Oxford, 1975) pp. 673–4.

7 Ibid. See also Sports Council, *Annual Report*, (Sports Council, London, 1978/9), Schedule III, p. 21.

8 Vamplew, *The Turf*.

9 G. Gibbs, *The Guardian* (13 June 1985); Football League, Report of the Committee Into Structure and Finance.

10 'And Now a Word From Our Sponsors', *Time Out*, 528, (30 May 1980).

11 R. Chesshyre and C. Brasher, 'Sponsorship, Who Benefits?', *Observer* (7 October 1979).

12 A. Cornelius, *Sunday Times Financial Section* (13 July 1980).

13 The Howell Committee has called for official control over these agencies.

14 Sports Council, *An Inquiry Into Sponsorship* (Sports Council, London, 1972); *Sponsorship – Who Needs it?* (Sports Council, London, 1978).

15 Howell Report. See also 'Lawn Tennis: Report of the Minister's Lawn Tennis Inquiry Committee', (the Smith Report) (Sports Council, London, 1980).

16 P. Ball and J. Taylor, 'The People in the Gucci Shoes', *Time Out* 531 (20 June 1980).

17 Smith Report.

18 Chesshyre and Brasher, 'Sponsorship – Who Benefits?'

19 'And Now a Word From Our Sponsors', *Time Out*.

20 *Sunday Times*, Week in Focus (18 August 1985).

21 J. Rhodda, 'Smoke Signal', *The Guardian*, 1 August 1978; J. Rhodda, 'IAC Attempt to Smoke Out Sponsors', *The Guardian* (no date); 'Fatal Mistake', *Sunday Times* (23 March 1980). See the Howell Report, p. 46, for details of the tobacco industry's support.

22 See H. H. Wilson, *Pressure Group* (Secker and Warburg, London, 1961) for an analysis of how important the breaking of the BBC's monopoly on

broadcasting was in the transition to consumer capitalism in the 1950s.

23 Chesshyre and Brasher, 'Sponsorship – Who Benefits?; D. Lehane, 'How to Advertise on BBC TV', *Sunday Times* (10 August 1980).

24 Inside Track, *Sunday Times* (21 April 1985).

25 Personal communications from the Football League, Professional Golfers' Association, Jockeys' Association of Great Britain, British Board of Boxing Control. See also Sloane, *Sport in the Market*.

26 H. Braverman, *Labour and Monopoly Capital*, (Monthly Review Press, London, 1974) ch. 19.

27 See, for example, J. Goldthorpe, et al., *The Affluent Worker: Industrial Attitudes and Behaviour* (Cambridge University Press, Cambridge, 1968); G. Friedmann, *The Anatomy of Work* (Free Pess, Glencoe, 1956), and *Industrial Society* (Free Press, Glencoe, 1955); T. Nicols and H. Beynon, *Workers Divided* (Fontana, London, 1976); H. Beynon, *Working For Ford* (Penguin, Harmondsworth, 1973); K. Roberts, *The Fragmentary Class Structure* (Heinemann, London, 1977).

28 Hunter Davies, *The Glory Game* (Weidenfeld and Nicolson, London, 1972).

29 Brookes, 'Cricket as a Vocation', S. Wagg, 'Well Brian: A Sociological Study of a Football Community', (M.Phil thesis, University of Leicester), ch. 2 (now published as *The Football World* (Harvester, London, 1984).

30 B. Dabscheck, 'Sport Equality: Labour Market Versus Product Market Control', *Journal of Industrial Relations*, 17 (1975); Sloane, *Sport in the Market*, and 'The Labour Market in Professional Football, *British Journal of Industrial Relations*, 17 (1969). See also P. J. Sloane, 'Restriction of Competition in Team Sports', *Bulletin of Economic Research*, 28 (1976); 'The Football Club as a Utility Maximizer', *Journal of Political Economy, 17 (2) (1971)*; P. Rivett, 'The Structure of League Football', *Operational Research Quarterly*, 26 (4) (1975); W. C. Neale, 'The Peculiar Economics of Professional Sports', *Quarterly Journal of Economics*, LXXVIII, (1), 1964.

31 Wagg, 'Well Brian', ch. 3.

32 J. Rhodda, *The Guardian* (29 March 1985).

33 Wagg, 'Well Brian'.

34 Brookes, 'Cricket as a Vocation'.

35 Ibid; Wagg, 'Well Brian'.

36 B. Dabscheck, 'Defensive Manchester: A History of the Professional Footballers' Association' (unpublished, Department of Industrial Relations, London School of Economics, 1978).

37 Z. Bauman, 'Industrialism, Consumerism and Power', *Theory, Culture and Society*, 3 (1983); M. Foucault, in C. Gordon, (ed.) *Power/Knowledge*, (Harvester, Brighton, 1980).

38 W. H. Martin and S. Mason, *Broad Patterns of Leisure Expenditure* (Sports Council, London, 1979) Definitions of what counts as equipment, and different methods of calculating expenditure, produce widely varying estimates.

39 J. Walvin, *The People's Game* (Allen Lane, London, 1975) pp. 48–9.

40 C. R. Hill, Spectrum *The Times* (12 February 1985).

41 'Report of the Royal Commission on Gambling', (HMSO, London, 1978).

42 For a review of ways of theorizing the body see B. Turner, *The Body and Society* (Basil Blackwell, Oxford, 1984).

43 M. Featherstone, 'The Body in Consumer Culture', *Theory, Culture and Society*, 1 (2), 1983.

44 P. Marsh, et al., *The Rules of Disorder* (Routledge and Kegan Paul, 1978).

Chapter 7

1 See for example, Glasgow University Media Group, *Bad News*, 1 (1976) and *More Bad News* 2 (Routledge and Kegan Paul, London, 1980); S. Hall, et al., 'The Unity of Current Affairs TV', *Cultural Studies* 9 (Spring, 1976); M. Tracey, *The Production of Political Television* (Routledge and Kegan Paul, London, 1977); P. Schlesinger, *Putting Reality Together* (Constable, London, 1978). There are exceptions. See, for example, P. Cohen and C. Gardner (eds), *It Ai'nt Half Racist Mum* (Comedia, London, 1982); J. Winship, *Advertising in Women's Magazines 1956–1974* (University of Birmingham, Centre for Contemporary Cultural Studies, 1980).

2 J. Curran and J. Tunstall, 'Mass Media and Leisure', in M. A. Smith et al., (eds), *Leisure and Society in Britain* (Allen Lane, London, 1973).

3 S. Hall, 'The Treatment of Football Hooliganism in the Press', in R. Ingham, et al., *Football Hooliganism* (Inter-Action Inprint, London, 1978).

4 The week surveyed was 27 October 1980–1 November 1980. The number of editions surveyed was 28.

5 72 main sports stories were identified. The method of selection may have somewhat discounted racing stories, since they tend mostly to be headlines, followed by extremely brief pieces hardly constituting a story in any real sense.

6 J. Tunstall, *Journalists at Work* (Constable, London, 1971).

7 A. C. H. Smith, 'Sporting Gestures', in R. Hoggart (ed), *Your Sunday Newspaper* (Penguin, Harmondsworth, 1967).

8 *BBC Handbook*, Appendix 11a, 'Programme Analysis 1977–8 TV Networks', p. 105, and Apendix 111a, 'Programme Analysis 1977–8 Radio'.

9 *TV Times*, citing official IBA figures, 13 July 1980.

10 BBC Audience Research Department, *The Public and Sport* (BBC, London, 1979).

11 B. P. Emmett, 'The Television and Radio Audience in Britain', in D. McQuail (ed.), *Sociology of Mass Communications* (Penguin, Harmondsworth, 1973). Emmet compares the BBC and ITV racing pattern from the mid-1950s to the early 1970s.

12 E. Buscombe, 'Ratings and Reality: Soccer as Showbiz', Spoilsports, *Time Out*, 426 (2 June 1978).

13 P. Golding and G. Murdock, 'Ideology and the Mass Media: The Question of Determination', in M. Barrett, et al. (eds), *Ideology and Cultural Production* (Croom Helm, London, 1979).

14 'Grandstand Gets The Key of the Door', *Radio Times* (10 October 1979); 'The World of Wooldridge', *Radio Times* (no date).

15 For a discussion of the economic determinants see G. Murdock and P. Golding, 'For a Political Economy of Mass Communications', *Socialist Register* (1973).

16 Tunstall, *Journalists at Work*, pp. 112–13. Racing correspondents, and possibly sports journalists specializing in the more middle-class sports, tend not to be working class. See Vamplew, *The Turf*.

17 Golding and Murdock, 'Ideology and the Mass Media'. For analyses stressing political and cultural factors, see: S. Chibnall, *Law and Order News* (Tavistock, London, 1977); Tracey, *The Making of Political Television*; Schlesinger, *Putting Reality Together*. See also P. Elliot, *The Making of a TV Series* (Constable, London, 1972).

18 S. Cohen and J. Young, *The Manufacture of News* (Constable, London, 1973). See, especially, the papers in this volume by Galtung and Ruge, and Hall's discussion of news photos.

19 J. Fiske and J. Hartley, *Reading Television* (Methuen, London, 1978) ch. 10.

20 R. Barthes, *Mythologies* (Jonathan Cape, London, 1972).

21 The front pages of all the national newspapers were analysed over the period 19 July 1980–4 August 1980.

22 E. Buscombe, 'Cultural and Televisual Codes in Two Title Sequences', *BFI Television Monograph No. 4: Football on Television, 1975*.

23 C. Barr, 'Comparing Styles: England v W. Germany', *BFI Television Monograph No. 4*; J. Wyver, 'Pulp on the Pampas: The Game as Light Entertainment, Spoilsports, *Time Out*, 426 (2 June 1978).

24 Barthes, *Mythologies*.

25 Barr, 'Comparing Styles', p. 51.

26 C. McArthur, 'Setting the Scene: *Radio Times* and *TV Times*', BFI, Television Mongraph No. 4; E. Buscombe & C. McArthur, 'Out of Bounds: The Off-Field Commentators', Spoilsports, *Time Out*, 426 (2 June 1978).

27 Schlesinger, *Putting Reality Together*; Tracey, *The Production of Political Television*.

28 Hall, 'The Treatment of Football Hooliganism'. See also G. Whannel, 'Football Crowd Behaviour and the Press', *Media, Culture and Society*, 1 (4), 1979.

29 The point is well made in the Glasgow work and by Golding and Murdock, 'Ideology and the Mass Media'.

30 'The State of Football', *Sportsnight*, BBC 1 TV, 15 October 1980.

31 *Thames Report*, ITV, 23 February 1980.

32 Hall, 'The Treatment of Football Hooliganism'. For uses of the 'deviancy amplification model' to explain how this occurs see: S. Cohen, *Folk Devils and Moral Panics* (Macgibbon and Kee, London, 1972); J. Young, *The Drug Takers* (Paladin, London, 1971). See also: S. Hall, et al., *Policing the Crisis* (Macmillan, London, 1978).

33 This conclusion is based upon an examination of the sports news photos in a survey of one week's editions.

34 Smith, 'Sporting Gestures'; Hall, 'The Treatment of Football Hooliganism'. For a different kind of assessment see: F. Inglis, *The Name of the Game* (Heinemann, London, 1977), ch. 5; F. W. Cozens and F. S. Stumpf, 'The Sports Page', in J. Talamini and C. H. Page, *Sport and Society* (Little Brown, Boston, 1973). Compare especially Inglis' eulogy for David Coleman with *Private Eye*'s column, 'Colemanballs'.

35 B. Bernstein, *Class, Codes and Control*, (Routledge and Kegan Paul, London, 1971), vol 1.

36 W. Labov, 'The Logic of Non-Standard English', *Georgetown Monographs in Language and Linguistics*, 22, (1969).

37 Martin Amis, 'Unideal Olympics, *Observer* (27 July 1980).

38 John Rhodda, 'That was no lady . . .', *The Guardian* (2 August 1980).

39 *Daily Express* (30 July 1978).

40 *The Guardian* (13 August 1980).

41 McArthur, 'Setting the Scene', p. 11.

42 G. Nowell Smith, 'Television-Football-The World', *Screen*, 19 (4), (Winter 1978/79).

43 All transmissions of the Moscow Olympic Games by BBC TV and ITV were video recorded and all coverage by the national press was examined with special reference to the way national identity was constructed.

44 See I. Jack, 'Comrade Popov Woos the Hardfaced West', *Sunday Times* (27 July 1980).

45 John Jackson, *Daily Mirror* (31 July 1980).

46 P. Fiddick, *The Guardian* (21 July 1980). See Denis Howell's letter on ITV's decision to cut back coverage, *The Guardian* (13 July 1980). See also the Controller of BBC1's reply to criticism of BBC's coverage: 'What a way to open the Olympics', *Radio Times* (9–15 August 1980).

47 *Olympic Report*, BBC 1 TV (2 August 1980).

48 Centre For Cultural Studies, *The Empire Strikes Back* (Hutchinson, London, 1982).

49 R. Williams, *Technology and Cultural Form* (Fontana, London, 1974).

Chapter 8

1 J. Hughes, 'The Socialization of the Body Within British Educational Institutions – A Historical View', (Dissertation in part fulfillment of M.Sc. (Econ.), Institute of Education, University of London, 1975).

2 J. Foster, *The Influence of Rudolf Laban* (Lepus Books, London, 1977). See R. Laban and F. C. Lawrence, *Effort* (MacDonald and Evans, London, 1947).

3 D. Finn, N. Grant and R. Johnson, 'Social Democracy, Education and The Crisis', *Cultural Studies* (University of Birmingham), 10 (1977).

4 J. Johnstone, 'The Development of the Movement Approach to the Teaching of Educational Gymnastics', *Bulletin of Physical Education* XIII (3) (1977); P. McIntosh, *PE in England Since 1800* (Bell and Son, London, 1968).

5 Ministry of Education, *PE in the Primary School*, Part 1, *Moving and Growing* (HMSO, London, 1952), and Part II, *Planning the Programme* (HMSO, London, 1953). Official acknowledgement of the centrality of Laban's ideas is given in the DES publication *Movement, Physical Education in the Primary Years* (HMSO, London, 1972), p. 16. Progressivist texts in movement usually do so as well, for example, see R. Morrison, *A Movement Approach to Educational Gymnastics*, 2nd edn (Dent, London, 1968). Some distance themselves somewhat, but are clearly in the same tradition: see, for example,

E. Mauldon and J. Layson, *Teaching Gymnastics*, 2nd edn (MacDonald and Evans, London, 1979).

6 J. Hughes, 'The Socialization of the Body Within British Educational Institutions – A Historical View'.

7 B. Bernstein, 'Class and Pedagogies: Visible and Invisible', *Class Codes and Control* (Routledge and Kegan Paul, London, 1975), vol III.

8 See the following attempts to overcome the status problem by elaborating the notion of 'movement' as a paradigm: G. F. Curl, 'An Attempt to Justify Human Movement as a Field of Study', J. D. Brooke and H. T. A. Whiting, *Human Movement – A Field of Study*, (Henry Kimpton, London, 1973); R. L. Groves, 'Towards a Dynamic and Objective Theory of Movement Studies', in J. Kane (ed.), *Movement Studies And Physical Education* (Routledge and Kegan Paul, London, 1977); P. H. Taylor, 'Curriculum in Transition: The Case of Physical Education, Association of Teachers in Colleges and Depts. of Education (ATCDE), *The Pursuit of Excellence in PE* (ATCDE, London, 1978). See also C. Crunden, 'The Uncomfortable Relation of Physical Education and Human Movement', *British Journal of PE*, 3 (1), (1973).

9 The wording of the 1944 Act is 'and it shall be the duty of the LEA...to contribute towards the spiritual, moral, mental and physical development of the community' cited in B. C. Cannon, 'Some Variations in the Teacher's Role', in P. W. Musgrave (ed.), *Sociology, History and Education* (Methuen, London, 1970). For a discussion of the Board of Education's action in 1926 when it eliminated all mention of subjects from the curriculum with the exception of practical subjects, see G. Grace, *Teachers, Ideology, and Control* (Routledge and Kegan Paul, London, 1978).

10 Schools Council, *Report of the Inquiry into Physical Education in Secondary Schools*, by J. Kane (Macmillan, London, 1974).

11 Among the numerous texts setting out the aims and objectives of physical education see the following official publications and texts by the better-known authorities in the profession: Department of Education and Science, *Movement, Physical Education in the Primary Years*; Ministry of Education, *Moving and Growing* and *Planning the Programme*; Morrison, *A Movement Approach to Educational Gymnastics*; N. Whitehead, 'Teacher Training Establishments and the Pursuit of Excellence', ATCDE, *The Pursuit of Excellence*; Report of the Working Party of Secretary of State for Scotland *Physical Education in Secondary Schools*, (HMSO, London, 1972), Curriculum Paper 12; British Association of Organisers and Lecturers in Physical Education (BAOPE), *Physical Education in Schools* (Methuen, London, 1970); P. McIntosh, *Fair Play* (Heinemann, London, 1979); R. E. Morgan, *Concerns and Values in Physical Education* (Bell, London, 1974) p. 75; A. D. Munrow, *Physical Education: A Discussion of Principles* (Bell and Son, London, 1972) p. 100; M. North, *Movement Education* (Temple Smith, London, 1973), pp. 56–7.

12 Working Party Report, *Physical Education in Secondary Schools*, p. 9. See also DES, *PE in the Primary School*, pp. 82–90. North's *Movement Education* similarly contains a strong condemnation of the 'anti-educational' effects of competition in physical education and school sport.

13 N. Whitehead and L. B. Hendry, *Teaching Physical Education in England*,

(Lepus Books, London, 1976) L. B. Hendry, *School, Sport and Leisure*, (Lepus Books, London, 1978), ch. 4; J. Yates, 'Psycho-social Aspects of the School Physical Education Programme', *Journal of Psycho-Social Aspects of Physical Education* (Dunfermline), (1975).

14 D. Glass, 'Education', in M. Ginsberg (ed.), *Law and Opinion in England in the Twentieth Century*, (Stevens, London, 1959); R. Williams, 'Education and British Society', in his *The Long Revolution*, (Pelican, London, 1975); R. Johnson, 'Education and Social Control in Early 19th Century England', *Past & Present*, 49 (1970) and his 'Notes on the Schooling of the English Working Class, 1780–1850 in R. Dale et al., *Schooling and Capitalism* (Open University, Milton Keynes, 1976).

15 The authors mentioned in note 13 above are exceptions.

16 Munrow, *Physical Education: A Discussion of Principles*.

17 Working Party Report, 'Middle Schools', *Physical Education in Secondary Schools*.

18 Ibid.

19 Ibid.

20 For the notion of a 'restricted code' in linguistic terms see B. Bernstein, *Class Codes and Control* 1 (Routledge and Kegan Paul, London, 1975), vol 1. For the notion that body language constitutes a restricted code see M. Douglas, *Natural Symbols* (Pantheon, London, 1982).

21 R. King, *School Organisation and Pupil Involvement* (Routledge and Kegan Paul, London, 1973).

22 J. Habermas, 'On Distorted Communication', in H. P. Dreitzel, *Recent Sociology*, No. 2 (Macmillan, New York, 1974) and 'Science and Technology as Ideology' in his *Towards a Rational Society* (Heinemann, London, 1971).

23 G. L. Underwood, 'The Use of Interaction Analysis and Videotape Recording in Studying Teacher Behaviour in Physical Education', in National Association of Teachers in Further and Higher Education *Evaluation in Physical Education* (NAFTHE, London, 1976).

24 E. Goffman, *Asylums* (Anchor, New York, 1961).

25 Ibid. See also Goffman's *Presentation of Self in Everyday Life* (Allen Lane, London, 1969).

26 These are taken from the official and professional texts cited above and an analysis of the content of photos in the major British physical education journal for teachers in schools, *The British Journal of Physical Education*, over the last 10 years.

27 W. H. Sheldon, et al., *The Varieties of Human Physique* (Harper and Brothers, New York, 1940).

28 Hendry, *School, Sport, and Leisure*, chap. 4.

29 See *Bulletin of Physical Education*, XVII (1), 1981.

30 Whitehead, 'Teacher Training Establishments', reviews the literature.

31 E. D. Saunders and K. S. Witherington, 'Extra-curricula Activities in the Secondary School', *British Journal of Physical Education*, 1 (1), 1970; C. Saunders, 'Pupils' Involvement in Physical Activities in Comprehensive Schools', *British Journal of Physical Education*, XV (3), (1979).

32 A. Gibbon, 'The Case for Physical Education: An Overview', *Bulletin of Physical Education*, 14 (3), 1978.

33 ATCDE, *The Pursuit of Excellence*, see especially the contribution by J. Kane, 'Some Psychological Aspects of Providing for the Gifted in Sport'.

34 J. M. Ross, 'The Physical Education Departments of 12 Comprehensive Schools', *British Journal of Physical Education* 4 (2), (1973).

35 'Report of the Central Advisory Council for Education (England)', (Newsom Report), 'Half Our Future' (HMSO, London, 1961) p. 48.

36 Saunders and Witherington, 'Extra-curricula Activities in the Secondary School'; Saunders, 'Pupils' Involvement in Physical Activities in Comprehensive Schools'.

37 I. Emmet, *Youth and Leisure in an Urban Sprawl* (Manchester University Press, Manchester, 1971) Central Advisory Council for Education (England), '15–18'. (The Crowther Report) (HMSO, London, 1960).

38 P. Corrigan, *Schooling the Smash Street Kids* (Macmillan, London, 1979); P. Willis, *Learning to Labour* (Saxon House, London, 1977); B. Sugarman, 'Involvement in Youth Culture, Academic Achievement and Conformity in School', *British Journal of Sociology*, XVIII (2) (1967); D. Hargreaves, *Social Relations in the Secondary School* (Routledge and Kegan Paul, London, 1967); C. Lacey, *Hightown Grammar* (Manchester University Press, Manchester, 1970).

39 G. Kalton, *The Public Schools* (Longman, London, 1966), ch. 7 shows the predominance of rugby compared with football in the middle-class-dominated private sector of education.

40 King, *School Organisation and Pupil Involvement*.

41 E. Anne Williams, 'Physical Education in the primary School – A Study of the Teachers Involved', *Bulletin of Physical Education*, XV (3), (1979).

42 King, *School Organisation and Pupil Involvement*.

43 *Daily Express* (30 July 1978).

44 S. Lopez, 'An Investigation of Reasons for Participation in Women's Football', *Bulletin of Physical Education*, XV (1), (1979).

45 M. Crowe, B.Ed Dissertation, University of Southampton, 1976, cited in Lopez, 'Reasons for Participation in Women's Football'.

46 Schools Council, *Report of the Inquiry Into PE in Secondary Schools*, ch. 5.

47 G. Wiener, 'Sex Differences in Mathematical Performance' and J. Harding, 'Sex Difference in Performance in Science Examinations', both in R. Deem (ed.), *Education for Women's Work* (Routledge and Kegan Paul, London, 1980).

48 The most widely circulated PE journal in this country, *The British Journal of PE*, shows virtually none.

49 D. Cherrington, 'Physical Education and the Immigrant Child', in ATCDE, *Physical Education an Integrating Force* (ATCDE, London, 1974).

50 Ibid.

51 Ibid.

52 E. Wood, 'Dysfunctional Aspects of West Indian Pupil Involvement in School Sport', *Bulletin of Physical Education*, XVI (2), (1980); P. Jones, 'An Evaluation of the Effects of Sport on the Integration of West Indian Children' (Ph.D Thesis, University of Surrey, 1977); E. Cashmore, Black Sportsmen, (Routledge and Kegan Paul, London, 1982); B. Carrington and E. Wood, 'Body Talk', *Multiracial Education*, 12 (1983).

53 M. Stone, *The Education of the Black Child in Britain*, (Fontana, London, 1981).
54 Carrington and Wood, 'Body Talk'.
55 'Interim Report of the Committee of Inquiry into Education of Children From Ethnic Minority Groups', (Rampton Report) (HMSO, London, 1981), Cmnd 8273.

Chapter 9

1 'Report of the Wolfenden Committee on Sport', 'Sport and the Community' (CCPR, London, 1960). Although it was formally a CCPR inquiry, to all intents and purposes Wolfenden carried official status. See also 'The Youth Service in England and Wales', (The Albermarle Report) (HMSO, London, 1960), Cmnd 729; Central Advisory Council for Education (England), '15–18' (The Crowther Report) (HMSO, London, 1960), part 1, ch. 4, 'Leisure Time Interests and Activities'; Central Advisory Council for Education (England), 'Half Our Future', (The Newsom Report), (HMSO, London, 1963).
2 The Wolfenden Report, p. 4.
3 Ibid, p. 6.
4 Ibid.
5 See, especially, the Albermarle Report, pp. 38, 42, 60 and 105.
6 The Wolfenden Report, p. 74. See also A. S. Travis, *The State and Leisure* (Sports Council, London, 1979).
7 For a discussion of the position of the various political parties at the time see D. Anthony, *A Strategy for British Sport* (Hurst and Co., London, 1980).
8 For details of these developments see C. Cockburn, *The Local State* (Pluto Press, London, 1977). On the concept of 'corporatism' and theories of corporatist development see: L. Panitch, 'The Development of Corporatism in Liberal Democracies', and B. Jessop, 'Corporatism, Parliamentarism and Social Democracy' both in P. Schmitter and G. Lehmbruch (eds), *Trends Towards Corporatist Intermediation* (Sage, London, 1979); L. Panitch, 'Recent Theorizations of Corporatism: Reflections on a Growth Industry', *British Journal of Sociology*, 31 (2), (1980).
9 H. J. Evans, *Service To Sport: The Story of the CCPR 1935–1972* (Sports Council, London, 1974).
10 Sports Council *Annual Reports*, *(SCAR)*, *1972/3–1983/84*.
11 For an analysis of the transition from Social Democracy to New Right 'authoritarian populism' see S. Hall and M. Jacques, *The Politics of Thatcherism* (Lawrence and Wishart, London, 1983).
12 C. Offe, Contradictions of the Welfare State (Hutchinson, London, 1984).
13 For the concepts of 'collective consumption' or 'social consumption', see M. Castells, 'Advanced Capitalism, Collective Consumption and Urban Contradiction', in L. Lindberg, et al. (eds), *Stress and Contradiction in Modern Capitalism* (Lexington Books, D. C. Heath and Co., 1975).
14 Sports Council, *Sport and the Community* (Sports Council, London, 1982), table 16, p. 21. See also C. Gratton and P. Taylor, 'Government Expenditure

(1), Local Authorities', *Leisure Management*, 5 (7), (July, 1985). For a discussion of the inadequacy of official statistics see S. Mennell, *Cultural Policy in Towns*, (Council of Europe, Strasbourg, 1976). See also Sports Council, *The Financing of Sport in the UK*, (Sports Council, London, 1983), Information Series 8; Travis, *The State and Leisure*.

15 Department of the Environment, 'Sport and Recreation' (The White Paper), (HMSO, London, 1975), Cmnd 6200.

16 Ibid.

17 Gratton and Taylor, 'Government Expenditure (1)'.

18 See, for example, Department of the Environment, *Recreation and Deprivation in Inner Urban Areas* (HMSO, London, 1977).

19 Cockburn, *The Local State*. For an account of the way the 'community approach' is implemented see Mennell, *Cultural Policy in Towns*.

20 See, especially, Sports Council, *The Report of the 12th Management Recreation Seminar* (Sports Council, London, 1980).

21 K. L. Oh and T. W. A. Whitfield, 'Leisure Centres: Excerpts From A National Survey', *Leisure Management*, 5 (6), (June, 1985).

22 'The 2nd Report From The House of Lords Select Committee on Sport and Leisure' (The Cobham Report), (HMSO, London, 1973).

23 M. Collins, 'Sport in Contemporary Society' (Sports Council, London, 1976), Sports Council Research Working Papers, 4.

24 *SCAR, 1976/7*.

25 Ibid.

26 *SCAR, 1979/80*.

27 *SCAR, 1981/2*, pp. 4–5. See also Sports Council, *Sport and the Community*.

28 *SCAR, 1981/2*, p. 18.

29 Ibid., p. 13.

30 *SCAR, 1982/83*, p. 12.

31 M. Rigg, *Action Sport Evaluation*, (Policy Studies Institute, London, 1985); S. Glyptis, 'The Freedom Trap', *Sport and Leisure* (Sports Council, London) (May–June 1985).

32 *SCAR, 1978/79*.

33 D. Ellis, Paper No. 5 in Sports Council, *12th Management Recreation Seminar*. See also R. Ingham, 'Football Clubs as a Focus for Community Participation', also in the *12th Management Recreation Seminar*.

34 *SCAR, 1983/84*, p. 24.

35 A. Leissner and J. Joslin, 'Area Team Community Work: Achievement and Crisis', in M. May and D. Jones (eds), *Community Work One*, (Routledge and Kegan Paul, London, 1974).

36 Department of the Environment, *Recreation and Deprivation in Inner Urban Areas*.

37 *SCAR, 1982/83*, p. 16.

38 White Paper on Sport and Recreation, para 62, p. 18.

39 Sports Council, *Report of the 12th Management Recreation Seminar*.

40 Notes on the Accounts, *SCAR, 1983/84*, p. 38.

41 Ibid.

42 *SCAR, 1981/82*, p. 18.

43 *SCAR, 1983/84*, p. 6.

44 C. Villiers (Sports Council), 'The Place/Need for Excellence in Sport', in Association of Teachers in Colleges and Departments of Education, *The Pursuit of Excellence in Sport and Physical Education* (ATCDE, London, 1977).

45 *SCAR, 1982/83*, pp. 19–20.

46 *SCAR, 1976/77*.

47 *SCAR, 1982/83*, p. 24; *SCAR, 1983/84*, p. 16.

48 *SCAR, 1979/80*.

49 *SCAR, 1982/83*, p. 16.

50 *The Times* (25 June 1985).

51 'A Royal Tilt', *The Guardian* (2 May 1979), 'Jeeps Answers the Prince', *The Guardian* (3 May 1979); J. Rodda, 'Howell Goes Back to Go Forward', *The Guardian* (23 November 1984).

52 C. Gratton and P. Taylor, 'Government Expenditure (2), Central Government', *Leisure Management*, 5 (8) (August 1985).

53 Travis, *The State and Leisure Provision*; Gratton and Taylor, 'Government Expenditure (1)' and 'Government Expenditure (2)'.

54 Sports Council, *Sport and the Community*, tables 15–16, p. 20. Sports Council targets set for 1981 were revised downwards in 1978.

55 A. J. Veal, 'Review of Sports Centre Studies (unpublished, Sports Council, London, 1981), and 'Leisure in England and Wales', *Leisure Studies* (May 1984).

56 Glyptis, 'The Freedom Trap; Rigg, *Action Sport Evaluation*.

57 E. Jones, 'Here Today, Where Tomorrow?', in Sports Council *Report of the 12th Management Recreation Seminar*.

58 See, especially, Glyptis' 'The Freedom Trap', which reports on the sports schemes for the unemployed and Rigg's *Action Sport Evaluation* for confirmation of this.

59 L. Melvern and R. Morgan, 'Now Cash Crisis Threatens to Halve Our Olympic Team', *Sunday Times* (16 March 1980).

60 'Government puts major hurdles in athletes' path to Moscow', 'Public Service Olympic move angers coach', *The Guardian* (3 March 1980); 'Thatcher steps up pressure on athletes', *The Guardian* (16 April 1980); 'Thatcher gags soldier athletes', *The Guardian* (17 July 1980).

61 *SCAR, 1979/80*.

62 See the Sports Council's statement on the issue in *SCAR, 1979/80*.

63 See *The Guardian* reports of 15 and 16 May 1981.

64 BBCTV, *Newsnight* (26 May 1981).

65 Ibid.

66 J. Rodda, 'AA Athletics Championships Held in N. Ireland', *The Guardian* (27 May 1981).

67 R. Rodwell, 'Cycling Grant Refused', *The Guardian* (9 July 1980).

68 See the Sports Council/Social Science Research Council, *Public Disorder and Sporting Events* (Sports Council, London, 1976) which, in contrast, attempts to adduce causes and exemplifies the social-democratic approach.

69 P. Hain, *Don't Play With Apartheid* (Allen and Unwin, London, 1971).

70 Sports Council, *Sport in South Africa* (Sports Council, London, 1980).

Chapter 10

1 Foucault's work, above all, has drawn attention to this point: see especially M. Foucault, *Discipline and Punish* (Allen Lane, London, 1976); *Power/Knowledge*, ed. C. Gordon, (Harvester, Brighton, 1980); *History of Sexuality* (Penguin, London, 1981), vol 1.

2 On the nature of British political development see W. Barrington Moore Jnr, *The Social Origins of Dictatorship and Democracy*, (Penguin, London, 1964); S. M. Lipset and S. Rokkan, 'Introduction' in their *Voting Systems and Party Alignments* (Free Press, New York, 1967); P. Anderson, 'Origins of the Present Crisis', *New Left Review*, 23 (1964); E. P. Thompson, *The Peculiarities of the English* in *The Poverty of Theory* (Merlin Press, London, 1978); R. Johnson, 'Barrington Moore, Perry Anderson and English Social Development', *Cultural Studies*, 9 (1976); H. F. Moorhouse, 'Political Incorporation', *Sociology*, 7 (3), (1973); G. Therborn, 'The Rule of Capital and the Rise of Democracy', *New Left Review*, 103 (1977).

3 R. Holt, *Sport and Society in Modern France 1920–1938*, (Macmillan, London, 1981).

4 Apparently, in 1913 English representatives attended the congress of workers' sports associations held under the aegis of the Bureau of the Socialist International to form the International Workers' Sports Association, D. A. Steinberg, 'The Workers' Sports Internationals', *Journal of Contemporary History*, 13 (1978).

5 Ibid.

6 C. Farman, *The General Strike* (Panther, London, 1974). The Police vs Strikers match at Plymouth was kicked off by the Chief Constable's wife.

7 J. Riordan, *Sport in Soviet Society* (Cambridge University Press, Cambridge, 1977); Sport Under Communism, (C. Hurst, London, 1978), 'Sport and Socialism', (unpublished paper for Colloque Internationale Pour Un Sport Ouvert La Vie, Paris, May, 1983).

8 Riordan, *Sport Under Communism*.

9 Steinberg, 'The Workers' Sports Internationals'.

10 Holt, *Sport and Society in Modern France*.

11 Foucault, *Power/Knowledge*.

12 M. Featherstone, 'The Body in Consumer Culture', *Theory, Culture and Society*, 1 (2), (1983).

13 Z. Bauman, 'Industrialism, Consumerism and Power', *Theory, Culture and Society*, 1 (3), (1983).

14 Foucault, *Powewr/Knowledge*, p. 57.

15 Bauman, 'Industrialism, Consumerism and Power'.

16 S. Hall, 'Notes on Deconstructing the Popular', in R. Samuel (ed.), *People's History and Socialist Theory*, (Routledge and Kegan Paul, London, 1981).

17 Bauman, 'Industrialism, Consumerism and Power'.

18 J. Habermas, *Legitimation Crisis* (Heinemann, London, 1976).

Index